ALSO BY EMILY BENEDEK

The Wind Won't Know Me

Beyond the Four Corners of the World

Beyond
the Four Corners
of the World

✳

A Navajo Woman's Journey

✳

EMILY BENEDEK

Alfred A. Knopf New York 1995

Portions of this work were originally published in
Newsweek and Redbook magazines.

Grateful acknowledgment is made to the following for permission to reprint previously
published material:
American Psychiatric Association and Robert L. Bergman: Excerpts from
"A School for Medicine Men" by Robert L. Bergman, M.D. (American Journal
of Psychiatry, 130: 6, June 1973), copyright © 1973 by the American Psychiatric
Association. Reprinted by permission of American Psychiatric Association and
Robert L. Bergman, M.D.
The University of Arizona Press: Navajo poetry excerpt from Blessingway,
translated by Leland C. Wyman (Tucson: The University of Arizona Press, 1970).
Reprinted by permission of The University of Arizona Press.

Library of Congress Cataloging-in-Publication Data
Benedek, Emily.
Beyond the four corners of the world: a Navajo woman's journey /
by Emily Benedek. — 1st ed.
p.   cm.
ISBN 0-679-42143-2
1. Bedonie, Ella.   2. Navajo Indians—Biography.   I. Title.
E99.N3B452   1995
979'.004972—dc20   94-46607
CIP

Manufactured in the United States of America
First Edition

For Jeffry Andresen

If you bring forth what is inside you,
what you bring forth will save you.

—*The Gospel According to Thomas*

Contents

✳

Contents

PART TWO

PART THREE

Contents

8 pages of photographs will be found following page 106

Introduction

The evening is perfumed with the thick scent of pine. The air is so clear and crisp I have the urge to gulp it, to fill my lungs with these fragrant breezes. The sun is setting over the horizon, a flaring globe that I can see for moments through the branches of the ponderosa pines, as they are jostled by the wind.

It is June 1985, and I have ventured out from New York City to this ochre-colored land of scrub and wildflowers to report a story for *Newsweek* magazine about a government-ordered plan to settle a boundary dispute between the Navajo and Hopi Indians of northeastern Arizona. I am sitting on the redwood deck of a lawyer who is helping the Navajos fight the law, which has led to the relocation of ten thousand sheepherders, many of whom speak no English, from the land on which they have lived for generations.

It is here that I first met Ella and Dennis Bedonie. Right away I noticed that there was something very unusual about Ella, a quality I had seen in few people. She radiated a sense of confidence that, I came to understand, was rooted in a deep faith. She spoke with a soft, soothing accent that was unfamiliar to me, but that I soon learned marked the speech of almost every Navajo. Ella was highly engaged in the talk that night, wherever it went, and she followed it with quick, bright eyes and a sharp humor. But sometimes, especially when she spoke of her parents, who live in a traditional manner that is largely unchanged from the time of their grandparents, she became very serious, almost worshipful in her respectfulness. Her voice lowered, her eyes even changed, as if instead of inscribing the images around her, they had suddenly reversed themselves, and now shone light and images outward.

Ella seemed comfortable with herself, at ease in her own skin, a quality so few people enjoy. That peacefulness marked her as someone people approach for comfort.

Ella's husband, Dennis, looked hauntingly like Sitting Bull, with broad cheekbones, acne-scarred skin, and flat nose. But whereas Ella seemed guileless, he was savvy. He said he had served in the military during the Vietnam era and returned home to discover that the Navajos were being told to move off part of their treaty reservation—land that to them was inviolable, was Mother.

"*Veni, vidi, vici,*" he said about the white man.

After my piece about the land dispute appeared in *Newsweek* in September of that year, I felt a persistent pull back out to that mysterious desert plateau of northern Arizona whose people had seemed at once so exotic yet familiar, troubled yet wise, calm yet emotional, but most of all committed—to the ways of their ancestors, to their culture. A few months later, I moved back to write a book, which was published in 1992 as *The Wind Won't Know Me: A History of the Navajo-Hopi Land Dispute*.

After the book came out, I asked Ella if she liked it. She said coyly, "It was good." And then she stopped. Trying to encourage her to be a bit more forthcoming, I prompted her with questions about different sections, whether she liked this episode or that.

"Yes," she said. Then more silence.

My spirits were steadily sinking, when she said: "Maybe

you could come back and write another book, this one about my dad."

This, I realized, was her answer to my question. The first book must have reflected her and her people in a way that was recognizable to her. And now she wanted to try again, this time to present a picture of the old ways for her grandkids, who will never know them in real life.

That's how this book started. It has evolved into a book about Ella's life, beginning with her birth in a world of ceremonies and spirits, and then following her abrupt departure at age six for a government boarding school, a different language, and a new world. It continues with her ten years of living with a Mormon foster family in California, then back home to confront the land dispute and relocation, to marry, and to earn a college degree. Woven through her story is her father's narrative of his own life and times, and embroidered into his story are the words of his own mother.

Stories about Indian people are fundamentally different from stories about other groups. For one thing, they are usually not best told through facts and figures, analyses of data, and a lot of policy talk from "experts." What is more interesting is to hear what Indian people say themselves, to observe what they do, and to note one's own feelings while among them. Navajo life is so different, it must be felt as much as apprehended through the intellect. The Navajos are truly religious people, and the world to them is made up of repeated revelations of the sacred. The philosopher Mircea Eliade has written a great deal about the transcendent part of religion—that which involves the apprehension of divinity. For the religious person, the sacred can be made manifest in any object:

> It could be said that the history of religions—from the most primitive to the most highly developed—is constituted by a great number of hierophanies, by manifestations of sacred realities. From the most elementary hierophany—e.g., manifesta-

tion of the sacred in some ordinary object, a stone or tree—to the supreme hierophany (which for a Christian, is the incarnation of God in Jesus Christ) there is no solution of continuity. In each case we are confronted by the same mysterious act— the manifestation of something of a wholly different order, a reality that does not belong to our world, in objects that are an integral part of our natural "profane" world.

Nonreligious people react with unease to those who suggest the world is full of sacred objects, sacred moments, as I did when I first arrived in the Southwest. This was thoroughly alien to the scientific, rational world in which I was educated, and in which I thought I worked. But as time went on, I saw that my comprehension—as well as the depth of my experience— was limited by my determination to analyze, and so remain detached from, what I saw in the ways to which I had become accustomed.

Looking back to the feelings that impelled me to return from New York to that vast, arid land to write one book, and then another, I now realize how much they were evoked by this Navajo view of the world as suffused with meaning, with the sacred. On that land, with those people, I sensed the presence of the divine, though I didn't know this in so many words, nor did I think too much about it. But the feeling stuck with me, and in this book I have tried to show something of it through Ella Bedonie, as she negotiates the distance between two realms—the sacred and the profane.

Her upbringing and her belief system are rooted in the sacred, but her American education, her college degree, and her life in the white world, with television, microwaves, coffee machines, and telephones, thrust her into the profane. In going back and forth between these two realms—sometimes by choice, sometimes by circumstance—she affords us insights into the nature of both.

In counterpoint to Ella's voice is that of her father, which is thoroughly imbued with the sacred. As much as possible, I have let the people speak for themselves, because their words have the poignancy and clarity that come from an open heart. I have also at times offered my own observations and the observations of scholars, to help a reader unaccustomed to this world better understand it.

Over time, I have become more and more convinced of the profound importance of stories in life. They are a complex indicator not only of events that take place, but through their color, their characters, cultural context, language, they provide all the information, subtle and polysemous, that one needs to be drawn into another world. Stories offer us a clear pathway to the imagination and the heart. As Eliade has put it, ". . . there is no other way of understanding a foreign mental universe than to place oneself *inside* it, at its very center, in order to progress from there to all the values it possesses." What better place to start than in the stories people tell one another?

The story of Ella Bedonie and her parents, Jack and Bessie Hatathlie, and the colossal changes that have come to their world in the last hundred years, is not just a story about Navajo Indian people, what they think, what they love, how they live their lives, how they view the environment, how they pray, what they think of white people, although these are all, of course, of great interest. Rather, I think this family's story has lessons for all of us, especially now in America.

One of the most difficult aspects of living in a society is working out a balance between being an individual, with his or her own needs, goals, and interests, and being a member of a group that holds expectations of us. Another balance that must be struck is that between our religious or ethnic tradition—we all have one, somewhere—and our membership in the larger community, in the outside world. Our challenge is learning how to remain concerned with ourselves, our own growth, prosperity, and happiness and the welfare of our immediate families, while also meeting our responsibilities to the larger group, our city or town or community.

The Navajo people have over the centuries developed a unique system for maintaining one's individuality while also remaining an important member of a vast social group—the clan. Every Navajo belongs to a family and a clan, and is related to other families and clans. These relations determine whom an individual may or may not marry, to whom he has responsibilities, and who has responsibilities toward him. This accords him a connection with a group that balances the facts of his existence—which is (or was traditionally) solitary and often lonely. In a way, the social responsibilities provide the security the Navajo individual needs to be alone. And the fact that he spends many hours alone—herding sheep, tending the cornfield—affords him many hours with his thoughts. Navajos place a great deal of importance on the views of every individual, a social value that fits nicely with the fact that Navajos have many of their own thoughts, the thoughts nurtured in their periods of isolation. Thus the community provides the counterbalance for solitude, even as it places importance on the products of that solitude.

How the Navajos remain Navajo and yet profit in their dealings with the outside world is more complicated, but it is accomplished through a tactic that is quintessentially Navajo: bringing into the culture whatever is seen to be useful in the outside world and in short order making it traditional. This technique eliminates the divisions and splits that have decimated much of Hopi society, for example, because of a rigid rejection on the part of some of anything that is not strictly traditional. Hopis who wish to accept the new are forced to see themselves as "moderns," which pushes them even further away from the traditional. The Navajos have moved on, accepting such useful items as the sheep and cows introduced by the Spanish, weaving and the cultivation of corn learned from the Pueblos, as well as the pickup truck, sewing machines, and other artifacts of modern life. These advances don't threaten the old order—they have become part of it.

The Navajos' story is also interesting to the extent that it is about assimilation. Every American is an immigrant or the descendant of immigrants—every American, that is, except the Native Americans. And every group that has come to this land has had to adapt to the new culture it meets. Every group must make decisions about the balance it wishes to achieve between maintaining the old ways—its religious or ethnic identity—and assimilating enough to be successful in the new world. But now, the influences of the outside world have become so powerful and pervasive—chiefly because of the ubiquitous media —that many groups, certainly including the Navajos, find their culture threatened at its roots. The old solution just described, of incorporating what is useful from outside into the traditional structure, may no longer be adequate. The Navajos, many of whom live as if it were still the nineteenth century, are now forced to examine the issues that have concerned immigrants through the years. How much of the old ways to preserve? How much to change? How ironic that the story of a Native American family one hundred years after the end of the Indian wars should be emblematic of the immigrant experience. (Indians even suffered the same indignities immigrants did when their real names were changed to ones more easily pronounceable by U.S. bureaucrats.) The story of the American Indians' struggles to find their place in the outside world is not so much a story of the United States as a melting pot, but more an issue of the pot boiling over, and bringing into its mix a group that has endeavored to stay apart.

Still, whatever struggles the Navajos may undergo to preserve their heritage, they continue to offer us an important lesson in the value of tradition, in a world where we tend increasingly to forget what tradition is. Every day, we see bits and pieces of many different cultures, but many of us hardly know our own well enough to get the kind of satisfaction that comes from the daily exercise of ritual and the daily contemplation of its meaning. These issues are relevant to Americans who are completely assimilated and yet long to feel connected to a religion or a group whose stories help explain who they are and where they came from. The lack of such a cultural identity reduces us to membership in the culture provided for us by the mass media, whose religion, when reduced down to its basics, is, as an actor once told me quite succinctly, "selling soap."

The Navajo people know that their tradition gives them strength and offers guidance; they understand the benefits of ritual, and rejoice in telling the stories of their forebears. In fact, almost every curing ceremony involves the recitation of the Navajo creation story. Healing comes in part from bringing to life—through stories—the lives of those who went before. The Navajos understand that the past is writ large in all of us, and that hearing the stories of the old ones helps us understand who we are, and thereby has the power to restore us.

Appreciating and celebrating the past does not have to mire us in the old-fashioned and out-of-date. To the contrary, perhaps only by reflecting on and coming to understand the importance of the past can we move beyond the limitations of the past. Traditional Navajo families are likely to be stronger and more successful than Navajo families who have either turned away from religion altogether or adopted Christianity. Their children are more likely to go on to college. Their native religion provides a foundation, a system of belief, upon which further growth can be based. Their religion, like most religions, also tells the Navajos who they are and what behavior is acceptable and what is not—it provides them with a guide and challenges them to create lives that suit their history and their cultural strivings.

Nonnative Americans, poised at the turn of the twenty-first century, are occupied with their own, apposite concerns. They are more and more interested in reconnecting with religion, more and more feeling the pull of the spiritual, and more and more concerned about the disappearance of community. Many of us, and many of our parents and grandparents, in trying to be "Americans," have severed ties with the past so thoroughly that we no longer know the stories and songs and ways of our ancestors. We live in suburban developments or apartment houses whose residents we may never know by name and who may never know us. How many of us sleep with the security of knowing there is someone nearby to help, and someone who will take care of us in our old age?

On a deeper level, without the stories of those who led the way, how can we tell our own tales? Only through others can we see ourselves. Mikhail Bakhtin, a twentieth-century Russian philosopher of human communication, put it this way:

> I am conscious of myself and become myself only while revealing myself for another, through another, and with the help of another. The most important acts constituting self-consciousness are determined by a relationship toward another consciousness (toward a *thou*). . . . The very being of man (both external and internal) is the *deepest communion. To be* means *to communicate.* . . . To be means to be for another, and through the other, for oneself. A person has no internal sovereign territory, he is wholly and always on the boundary: looking inside himself, he looks *into the eyes of another* or *with the eyes of another.* . . . I cannot imagine without another, I cannot become myself without another; I must find myself in another by finding another in myself (in mutual reflection and mutual acceptance).

We are nothing without the others who preceded us, and without those around us. With these people, we come to an understanding of who we are. Forming the stories of who we are, one could argue, is a central imperative.

Ella is attempting what few Navajos have done successfully. She is a modern, college-educated woman married to a man who also holds a college degree. Yet she is also a traditional Navajo who, as eldest daughter in this matrilineal culture, is heir not only to her parents' possessions but also to their ancient cultural and religious knowledge.

Ella's attempt to live with one foot in each culture has not been without its grave difficulties. Several years ago, after moving from the reservation to Flagstaff, a nearby town, hoping it would offer her family better opportunities, she watched helplessly as her eldest son became involved in a gang, eventually dropped out of school, and was badly hurt in a gang fight. For months afterward, she didn't know where he was, though she had been given the terrifying reassurance by the gang leader that her son was receiving "the medical care he needs." In the middle of it all, she was diagnosed with breast cancer.

She moved back to the reservation, chastened, believing the gods had delivered a clear warning to her about the perils of abandoning her land and her tradition. Within the next year, it seemed, the gods had forgiven her. Her son eventually returned and went on to college, and her breast cancer went into remission.

Although that chapter of her life seems to have ended well, Ella will be faced for the rest of her days with questions about what balance to strike between tradition and the outside world. She has been given a promising legacy: her people have been designated the "most adaptable" Indians in the country. The Navajos have survived war, captivity, disease, and subjugation, yet are a vital, populous tribe of 200,000.

The Navajos have developed unique methods of retaining the old while adapting the new—it is this strategy that some observers credit with their cultural success. Ella must forge her own path within that tradition, must come up with her own solutions to the conflicts of old and new—problems made more acute by her education, the ever-encroaching tides of the outside world, and the deepest of ties to her tribe.

New York City, 1995   E.B.

Part One

1

"My Corn Extends Its Hand to Me"

Ella Bedonie steps between the corn plants, her feet sinking into the furrows of red, dry dirt. The plants are as tall as she is, their stalks as thick as bamboo, long leaves reaching out to the sun like the arms of supplicants. Green of all shades— chartreuse, Kelly, beryl, citron—shiny fronds waving about her, the corn like dancers, naiads in the forest, pointing to springs, to the sun, to the spirits. Ella reaches up between the shiny, rustling leaves to the golden plumage ripening in the sun. Dry and layered like wheat, the tufts rise from the rich dark plants with their precious pollen. The plants give only a teaspoon of pollen each day, so Ella will return day after day for weeks until she has harvested it all. Then she will trade it with the medicine men who prize it for their healing ceremonies.

Ella shakes the top of a plant into her bowl—a colander into which she's laid a white cloth anchored with two quarters. When the plant has given up its small offering, she moves to the next, shaking the stalk just below the top, shaking, shaking, careful not to break it.

The sun beats on her arms, her hair, her feet. As she moves to the plants, their leaves seem to wrap themselves around her in welcome. They appear like dancing Yei-bi-cheis, figures of Navajo gods, almost stepping from their posts in the garden to walk with her here on the desert floor. Puffs of pollen swirl into the clear air, sweet in the nose and mouth, yellow as marigolds.

An airplane passes overhead. Its shadow cuts across the ballet of leaves and sunlight. Ella looks up. Above her, the sky is huge—powder blue and stippled with clouds rolling toward the San Francisco Peaks.

"My cousin used to tell me that those clouds came from the gods shearing sheep up there, and I believed him," she says. "I used to look up there all the time and think, 'Boy, the gods are doing a lot of shearing.' " Her laugh bubbles up from her like water from the springs nearby. She tips her head to the side, thinking about the joke that fooled her.

"Okay, then," says Ella, heading across the long rows of tilled earth, the dirt filling her sandals. Her face eases into a peaceful oval of solemnity. She has been transported by this cornfield, filled with the plants that grow inexplicably from the dust, the plants that remind her of the songs she was taught as a child by her father, the songs that tell her about the Navajos' origins, their beliefs, the care of the plants.

> *The group of roots enter the ground*
> *Several kernels sprouted in one spot*
> *It starts out on opposite sides*
> *Its roots go down, the leaves come up*
> *It starts out from below*
> *One plant appears, two plants appear, three appear,*
> *Four appear*
> *Now the corn is green*
> *My corn extends its hand to me*
> *From the very center of wide corn field*
> *My corn extends its hand to me*
> *Now your White Corn Boy, my corn, extends his hand to me*

Dressed in fabrics, your boy, my corn, extends his hand to me
Dressed in jewels, your boy, my corn, extends his hand to me
Now your long life happiness boy, my corn, extends his hand to me
My corn extends his hand to me
From the very center of vacant cornfield
My corn extends its hand to me
Now your Yellow Corn Girl, my corn, extends her hand to me
Dressed in jewels, your girl, my corn, extends her hand to me
Dressed in fabrics, your girl, my corn, extends her hand to me
Now your long life girl, my corn, extends her hand to me
My corn extends her hand to me
My corn shows love for me
My corn shows love for me
My corn now indeed listens
My corn leaves are blowing in the same direction

"The Indian way is really, really simple," says Ella. "You look at things in a good way, understanding that everything has a meaning and everything has a purpose in this life, and that if you sit down and try to understand, all these things will come to you. They'll talk to you through the wind, even the rocks. That to us is like a meditation; you can get healing from these things, just like talking to medicinal plants, asking them for their help because they're individual plants, and they have a name, and they're like individual people. And you talk to them and ask them for their help.

"A lot of times you go to these herb stores and you buy your herbs [and ingest them] and I guess it works for [Anglo] people like that. But for Indian people, you have to go to that individual herb and make that offering and tell them the purpose, the reason why you're there and then take it. When you're done with it, you bring back the plants, and lay them down with an offering again. And right there, it's showing respect for plant life."

The Indian way also requires one antecedent understanding.

Ella says, "You have to have that belief that there is something greater, there's something that is a powerful force called the Creator. You look at the changing seasons—why would they change and what makes them change? You see birth, you see generations being born all the time. And you see plant life. You plant something and you watch it grow. You watch the buds come and you watch the flowers, and then you have food, you have corn. And looking at those things, thinking about those things, that's when you realize there is something greater, there is a powerful force around you that makes these miracles happen. You have to get your mind at that level, to relate to everything around you.

"You have to believe that before you can even begin to think, 'This plant is going to talk to me; this rock is going to talk to me.' You have to put your mind at that level, a real simple level. You have to sit there and think, 'I'm no greater than anybody else, I'm just a simple person, and I want to be able to get this knowledge, and I want to be able to relate to everything around me.' Everything can be made simple, and you just talk to whatever's around."

✳

The traditional land of the Navajos is bounded by four sacred mountains—in the west by the San Francisco Peaks near Flagstaff, Arizona, in the south by Mount Taylor and the Zuni Mountains in central New Mexico, in the north by the La Plata Mountains of Colorado, in the east by Pelado Peak near Jemez, New Mexico. The twenty-five-thousand-square-mile Navajo reservation today pretty well covers the original territory of Dinetah—Land of the Dine, the People, as the Navajos call themselves. The reservation occupies about one-eighth the area of Arizona, in its northeastern corner, and stretches into New Mexico and Utah—the region known as the Four Corners, because it is here that the state borders of Utah, New Mexico, Arizona, and Colorado all converge. Rare among American Indian people, the Navajos still occupy most of their land in its original location. (In contrast to the mavens of political correctness in universities and the media, the Navajos variously refer to themselves as Indians or Native Americans. They do not consider "Indian" a pejorative term. And Navajo women refer to each other as "ladies"—a word they do not find offensive.)

"My dad says when you make a fist, your knuckles represent the four sacred mountains, and the whole hand represents Mother Earth," says Ella. "He says that's why you should never use your fist to hit another person, because it is holy."

Ella's mother and father, Jack and Bessie Hatathlie, sixty-five and sixty-three respectively, live twenty miles from here. They run livestock and tend their cornfields—one adjacent to Ella's, as well as two more, tucked into fertile, naturally irrigated patches of the desert near their home. Jack and Bessie live for the most part in the nineteenth century, in the fashion of their parents and grandparents. The Hatathlies' camp sits three hundred yards from State Highway 264, the main road that connects Tuba City with the Hopi mesas, on which, in a dozen villages, live about six thousand Hopi Indians. The Navajos and Hopis, different tribes with different ancestries and histories, live in close proximity here, the result of their prehistorical migrations, encroachment of white settlers, and confused U.S. Indian policy.

The Hatathlie camp consists of three hogans—the round, one-room Navajo dwellings, typically made of mud or wood or stone—and the main house, which is rectangular, made of concrete blocks, with a sloped roof and an open porch in front. The house has several glass windows that are almost always cracked, a result, the family says, of military planes breaking the sound barrier. The living room is furnished with plaid couches, a wooden bureau, and a wood-burning stove that up until a few years ago was an oil barrel cut in half, with a smoke pipe extending out the wall of the house.

On the walls are shelves to hold the children's school trophies and mementos, as well as studio photos of the children and grandchildren, and the floor is covered with linoleum. Jack and Bessie have their own bedroom, which is decorated with beaded buckskin pouches, strands of beaver fur, ceremonial objects like fans made of eagle feathers, and family photographs. They have a double bed with metal spring and mattress. Mattresses are a fairly recent development; Ella grew up sleeping on sheepskins on the floor. Also standing in this room is Bessie's loom, on which she makes fine Navajo rugs. She has a large closet in which she stores her clothes and the precious items she wants to keep away from exploring children and grandchildren. A second bedroom is for the children, but if all the family should come home at once, several must sleep on the couches in the living room, in the one other hogan that is habitable, or in their cars.

There is no electricity, running water, or central heating. The kitchen has a dry sink, a broken propane stove, a broken propane refrigerator, and a table with dinette chairs. Waste from the sink passes out of the house through a hose and into the sand. Large white plastic buckets hold water, which is used for cooking and cleaning. An enamel pan of water stands near the door for daily hand and face washing. A wooden outhouse stands several hundred feet from the front door.

Ella once brought home a friend from college, a white woman who was studying to become a social worker. Ella asked her, "Do you think my family's really poor?" And the young woman said yes. According to Ella, she said, "I look at your family and I think that they're really poor. You don't have very much, and it seems your house is really in need of repair." Ella says, "We reminded her of people living in Mexico who are barely making a living. She said, 'Sometimes I think you're below poverty level. People on welfare in Flagstaff would probably live better than you.' That was what she told me. She was from Iowa."

This is probably the reaction most visitors would have. No

bathroom, no showers, no running water to wash the dishes. Concrete floors, no lights, no air conditioning. And in fact, welfare housing in Flagstaff consists of new, wooden homes with carpet, electricity, plumbing, modern kitchens, and small, neat backyards.

But Bessie does not want a modern house. In fact, she considers indoor plumbing an abomination. She told Ella, "I can't imagine myself going to the bathroom in my own house. I can't imagine doing that because in the Navajo way, there is a lot of respect for homes. A hogan is composed of the earth and also of the heavens. The top of the hogan is the heavens. And then the pillars that hold up the homes are the gods that represent the Navajos. It's a very holy place. That's where you raise your children. It's a very spiritual place, and you pray in there. And you have your house built so that the gods can visit you every morning and look around in your house. You have a lot of ceremonies in your house. I can't imagine going to the bathroom in it."

Where visitors see poverty, the Navajos see plenty. They have less desire for material goods because their life is imbued with the experience of the sacred. They are inside life, not outside life, in a way unknown to any but the very religious. A visitor can sense it at times, in whiffs—for it is a foreign scent, unfamiliar to those who live in a society that disavows both the need for and the existence of meaning in the world. In the Navajo world, the gods are close. This offers peril but also the deepest satisfactions, for when the gods are nearby, and their commandments are clear, life is perfumed with purpose.

As the religious historian Mircea Eliade puts it, "The world exists because it was created by the gods, and . . . the existence of the world itself 'means' something, 'wants to say' something, that the world is neither mute nor opaque, that it is not an inert thing without purpose or significance. For religious man, the cosmos is proof of its sanctity, since the cosmos was created by the gods and the gods show themselves to men through cosmic life." The Navajos are surrounded by the experience— not simply the idea—of the divine.

Contemplatives endeavor as much as anyone in the modern world to experience the divine. Nevertheless, they must make an effort to do so. Says one cloistered nun from the Sisters of the Visitation, an order founded in France in 1610, "No matter what we do in the context of our day, we try to make that prayerful, to make every action have a prayerful intentionality behind it." The Navajos don't "try" to create prayerful intentionality. Everything they do is filled with prayer; their gods are not hidden from them. They live in an intrinsically sacred world. This reality creates a tremendous difference in the quality of Navajo life, and in part explains why sections of white society are fascinated by American Indians: they are drawn by the Indians' reverence.

The Hatathlie camp sits on plains land that stretches as far as the eye can see. A handful of cottonwood trees rise from the sand to provide shade. Reservation dogs—a small shepherd mix—and cats play and sleep around the house. Siamese cats are a special favorite among Navajos, and sometimes the male Siamese are loaned from family to family for breeding purposes. A ragtag herd of woolly sheep and long-haired goats rumble nearby and settle in the shade of one of the hogans.

That is the world into which Ella was born. A world of spirits and ceremonies, of long summer evenings dancing and visiting with neighbors around the bonfires of squaw dances, healing ceremonies that seek to lift malevolent spirits from the afflicted. A world of back-breaking labor herding sheep and growing corn, hauling water and wood. A world of delicate and profound physical beauty—immense stretches of spare grassland that drop, suddenly, into rainbow-colored box canyons. Elsewhere, forests and mountains, lakes, cliffs, then more canyon lands. Everywhere, lunar elevations, mesas, conical piles of cinder from ancient now-extinguished volcanoes. Then rock formations in the shapes of ships, ghosts, arches, wind holes. This is the world that offered her her first language—Navajo—and her first system of thought, philosophy, and belief.

But Ella left this land in the early 1950s as a little girl and journeyed toward life in the white world. Hers is the first generation of Navajo children gathered up at age six and bused to government-run boarding schools—removed from their families and raised in institutions for years at a time. Little by little, the new ways began to influence Ella, the new language to change her and the way she thought. With education came a new way of life and the questioning of traditional belief. Learning the English language, with its technical words and its analytic thinking, opened worlds and thoughts the Navajo language did not admit. It was a painful struggle; the two systems seemed so opposed that Ella sometimes wondered if she would ever learn English, ever learn the Anglos' logic. But she persevered, eventually earning a college degree in anthropology.

Once she questioned the power of the Navajo pantheon, Ella found herself in a strange land, a land no longer solid and complete, inclusive, answering all questions. As the years went by, Ella abandoned the Christianity she had been taught and returned to Navajo beliefs and explanations. Or rather, she realized they had never left her. However, she also realized she had become irretrievably accustomed to the conveniences of modern life.

Now Ella and her husband, Dennis, also a college graduate, are lodged between worlds—Navajo and white, religious and secular, traditional and modern. They want their children to benefit from modern education, but want them also to learn the traditional ways. They want them to believe the white world is open, but also to be proud that they are Navajos. They want them to walk easily in the land of the white man, but also to avoid drugs and alcoholism, to resist the lure of materialism and unbridled ambition. They are trying to find a balance between the tradition that nourishes their souls and the dominant culture through which they provide the material needs of their families.

Tuba City, the Navajo town of six thousand in which they live, mirrors this conflict. One sees modern pickup trucks whose beds are loaded with Navajo grandmothers in traditional dress and jewelry, their hair covered with bright kerchiefs; Navajo men dressed like cowboys in Wrangler jeans and white straw cowboy hats rounding up their livestock or heading off for the all-Indian rodeos. The dusty soil is littered with discarded Coke cans and ancient pottery shards; children herd sheep on horseback with Walkmans pumping rock 'n' roll into their ears. Symbols of traditional life exist side by side with modern artifacts here, revealing over and over the meeting of cultures, Navajo and Anglo, and eras—nineteenth and twentieth centuries—that drives Navajo life.

"I could never live as a totally Navajo person," Ella says. "I would miss the conveniences. I would miss TV; I'd miss my soap operas." Ella laughs. "I'd miss taking a shower, washing my hair, and changing clothes every day."

Nevertheless, breaking with her past entirely is impossible. "You know, if I tried to become a totally white person, if I said, 'I'm never going to come back to the reservation,' just cut all ties, I'd probably feel lonely all the time."

2

"The One Who Was Really Light's Wife"

The sun is red, glowering over the horizon, impossibly large, promising another hot, dry day. Ella has been gathering pollen for several hours. Nearby, in the shade of a cottonwood tree, Ella's grandmother tends a fire and turns strips of mutton sizzling on a grill. Around them on all sides are fields, worked by different families, of corn, beans, melon, squash. The wide row of gardens stretches between U.S. Highway 160 all the way up to a ridge of dun-colored cliffs that marks the start of the Moencopi Plateau. The highway runs northeast from Tuba City to Cow Springs, Kayenta, and Mexican Water.

Ella walks to the fire, murmurs a few words in Navajo to her father's mother, Rena Williams, and gently takes the utensil from her. Rena is ninety-two, a small woman now and frail, with watery eyes. She sits with her feet folded beneath her, dressed in the traditional Navajo women's garb, a layered satin skirt, velvet blouse, and turquoise necklace. Her hair is pulled back into a *tsiyeel*, a figure-eight-shaped bun worn by men and women, tied with a skein of white yarn.

Ella steps to her truck, gathers paper plates and napkins, returns to the fire. She forks the long, twisted strips of roasted meat from the grill onto a plate, sprinkles the meat with salt from a metal shaker, and places the plate on a blanket she has spread on the ground. She opens a Tupperware bowl, in which rests a ball of kneaded dough, perfectly smooth, puffed like a pillow. She grabs a handful of dough, shapes the lump into a ball, then a pancake, and proceeds to flap it from hand to hand until she has made a six-inch round, like a pizza crust. She drops it on the metal grill to roast. Ella twists off several more pieces of dough and flips the rounds onto the grill. She removes a blue enamel coffeepot from the flame and sets it onto a rock.

The breeze is hot, the smells of dust and corn mixing with the roasting meat and the burning juniper wood. Ella's grandmother is happy down in the fields, happier here than in the ranch home the government built for her in Tuba City. The house is too big, too angular, too noisy, nothing like the old hogan in which she used to live, the nearest neighbor a mile or so away. "The floor is too hard; it hurts my feet," she says of the poured concrete floors covered with wall-to-wall carpeting. Rena prefers the soft red dirt floors, covered with blankets, of her old home. "There's too much light," she says of the house with the large bay windows. Her hogan had small windows, placed high, for just a peek of the sky. But the authorities don't understand that she prefers a mud hut to a three-bedroom house.

Rena did not choose to move; the government told her she must. Her old hogan was situated on land the government says now belongs to the neighboring Hopi tribe. Because Rena is so old, she didn't have the strength to fight, so she moved into the house the government built for her on Navajo land. Ella's parents, Bessie and Jack, are in the same position, but they have refused to move.

Rena is so uncomfortable in her new home, however, that she tells Ella she wants to stay down here in the fields in one of the open shacks the farmers have built for shade during the long hot days when they try to keep the crows away from their crops. Rena would like to bring down her blankets and sleep here, where she can hear the plants, the animals, the birds, where she can walk on the earth, feel it under her feet, smell the wind and the rain.

The aroma of mutton wafting over the fields also makes Rena happy. The Navajos acquired sheep from the Spaniards in the early seventeenth century and prize them highly, for sheep provide meat for food, hides for bedding and clothes, and wool for their famous weaving. They are like money in the bank—good for food, for cash, for wool. With the sheep, life is ensured. Caring for the sheep requires the cooperation of all family members and thus forms the basis of family unity and individual responsibility. The herds even reflect the family— every child gets lambs when he or she is old enough to tend them, and watches as his or her subherd grows with the rest. The sheep herds also reflect alliances between families. A man will take his subherd with him and join it with his wife's herd, usually not at the beginning of his marriage, but after he feels a part of his wife's family, after the arrival of their first children. A Navajo man customarily moves to his wife's land.

Rena can no longer tend sheep; her new house lot has no room for livestock. This makes her feel lonely, without purpose. But here, smelling the mutton, she imagines the old days.

Rena is known among the old Navajos as "The One Who Was Really Light's Wife," because her husband, Joe, had light, almost white skin. Most of the elderly Navajos have Navajo names for one another, like Hosteen, Kee, Hoskie, Atsitty, Tso, Bahe, but they are now known by the English names given to them by missionaries or by U.S. census takers when they first came out to the reservation in the early twentieth century— names like Laila, Ruby, Esther, Nora, Eula, Nathan, Ambrose, Michael, Sam.

Ella's mother has several different names in the tribal records—Emily Atcitty, Bessie Zahne, Emily Zahne, and Bessie Emily Hunter. She was known as Emily for a long time; now she is Bessie.

The next generation, Ella and her siblings, those born in the

Bureau of Indian Affairs (BIA) hospitals, were named by the Anglo nurses who filled out the birth certificates for the non-English-speaking mothers. A few attempts were made to find spellings for Navajo names. Ella was given her name, she thinks, because her grandmother's census name was Stella. Ella has two brothers named Fred as a result of being named by nurses, so the family calls one Fred, the other Freddie. The Navajos were given new, English names, just as immigrants to Ellis Island with unpronounceable names from Russia or Eastern Europe were given new names—or mixed-up, Anglicized versions of their own. Navajos were treated like immigrants in their own land.

Ella is a member of the first generation of Navajo women to put names of their own choosing on their children's birth certificates. Most Navajo women also give Navajo names to their children, as well as nicknames, by which they are known.

Rena eats her meat slowly, carefully, savoring each bit that she pulls with her fingers from the twisted rope of meat. She chews on the fragrant tortillas Ella has made and washes them down with heavily sugared coffee. When Rena is finished, she dozes in the warm afternoon breeze.

Ella runs her fingers through the corn pollen, lifting out dried worms, bugs, and other scraps. For her half-day's work, she has collected about a cup of pollen. She tries to get to the fields in the morning, because she gathers more than if she waits until the afternoon. She wonders if the afternoon yield is less because the bees gather the pollen in the mornings. The corn will produce pollen for about a month, starting now in June, when the cobs begin to form. She will save some of the pollen for blessing her home and her children, and she will trade the rest to the medicine men.

"That pollen represents life," says Ella. "And you only take just a little bit when you're going to pray with it. You put a little dab in your mouth, and then you put it on your head; that pollen is the connection between Mother Earth and your

Father the Sky. You're in the middle and you're a child of the Holy People. It really means a lot to the medicine people. They use it as offerings for the Holy People. They pray with it, and sometimes they use it for sand paintings. It's very scarce because a lot of people don't really bother [to gather] it."

The Navajos call their deities the Holy People, though they are not "holy" in the sense of possessing virtue or moral sanctity. Nor are they benevolent protectors or guides. Rather, they are powerful and dangerous. The Navajos are ever trying to maintain good ties with the Holy People—or at least stay away from them. The Holy People for the most part let humans live out their lives without much notice—unless they violate taboos. And then the Holy People can exact punishment by causing illness. However, they can also reverse their actions—if appealed to properly, the Holy People can be convinced to remove the illness or imbalance they have caused. The Navajos strongly believe the Holy People must be thanked or propitiated at the appropriate times.

A mild breeze has picked up, rustling the corn, which raises a clatter like polite applause. Ella looks toward Rena and says, "My grandma says she wants to have a ceremony. She's been having bad dreams. She says that somebody's touching her at night, on her leg. Somebody's trying to move her leg."

Ella is quiet for a moment, then continues. "Her grandkids say she's imagining it, nobody's touching her ankle. But my grandma told me she knows who it is. She recognizes the hand; it's a big hand. It's his hand. He's touching her ankle."

Rena means her husband, Joe, who recently died at a nursing home in Blanding, Utah. Rena has been having nightmares about him, that he has come to get her, pull her along with him to the other world.

Ella says, "She told me, 'I know that sometimes when that happens, that whatever it is, the spirit might even take your spirit and take you away.' "

Navajos have many taboos about the dead and fear the dead

profoundly. In the old days, a dead person's shoes were put on the wrong feet so the spirit couldn't track its way back to the living, and the face was painted red. On a corpse, rings are shifted from the ring fingers to the forefingers, so the spirit, if it starts to wander around, can be identified. A hogan is abandoned if someone dies in it.

Rena is not ready to travel to the other side. She wants to remain here as long as she can, and therefore her dreams rattle her. Joe, once a powerful medicine man, was known to dabble in witchcraft. He was a gambler who people believed said prayers over the cards to help him win. And he won. He was a powerful man who lived a wild life, and this makes Rena worry.

Rena wants to have a ceremony to relieve her of her husband's spirit. A medicine man will sit with her in a hogan, chanting and singing prayers all night over her, trying to call up the powers of the Holy People to drive away the spirit of the dead. In the Navajo way, ritual knowledge—the recitation of prayer—has power. Performance of the proper ceremonies in the proper way compels the gods to cure the patient.

Ceremonies are performed on the reservation every day of the year in all areas. Although Navajos make use of modern medicine to help cure them of sickness, they rely on traditional curing as well. Often a patient will follow a course of treatment in both disciplines. Most medical doctors realize that the Navajo patients do better if they are also tended by medicine men, and cooperate with the family if they wish a medicine man to visit the patient in the hospital.

3

"This Is Where I Am Tucked into the Land"

Ella's father and mother, Jack and Bessie, are sitting in front of their house, scraping kernels off the corncobs they have harvested. For several weeks, the cobs have been drying on the roof of the ramada. Now the corn has been gathered from the roof, and Jack and Bessie are separating the cobs by color—red, blue, yellow, and white—and storing it in barrels. The corn will be boiled in soup or ground to make cornmeal. Jack and Bessie talk quietly as they work. The dryness of the air and the placid rolling of the land create a feeling of absolute stillness. It is quiet as it never can be in the outside world, so quiet it makes your ears pound at first. Noises have no echoes; it seems they are swallowed up by the earth. Sitting in the sun, grinding corn, pulling kernels off the cobs, or cooking, a visitor feels held, moored. When showing a visitor his home, one old Navajo said, "This is where I am tucked into the land."

To the west in the distance, ever present, are the three triangles of the San Francisco Peaks, a former volcano that is sacred to Navajos and Hopi alike. For the Navajos it describes the western boundary of Dinetah, and on its sides grow sacred herbs and plants. The Hopis believe their gods—or Kachinas

—winter on the summit. Over the Peaks, the clouds are often roiled in a steaming, angry mass where they churn for a time, often dissipating before they can deliver their rain to the dry cornfields of the reservations. The storms usually arrive twice a year, in January and July, causing flooding and creating mud soup out of dirt roads. At other times, when rain is but a dream, cumulous clouds float in the blue sky like boats out for a sunny afternoon sail.

Bessie dresses like all the other Navajo women who live around her—in the layered full skirts and velveteen blouses whose style the Navajo women picked up from white frontier women. Bessie also wears silver and turquoise jewelry and sturdy shoes. Her long black hair is pulled up into the traditional Navajo *tsiyeel,* and tied with a thick clump of white yarn. Bessie has a wide face with high cheekbones, and old photographs reveal her as unusually beautiful. Now her expression is grim, tired. She rarely laughs. Her long black hair is thinning on top of her head.

One of her worries is her sheep herd. The government has reduced her permit level gradually over the years, so that her herds have been reduced from hundreds to fewer than ten, leaving her now not with a herd but a flock of pets. The old people speak of the days when the grasslands were filled with so many sheep they looked like cotton fields. The flowers were knee-high. The gods rewarded the Navajos for taking care of their sheep by providing rain, which made the grass grow. But the white men thought differently. Scientists determined the rain didn't come because there were uncontrollable cycles of drought, and that the livestock was grossly overgrazing the dry land. In the thirties, the government initiated the first of many drastic and highly traumatic livestock reductions. The draconian restrictions continue to this day. That is why most Navajo men must find work off the reservation to feed their families. The grassland has recovered somewhat, so that it can accommodate more sheep, but the government keeps livestock levels below capacity in the interest of preservation.

Jack wears jeans and cowboy or button-down shirts. His hair is cut short, in the style he learned in the fifties as a member of a railroad track crew, and he wears either a cowboy hat or a baseball cap. He is a cheerful man, and loves to laugh and tell stories. Both Jack and Bessie wear glasses with Polaroid lenses. The sun on this land is ever-present, and it damages unprotected eyes.

Neither Jack nor Bessie ever attended school, though they have learned to sign their names. When Bessie shops at Basha's grocery store in Tuba City, she asks a clerk to write out a check for the proper amount. She then signs it. She keeps the receipt, and at the end of the month Ella balances her checkbook. Bessie has a credit card too, which she seldom uses. Ella has instructed her not to charge more than $20 on it. Every month, Ella also balances her father's checkbook and writes out checks to pay his bills. Bessie has her own checking account, into which she receives payments from Jack's Social Security.

Although Jack can't write, he leaves messages for Ella by drawing pictures. For example, if he's going away for a day and he wants Ella to look after his livestock for him, he'll leave her a note with a picture of a sun with rays—this means morning. Then he'll draw a calf and a bottle, a chicken and a feed bag, and a corral, filled with sheep, whose gate swings open. This means he would like Ella to go to his house to bottle-feed the calf, pour grain for the chickens, and let the sheep out of the corral. If he's going to be gone another day, he'll draw a line, then the calf again, and the sheep corral with its gate closed, so she'll make sure to pen up the animals for him at night.

Sometimes if he needs money, he'll leave a note for Ella asking for a loan. She has taught him to write the dollar sign, and he knows numbers. Ella also at times leaves notes for him in which she asks to borrow money. One day in the middle of August, Ella left her dad a note showing a schoolhouse, a pair of pants, a shirt, and a sock. She wrote the amount of money she needed, and drew a picture of the famous hole in the rock in Window Rock, the Navajo capital, and a float from a parade. And she added three "number" signs—"###." That meant she would pay him back on the third day of September, the month when the Navajo Fair takes place in Window Rock. She needed to borrow money to buy her daughter, Nell, some school clothes.

Unfortunately, the day she left him this note, he left her a note at her house with a picture of his tractor and a dollar figure—he needed money for his monthly payment. Both had found themselves short before the end of the month. "He was just laughing about it," she said. "Same day, we're both broke."

Bessie's pocketbook is her file cabinet. In it, wrapped in a rubber band, are all the official communications she gets from the government, such as notices about livestock fees, notices that her stock has increased over her permit level, and so on. (Navajos pay the government for grazing rights, and the number of animals they can run is regulated by the government, a pair of facts the Navajos find hard to comprehend.) In her handbag, Bessie also carries cards with her children's birthdates, Social Security numbers, and census numbers. She can't read any of them, but she knows where they are if she needs them. Her children can read the letters to her, because all but one has graduated from high school, most have taken college courses or completed training, three have undergraduate college degrees, and a fourth, the youngest and most scholarly, is currently enrolled as an engineering student at the University of Arizona.

Ella says that her mother knows by the look of the papers what they're for and which she can throw away. "I don't know why she keeps them in there, but she says, 'You never know when they'll ask you.' "

✳

It is unclear how long the Navajos have lived in the Southwest. The structures their ancestors made (and that the Navajos still make today)—huts of wood and mud—deteriorated rapidly, leaving behind little material for reliable dating. It is generally believed that the people who would become Native Americans migrated from Asia to Canada when the Bering Strait was still a landmass, and made their way south, in different groups, in waves, each pushing the other farther, until the different tribes populated all of North, South, and Central America. The earliest archaeological site generally attributed to the Navajos dates to 1541 and is near Gobernador Knob in northern New Mexico— one of the sacred mountain ranges of Dinetah.

Some anthropologists believe the Dine may have entered the Southwest as early as A.D. 800, while others maintain they arrived as late as the Spanish in the mid-1500s. Their route of entry is also a matter of debate, some believing they came down through the Rockies, others that they first went south to the Great Plains and then west, still others that they entered from the northern Great Plains. But what is known is that the people who appeared around the Pueblo people, with long hair, ill-clad in skins and woven plant fibers, were impoverished hunter-gatherers, descendants of the Athabaskan people who still live in Canada and Alaska, and that they were "among the most primitive tribes on the continent." Before the arrival of the Europeans, the Athabaskans lived in the north woods, where they hunted caribou and moose and trapped fish. "Their homes were shelters of poles, covered with bark and earth. Most of them made no pottery or baskets. They led a wandering life, with little organized government. Their ceremonies were only the few, irregular ones which called the wild game. Their medicine men were solitary visionaries, with no established ritual."

But the Athabaskans possessed a wide imagination and openness to the new that led them to learn quickly from the other cultures they encountered during their migrations. Their meeting with the ancient Pueblo people had a profound impact on their culture, for it is believed that from the Pueblos the Navajos learned to plant corn and learned or relearned to weave.

Eventually, over years of contact and intermarriage, the Navajos would adopt elements of the Pueblos' elaborate ceremonial system and learn production of such items as pottery, pipes, and canteens. The meeting with this continent's "original apartment dwellers," the Pueblos, is recorded in Navajo myth as awe-inspiring—people living in grand, mysterious, multiroomed stone houses built into canyon walls, growing fields of corn, with a religious system full of costume, drama, and parade.

Eventually, the Navajos too began to settle down as farmers, separating from their more warlike cousins the Apaches. They were named by the Spanish the *Apaches de Navaju*, from Tewa words—*Apachu*, meaning "enemy" or "stranger," and *navahu*, meaning "a large arroyo in which there are planted fields." The Spanish knew them as "very great farmers" (*muy grandes labradores*).

In the late sixteenth and early seventeenth centuries, the Navajos also gained knowledge from the Spanish, particularly about the precious horses, oxen, and sheep the latter brought with them, animals that would transform the life of the Navajos. From the Spaniards the Navajos learned to herd livestock, ride horses, and make silver jewelry.

Poor in material culture, the Navajos developed a rich symbolism in their religious system and a deep appreciation of knowledge. They appropriated from the people they encountered whatever they found useful—customs, ideas, technology, myth. The Navajos didn't take the objects they admired (except the livestock); they took the methods of production, the ideas, the skills, and made new products or adapted ideas until they were uniquely their own. This ability has given them a reputation as a most flexible people, people who can learn any skill they are shown, and who can survive any deprivation. They are really a composite of people—influenced in both blood and learning by all the cultures they met and married into during their journey to and around the Southwest.

Ruth Underhill describes the People around A.D. 1500:

From . . . hints of myth and fact, it is possible to realize the hardy mixture comprising the Navajo tribe—huntsmen from the north, used to privation and fighting; civilized Pueblo farmers, trained to industry; wild warlike Utes; and wanderers from the western desert, skilled in basket making and the finding of food! Every way of life was represented among them, every physical form and every mental attitude. It is no wonder that such people were open to new suggestions and had the energy to try everything. Here was no settled group of conservatives moving along the same channels for centuries. Considering this background, it is not surprising that the Navajos, within the next few hundred years, remade their way of life not only once [after the arrival of the Spaniards] but twice [the second after their capture, imprisonment, and release from Fort Sumner at the end of the Indian wars]. They found new ways to support themselves and evolved a new mythology, with pageantry as magnificent as any known to Indians. And the Navajos are still changing.

Although they are known for their remarkable adaptability and have shown great interest throughout their history in absorbing into their culture whatever they found useful in others while maintaining what is essentially Navajo, now that the children are uniformly educated in the white men's schools, change is taking place at a far faster rate. Today there are ceremonies so sacred that only those who have never attended school may observe them. "The ceremonies are too strong," says Ella. "If you've gone to school, the old people say, you are too fragile to see them."

The old people see that the young ones have been changed by their education. Their thinking is different—weaker on spiritual matters but stronger in matters of technology, the particular gift of the white man. Jack and Bessie know that education will help their children get jobs so they can support their families, and they have encouraged their children to complete high school and go on to college. But they also believe that knowledge of the white ways has hurt their children by taking them away from Navajo spiritual life. Scientific, rational thinking and the doubt it has engendered and elevated, some might say, into a belief in and of itself, have weakened the Navajo way of thinking.

But if the old people keep the young ones away from certain rites, they would seem in effect to be willing those ceremonies to disappear. This satisfies some Navajo prophecies, which hold that this world will inevitably be replaced by another—in the pattern established in the stories of the Creation. The current world already constitutes its fifth incarnation (fourth in some versions).

The older people seem somewhat resigned to the new rate of change, in part because of the prophecies, but also because they know they cannot fight the U.S. government when it says the children must go to school. At first, they did. Around the turn of the century, both Navajos and Hopis hid their children from the school man. But government agents then sent the parents to prison and tracked down the children, until the Indians realized this was a fight they could not win.

4

"My Mom Always Says,
'Never Trust a White Person' "

Ella pushes back her dinette chair and walks across the kitchen
to the Mr. Coffee machine, scoops a few tablespoonfuls from
a red bag marked "Gourmet Coffee" into a paper filter, slides
the filter mechanism into the machine and flips the switch. She
stands in the kitchen of the trailer in Tuba City in which she
and her husband and three children live, a few minutes' drive
from the cornfield, twenty minutes from her parents' place.

Ella returns to the table and sits down. She is forty years
old, short, about five feet two, and walks with a slight limp as
the result of a congenital hip displacement. Her face is wide,
with high cheekbones, brilliant white teeth, and movie-star
eyes. Her skin is light brown, her lips gracefully sculpted and
the color of berries. She wears white pants, a white and pastel
short-sleeved blouse, a snowflake pendant at her throat, and
ruby-red pumps. Her hair is cut short and permed into waves.
Ella's eyes are by turns watchful and merry.

Outside, row after row of white trailers sit on cul-de-sacs
that are sprinkled with basketball hoops and small gardens.
Tuba City is one of a handful of urban areas on the Navajo
reservation where people live in modern houses on suburban-

looking streets, or in trailer parks, with electricity, running water, and TV. The town, the center of commerce and administration for the reservation's western half, lies sixty miles south of the Glen Canyon Dam and the southern tip of Lake Powell, and eighty miles north of Flagstaff. It boasts gas stations and supermarkets, schools, a bank, movie theater, restaurants, and a post office.

"I brought my mom some of this coffee," Ella says, "and I made it in her old enamel pot. The first time my mom tasted it, she spit it out on the ground. She thought the coffee had gone bad. Then I told her it was *gourmet* coffee. I saw her a few minutes later pouring herself another cup, and tasting it, kind of tentative-like. Later on, I heard her tell a friend of hers she was drinking *gourmet coffee*." Ella laughs.

Ella's trailer development is set up on the top of a hill overlooking the center of town, the old Bureau of Indian Affairs compound. Nearby is the original BIA boarding school, a massive, forbidding red brick edifice, now abandoned, in which Ella received her first, unhappy introductions to the ways of white people. The school was built along a street now shaded by large cottonwood trees and lined with red brick Victorian houses sporting white painted porches. Driving into the BIA compound is like passing into a town from Kansas that has been dropped, intact, by a strong tornado, in the middle of the desert. It feels like a back lot on a movie set, so different are its buildings from the rest of those in Tuba City, so different is its landscaping, for nowhere else in town are there seeded lawns and mature trees. Now the compound includes a primary day school, a hospital, housing for the doctors and teachers, and tribal legal offices.

Ella's windowsill is covered with small ceramic and metal animal figures. The Navajos place a great value on animals, in part because of their importance in the Creation myths. The figures are rounded and serene, different from the Zuni fetishes they resemble, also carved models of animals, but more artistic, symbolic, often decorated with bits of coral or jet or crystal. The fetishes are believed to carry powers characteristic of the species they depict. A mountain lion, for example, set up high, will protect you from your enemies.

On the kitchen walls Ella has hung traditional Navajo domestic utensils: a thick bunch of stiff grasses from the broom plant, tied in the middle, which makes up a traditional Navajo hairbrush, and stirring sticks, for corn mush, made from twigs of the black greasewood tree. Navajo legends maintain that hunger won't enter a home that has stirring sticks; the hunger is afraid of the sticks, which it perceives as arrows that can kill it.

"My mom always says, 'Never trust a white person,' " comments Ella. "She says when you go to school, the white man teaches you to think with your head, and then you eventually forget how to think with your heart. And when that comes about, that's when you start losing your identity as an Indian, and you start feeling ashamed of your people and ashamed to speak your own language. That's when the damage has been done, when you really start thinking with your head instead of your heart.

"But then my dad says, 'There are a lot of white people who have deep hearts, and they know how to think with their hearts.'

"My mom always says, 'Well, I never trusted a white person because it seems like no matter how hard I try, I've always found something I didn't like in them. There was always something that they wanted to take from me. And they never gave me anything back.' "

Jack has spent much of his life working with whites. He recently retired from the Navajo Power Plant in Page, Arizona, where he earned $24,000 a year as a custodian. That salary put his income at three or four times that of the Navajo median, and he appreciated the benefits that contact with whites brought him and his family. He even likes TV, says Ella, especially boxing and wrestling, and animal cartoons, because it reminds him of the Creation stories.

Bessie does not like the TV. She believes it causes nightmares and sleepwalking in children. She thinks that watching soap operas leads to divorce because people pattern their lives on the meaningless interactions they see on the screen. When Bessie is at Ella's house, she will sometimes watch nature shows on the PBS station, but if she should later become sick, she'll likely blame the television for having shown her a picture of an animal that is taboo for Navajos. Bessie's world is dominated by the myths and stories and beliefs she was brought up with, and this way of looking at the world insulates her somewhat from the ways of the white man. Her very language prevents her from understanding certain concepts (primarily those applying to business, law, or technology).

Bessie has had less contact with whites than Jack, yet she bears a lasting distrust. She won't even go to the Indian Health Service Hospital in Tuba City, where the Navajos get free health care. She thinks the doctors make you sicker. Ella says that the only reason Bessie gave birth to her babies in the hospital is that Jack packed her up and drove her there.

Bessie does not like the education her children are getting in the white man's schools. Ella says, "She said, 'Why do you want to learn about the white man's history? Why do you want to know about the wars the white man has? The white man's afraid to teach history the way it should be taught. The way he is, even today, he is trying to get rid of the Indian person because the Indian person has always been on this land.' "

Ella says, "Sometimes I wonder, how does she know all these things? How does she know these things are being taught in school? And I asked her that, and she said, 'I hear you talk about it. When the children bring their homework home, and just by looking through the pages, I see, and I ask them, 'What is this?' And they'll respond and say, 'That was a certain war and that happened here in the U.S.' And my mom tells me, 'I see the things the white man teaches in you, a lot of the things they do and the way they are, I see it in you, so that's how I know.' "

Although pieces of the modern world impinge on them every day through the televisions in their children's homes, the magazines stacked in stores, news on the Navajo Nation's radio station, their grandchildren's homework, in the end these things affect Jack and Bessie very little. They are not interested in the modern world; they prefer to keep their distance from it.

"I once asked my mom, 'What is a human being?' " says Ella. "And she said, 'A human being is a person that thinks with his heart, that thinks [of] good all the time, that has respect for life around him, that has respect for even the smallest rock. A human being is a person that thinks that the rock will talk to him and teach him a lesson—the smallest thing that Mother Nature has made available for us. A human being must understand why we are here on earth, why the plants are growing, why we have the four seasons, why we have the heavens. That is a human being, somebody that understands nature, somebody that thinks he's not any better than anybody else, that thinks that everybody is equal no matter what color they are or what language they speak. That is a human being.' "

Bessie also told Ella that since she is a teacher, she should focus on teaching white people how to be human beings.

"Maybe the white man's way of teaching is not for the Indian people," she told Ella. "Maybe you can start a school where you teach white children how to be Indian children. When you start teaching white children how to think like Indians, maybe we'll have human beings again. Then maybe your children and the white children will learn how to get along in this world. Maybe their world will be better than the way things are today. Seems like human beings—five-fingered people—are fighting among each other. In our legends that wasn't supposed to be. It is one of our prophecies: when these things get started, there's going to be an end to life."

Ella goes on: "My mom says, 'I don't want life to end. I

want my children to grow and reproduce. And I want my children to be able to get along with the white children, to be able to live like human beings and learn how to share and get along.' "

＊

Although Bessie says she has never met a white person who hasn't tried to take something from her, she is the not-infrequent recipient of charity from various groups, whose members send food, clothes, and other supplies to the reservation. Bessie recently received boxes of supplies from a group of women in Salt Lake City, Utah, who are interested in helping out the Navajo elderly. The sponsoring groups tried to find out what Bessie and others needed, but communication is sometimes difficult. In one package, they sent her Vicks VapoRub, aspirin, Band-Aids, Noxzema, and panty hose. Bessie has no need for panty hose—she wears socks and sturdy shoes. But, waste not, want not: she used the nylons to tie up the sheep.

Bessie let the women know she would like some socks, and they sent her woolen socks, which Bessie put in the clothes washer and dryer at the laundromat in town. They shrank to children's size, so Bessie undid them and used the yarn for her weaving.

Navajo skirts are layered and flounced, and require quite a bit of material. When Ella told the Utah women that each skirt requires about six yards, they were flabbergasted and wanted to know what the skirts looked like. The Navajo women wear blouses made of velveteen, which require two yards. Ella wrote to the Utah women to let them know her mother's favorite colors: blue, turquoise, brown, and purple. To help out, Ella makes a lot of her mother's clothing with her electric sewing machine.

The women sent the packages UPS, which doesn't deliver to the remote campsites of the reservation, so the packages were routed to Flagstaff, a ninety-minute drive, where Ella and her husband Dennis tried to track them down, but failed to find them. The packages were eventually returned to the senders. This generated a few telephone calls, during which the Utah women tried to find out more about the Navajos.

They want to know what kind of shoes Bessie wore.

Recalls Ella, "I told them my mom prefers tennis shoes, black tennis shoes. And the lady was surprised; she said, 'Well, what does she wear when she goes out?' And I said tennis shoes!" Ella laughs. "And she said, 'What about leather shoes?' and I said, 'She prefers tennis shoes, the kind you buy for $2.99 or $3.99 at K Mart.' "

The women seemed to have no idea of Bessie's way of life, or of the fact that her feet seldom touched anything that was not blown with red dust. They told Ella they had been to Sears and found some nice pumps on sale. Wouldn't she like a pair of pumps for a special occasion? All Ella could do was laugh.

"They asked what kind of hair stuff does she use. And I said, 'Send her a skein of white yarn from the store, the real thin kind, or you can send her a skein of beige. She uses that to tie her hair.' I said, 'You can send her rubber bands too, 'cause the grandkids, they tie their hair with rubber bands and [use] a steel brush, like the kind you find at animal stores, that's the kind they use.' Bessie uses yucca to wash her hair, and sometimes shampoo, if she showers at Ella's place. The Navajo women used to use Borax, the laundry detergent, which caused many of them to lose hair on the tops of their heads.

"Oh, they wanted to know what kind of stationery she liked too.

"I said, 'My mom don't read and write.' I said, 'If you send her stationery, she'll probably use it to light the fire.' " Ella laughs again. "The woman just laughed on the other line.

"Oh, they wanted to know what kind of scent she likes—perfume. And I said the only time she uses perfume is when it's really hot and there are a lot of mosquitoes and she has to herd sheep. She puts perfume on when she goes out so the mosquitoes don't bother her. Or, I said, she puts it on the dogs and the cats so the mosquitoes won't bother them. The lady was really laughing then.

"Then she asked what kind of china would she like. And I told her she likes the plated kind, the enamel kind, cast-iron dishes."

Finally, boxes did arrive, in care of some Mormon college students driving this way. The women had also sent along water jugs and coolers, which Ella had informed them were much prized by the Navajos for keeping water and soda pop cool for a few hours. Ella was surprised to see that they sent Coleman ice chests and water jugs, very expensive, good-quality items.

"I told my mom, 'You have to really be careful of these; they're real expensive stuff. They're really expensive, you have to really take care of them.' " So Bessie put them in her closet, with her other treasured possessions. Bessie has a trunk into which she places special items. In it she has some china cups sent by an acquaintance, some small animal models, and a copy of *The Color Purple*, signed by its author, Alice Walker, who gave Bessie the book after buying a rug from her.

Some food items sent by the Utah ladies met with great suspicion from Bessie, as does most unfamiliar food. Pasta went immediately to Ella, who brought it to work as art supplies for her students. (Ella disapproves of the kids using corn for art, because corn should be treated with respect and not wasted.) "These people don't eat pasta," she said about the traditional people like her mother. But Ella likes trying new food, and she boiled up some of the noodles her students didn't spray-paint. They were greenish.

"It tasted awful. I think they were natural foods or something," she said.

The Utah women also sent dried peas and beans, some of which went to the sheep. They also sent bulk flour that wasn't otherwise identified. Bessie mixed some of it with their regular Blue Bird white flour. The rest they gave to their Hopi friend Rita, who lives in the nearby Hopi village of Moencopi. "We gave it to Rita to figure out," said Ella.

Bessie was grateful for some canned goods and soybean oil, which the Navajo women use to fry bread—they are substituting oil now for the lard they formerly used. But the most inappropriate offering in the care package was perhaps the most poignant.

Ella says, "They sent her this real weird-looking jacket, really weird. It's a brand-new jacket. I guess it's one of those fashion, designer jackets. It doesn't look like anything you would wear here. It said, 'Made in Italy.' It's pigskin, like leather. I thought it was really nice, but I wouldn't wear it. They would have thought I was Hollywood or something.

"Nell says it was ugly. But it had a fur collar. I took that fur off and gave it to this Anglo friend of mine."

Ella gave the jacket to her mother, minus the fur collar. After inspecting it thoroughly, Bessie knew just what to do with it. She spread it out on the bottom of a box, which she placed in the sheep corral. This was winter, and the lambs were coming. After they were born, they were separated from the sheep and placed in the box, where they snuggled up against the pigskin jacket imported from Italy.

5

"There's No Such Thing as Love, at Least Romantic Love"

"What is the Navajo concept of love?" I ask Ella.

Ella bursts into laughter. We are sitting in the living room of her trailer. She laughs and laughs again. She looks me right in the eye, adjusts her glasses, shakes her head, then says, "Well, how would I put it? The Navajo concept of love. Hmm." She pauses, then says, "There's no such thing as love, at least romantic love." She looks at me again and laughs gleefully.

Ella's twelve-year-old daughter, Danielle, known as Nell, opens the front door and walks in. She has long black hair and light skin, like her mother. Her bangs are teased and sprayed and stand up several inches—the style of the moment on the reservation. Last year her hair was permed and wavy. Navajo girls all gave each other home perms, which not only made their hair curly but turned it several shades lighter. Nell has now let the wave grow out, and her hair is once again straight and shiny black. She wears khaki shorts, a matching V-necked tee-shirt and sandals. In the last months, her appearance has changed dramatically from that of a kittenish young girl to a teenager. Her features are slightly out of proportion; her face has been changing so much in the last year that symmetry has not quite kept up. Her voice is still that of a little girl, however, high-pitched and inflected with a careful, childlike pronunciation. She is carrying a paper bag from Taco Bell and a large soft drink. Her facial expressions have lately become those of classic adolescence—baleful aggravation and astonishment, usually directed at the doltish remarks of parents or other adults. Her brother Kimo, twenty-one, is now in Tucson, attending college, and Buzz, eighteen, is just finishing Tuba City high school.

Nell stands at the counter and pulls from the paper bag a box of nachos. She opens the box delicately, careful not to get a drop of grease on anything but her fingertips. Nell is a very fastidious girl who spends a good portion of the day in the shower or before the bathroom mirror. When she spotted her first pimple last fall, Ella tells me, she refused to go to school.

"Nell, what is love to you?" her mother asks, unable to hold back her mirth.

Nell's eyes grow wide; she looks her mother straight in the face and says, "Gaaa, Mom. I'm not answering that question." After a few moments, she says, "I don't know; I just hear the word all the time."

Ella asks her, "What do you think love is between Daddy and me?"

"Pfaaw," says Nell, without missing a beat. "There isn't any love at all." She looks over at her mother to check her reaction to this tease. Her mother laughs harder, looking at me.

"I don't know," says Nell, "being friends?"

"When you think about having a boyfriend, what feelings do you have?" I ask Nell.

Nell pauses for about a minute, looks irritated. "I don't understand the question."

"She doesn't have a boyfriend yet, so she doesn't know," says Ella. "She's scared of boys."

Nell is a powwow dancer, and has competed in the pan-Indian dancing competitions since she was six years old.

Powwows provide an opportunity for Indians of all ages and tribes to meet and dance traditional steps and in traditional costumes. In the summer, powwows take place every weekend across the country and in Canada. The youngsters can choose to dance whatever style they want—northern, southern, fancy, traditional. Nell began as a fancy shawl dancer, and now is a jingle dancer, a style she learned from the Ojibway people of Canada after a visit there last summer.

Ella makes all Nell's costumes on her sewing machine, and used to bead her moccasins and leggings as well, though Nell is now doing her own beading. Powwow dancers are judged on their dress, their dancing style, and their knowledge of the songs. Nell spends hours watching videotapes of powwows, learning dance steps, memorizing different songs, getting tips on beading and sewing and decorating costumes. All Nell's work and preparation has paid off: she has just been selected as Western Agency Powwow Princess, a distinction that allows her to wear the beaded Western Agency crown for a year to all her powwows and to make presentations and appearances across the reservation.

Ella explains that at a recent local powwow, the head male dancer was supposed to dance with the head lady dancer, who was Nell, in the owl dance, which required them to hold hands. The man, who was about thirty, approached Ella to say with some bewilderment that he couldn't find Nell.

"She was scared of him," says Ella.

"Oh, Mom, he smelled," Nell says.

"What did he smell like?" asks Ella.

"He smelled like a man."

"I told her it was an honor for them to ask her to be the head lady dancer," says Ella, trying to stop giggling. "And if he's the head man dancer, she should dance with him. She's not going home with him." Ella speaks with a warm understanding of her daughter. She teases her, but with restraint. Although she and Dennis keep a very close watch on their daughter to protect her from the many threats they perceive around her—alcohol, drugs, gangs, friends who have not been brought up in traditional families—they never criticize her personality or who she is. One might say she was spoiled, if she weren't so determined to be a good and faithful daughter. As the only daughter, and the daughter of an eldest daughter, she, like Ella, is heir to the family's teachings—its knowledge of Navajo ways. Navajo culture is matrilineal and matrilocal. Inheritance passes through the women.

Nell was a much-desired child. In fact, Ella was told not to have another child after Buzz, her second son. However, Ella became pregnant again, and after a difficult birth, delivered a daughter. Nell has always been treated as a great gift by her parents, and her name, Danielle, is a special one—a combination of Dan, Dennis's nickname, and Ella.

"Have you ever had a crush?" I ask her.

"I don't know what a crush is."

And with that, Nell brings the discussion of love to a close. She eats her nachos, and changes the subject. I suspect the issue of boys is becoming more important in her life. Her mother told me that last fall she got so mad at a boy who was flirting with her that she wound up and punched him.

The trailer door, which opens with the sound of plastic peeling, opens again, and Dennis, who is forty-two, walks in. His face breaks into a large grin. He is of medium height and build, with dark skin, long, jet-black hair and warm, merry brown eyes. He has a savvy grace. He is a counselor at the Tuba City elementary school and is much loved and respected by the children. He is cool, though, too. He keeps up with what's happening on the reservation as well as in the outside culture. He wears a leather jacket and a Washington Redskins cap.

Dennis is a generous father and a hard worker, who always has plans and ambitions and projects afoot. Last summer, he was a disc jockey at a local radio station, mixing tapes of his favorite sixties music at home and bringing them into work and introducing the songs with a smooth, informed patter.

Today he's planning to drive Buzz to the mall in Flagstaff. Buzz and his girlfriend, Sonya, have an appointment tomorrow to sit for a photographic portrait at Basha's supermarket, and Buzz wants to buy a new silk shirt. Ella's living room is hung with studio portraits of her children, nieces, and nephews. Navajos love displaying photographs of their families.

When his kids want something, Dennis tries to provide. He encourages them to explore their own interests, though he urges them away from alcohol and drugs, a scourge on the reservation that leads to one or two deaths every weekend, mostly by drunken pedestrians getting hit by cars. A Vietnam veteran, he had his own bouts with alcohol, and he knows liquor is problematic for many Indian people. After he graduated from Northern Arizona University in 1986, and after landing a job as a counselor for a Navajo agency that oversees the care of handicapped Navajo children, Dennis reveled in his ability to provide for his children, buying bikes and televisions and stereos and clothes. Today he is a counselor for "at risk" children at Tuba City elementary school—children who are at risk of dropping out or at risk of abuse at home. Because he was raised in Flagstaff, and both of his parents had some education, he is much savvier than Ella in the ways of the outside world. He likes rock 'n' roll and has a pretty good collection of oldies, sixties hits. Ella laughingly admits she can't tell one from the other.

"I asked Danielle, 'What is love to you?' " Ella tells Dennis, looking interested in his reaction, but again dissolving in laughter. " 'What is love between Daddy and me?' And then she just laughed."

Nell says, "Love doesn't look right with you guys. It looks better with younger people, not old people like you."

＊

"Come on," says Ella. "Let's go see Harry Williams."

Ella loves going out on adventures, and loves especially to

visit relatives. Harry Williams is the chapter president of Coal Mine Mesa, and a clan relative who was brought up with Ella's father. The Navajo reservation is divided into 110 chapters, or communities, each of which has its own local officials, who run the chapter house, which provides showers, classrooms, and jobs, like ten-day weaving projects, or opportunities to acquire and plant fruit trees. In addition to electing its own officers, each chapter also sends delegates to the Navajo Tribal Council, which operates like the U.S. Congress in the three-branch system of the Navajo tribal government.

A clan is a grouping of families with a common ancestry. One's clan determines whom one can marry and whom one cannot, and it defines familial responsibilities. Clan relations also determine whom one can tease and be teased by. They indicate the obligations and responsibilities that order traditional Navajo life. The kin relations define who is a relative, and the golden rule in Navajo life applies, most significantly, to relatives.

A child takes the clan of his mother. He is "born for" the clan of his father. One is not permitted to marry someone who is a member of one's own clan or one's father's clan. Teasing is allowed toward (and from) members of a clan you are allowed to marry into. For example, Ella knows a man who has a field near hers who is the same clan as her father's paternal grandfather. This is a clan into which she could marry if she weren't already married. If she is in the field too long working beside this man, Ella's father will tease her by saying, "You'd better go home and start making tortillas." The bread he refers to is called in-law bread. It would be offered as a payment by the woman for the occasion of having sneaked looks at this man.

When Ella and Nell are at a powwow, Ella will tease her daughter about men who are members of her grandfather's clan. "I tease Nell with people that belong to my father's clan, the clan that I was born for," says Ella, "which is the Salt Clan. When we go to powwows, there are several people that I call 'father,' because they belong to the Salt Clan. And I'll tease her, 'Don't be looking at my father, that's why you keep getting out of step.' Or I tell her, 'Don't keep looking at my dad, he's worth a lot of tortillas.' So I tease her that way so she knows that that person is her *che'*—grandfather—by clan. And that it's okay if she marries into that clan."

Through this kind of teasing, children learn whom they may associate with, whom they may marry, and what their responsibilities are toward different family members.

Harry's house is only a few miles from Ella's place. We drive carefully through the winding streets, because after dark one must be on the lookout for drunk drivers here. Although we peer through the headlights for danger, the air is calm, the rolling dirt roads quiet, the shadows soft. Harry's home is large, brown, with a peaked roof. Inside the metal screen door, it has the feel of the houses of many upwardly mobile Navajos. It is furnished with couches and stuffed chairs and dark wood shelves displaying trophies and Indian crafts. The rooms are carpeted with shag rugs and decorated with portraits of family members. Yellows and browns predominate. The walls are finished with thin wood paneling, the house roomy and neat.

Harry Williams shows us to a small den, whose main wall is hung with a Navajo rug. We sit down, and Ella asks him what love means to a Navajo.

Harry is a barrel-chested man of medium height. His face is gentle, his hands chubby and expressive. He smiles, looks embarrassed, laughs with Ella. He won't speak until Ella prompts him again.

"In the traditional way, I guess," he says, "there's really no such thing as love, [the way] the white man says. Love is how you provide." Harry speaks slowly, in a low, gentle voice, and stops at the faintest sign of interruption.

"You have to depend on one another to make a living for your kids and yourself, make sure that you have a place to live, make sure there's fire, that there's water, make sure there's food and that you live in harmony. I don't think in the earlier days there was such a thing as hugging and kissing and things like that. It's just that you make a living together, have faith in one another, respect one another, trust one another. That's all that really mattered."

In accord with this philosophy of marriage, people didn't choose their own mates; marriages were arranged by relatives, usually grandmothers. In the old days, men could take more than one wife, as long as they could support their separate families. Harry won't say much beyond this, though he says that there always were cases in which a couple happened to get along very well together. They would show their closeness by doing things together. "They would herd sheep together all the time. But they're not out there kissing one another in public."

Harry does say that bonds between parents and children are immensely strong. "I would say the majority of white people say once you're eighteen, you're on your own. They'll kick you out the door—'Go find a place to live and whatever.' But us Indians, like me, I'm fifty-four years old. When I get a headache, I go over to my mother." Harry laughs. "And I want her approval on certain things, like [I would] a medicine man.

"As long as your mother or father is alive, you really don't have no say-so. Until they're both gone. And then you have the say-so. And that's just the way it goes. If they're still alive, you still have to get their approval, even if you're eighty years old and your mother's a hundred years old. You'll go over there and make sure they're aware of what you're going to do. I still go to my mother for advice." He laughs heartily but shyly. He looks slightly embarrassed by his admission.

✳

Later that night, after a dinner of oven-broiled chicken rubbed with salt, salad, and corn, Ella talks once again about love.

"It's like Harry said," says Ella. "You show love by taking care of one another."

"Respect, reciprocal respect," says Dennis, sitting on the

sofa in the living room. Behind him, the walls are decorated with a large photograph of Nell, at age six, dancing, and a portrait of Kimo, their eldest boy, and his Hopi girlfriend, both of whom are in college in Tucson. Also hanging on the wall paneling is an oil painting of a Navajo medicine man, and some Hopi baskets. On another wall are hung several cradleboards from different tribes, a collection Ella is building. There are also several beautiful large fans made of eagle feathers, with beaded handles, fans that Dennis uses for peyote meetings and when he serves as master of ceremonies at powwows. The living room is filled with plants. Of course, this being an American home, a huge television sits in front of the sofa.

"What about that tingly feeling?"

"I think the feelings are there," says Dennis. "We just don't say things like, 'I love you from the bottom of my heart.' " He rolls his eyes.

"Dennis and I were talking about it; we've been together for twenty years," says Ella. "That's a long time." Dennis giggles. Ella adds, "We're going to have to have a good fight before twenty-one comes around."

"You've never had a fight?"

"Nope," says Ella. "None. That's why our kids say we have a boring marriage. Nothing exciting. I guess their friends talk about their parents fighting. Buzz says, 'You guys are so boring. You don't even get mad, and you don't even argue.' He says, 'My friends' parents, they beat each other up.' "

"Why don't you fight?"

"I don't know. I guess we communicate pretty well."

Ella and Dennis are immensely respectful of each other. They don't interrupt; one listens carefully while the other speaks. The Navajos understand the art of conversation better than most Anglos. They know how to listen. They don't reply immediately. They think about what they've heard and sometimes say nothing. Later, they may come back to you and offer a comment. Weeks or months later, they might let you know that they've been thinking about what you said and may then offer a thought. They think first, talk later.

"That love concept," says Dennis, "We don't have a word for it like the white man uses it. But it's there. It includes just being there for the other person, companionship. Just doing things together, that love is there."

Over the past twenty years, the longest they have been separated was four days when Dennis went to a conference in Minneapolis. During that time, Ella asked Nell to sleep with her. "I wasn't exactly lonely," she says, "but that companionship wasn't there. I had my kids, but he wasn't there. We've always been together; we do everything together. In some families, one person goes to Flagstaff and does the shopping herself. We always do things together. I guess we depend on one another. When I need something or when I have a bad dream, I tell Dennis. The other night, I fell off the bed," Ella breaks into laughter. "And I didn't know I'd fallen off the bed. Dennis said, 'Get back on the bed.' "

Dennis says, " 'Geez, what are you doing,' I thought."

"It was really weird," says Ella. "I'm not used to working full time, and I am exhausted when I come home from work. It seems like my blood is really weak. I just lie down, and the kids do everything. Nell will be getting something ready to eat, and Buzz will clean up. The kids in the school were really hyper around that time because we had a lot of rain. And I was in the classroom with them most of the time by myself. So I was just really tired.

"I was sleeping at the edge of the bed, I guess, and I must have turned. The next day I thought about it. I thought I dreamt I fell off the bed. And for some reason, I kept thinking about it, which is really unusual. And I didn't say anything about it until Dennis asked me, 'Did you know you fell off the bed last night?' " Ella laughs.

"And then the rest of the night I lay in a really weird way, with my legs under me and my butt in the air like a little kid.

I did that when I was a child; I remember it was very comfortable for me, sleeping like that."

Ella brings the conversation back to love. "We're like security for one another."

"And in the Navajo way, there is no such thing as flowers and candy and romantic candle-lit dinners?"

"One time he said *that* to me," says Ella. "He brought me some flowers. I guess he wanted to see what I would say when he said, 'I love you, and that's why I brought you some flowers.' "

Ella stops, blinks, laughs again. "I looked at him and started laughing." Ella laughs uproariously.

"She started laughing," says Dennis, looking a tad deflated. "I was doing it in a way to say white people do this; I wonder how it would make Ella feel?"

"Because, you know," says Ella, giggling, "we're always imitating white people."

Ella is joking, but she's also telling the truth. She knows that although she is deeply rooted in her own culture, she is always looking at herself through another lens, the lens of the white man.

Neither of them mentions that part of what holds them together is the tradition that binds them, the tradition that led to their arranged marriage when Ella was twenty and Dennis twenty-two, the teachings that offer them guidance, and the family that surrounds them and offers them help. But the new generation is different. Although Ella's children were brought up with the same ethics, with the same values, they are closer to the Anglo world. Their first language was English, and therefore their minds are organized around a very different logic and system of thought than are Ella's and her parents'. Further, they have attended Anglo schools for much of their lives, whereas Dennis and Ella lived in Phoenix and Flagstaff for work and school, and have grown up in the white world. And so, also, love is different. Buzz and his girlfriend "have their little love quarrels, stuff like that," says Ella.

" 'Do you love me?' 'You don't love me.' They say that to each other all the time," says Dennis. "TV, that's their generation."

✳

"In the Anglo way," Ella says, "when you speak to your children, you say, 'I love you.' It's like that; it's something that's said in the open all the time. In our way, you show your love to your children not by calling them by name, but by saying *shiyazhe*, 'my little one', and when you say that, you're looking at a mirror of yourself. Because that person came from you. You're looking at a mirror of your inner self when you say *shiyazhe* or *sheewe*, which means 'my baby.' They say when you use those words—*sheewe, shiyazhe*—that whatever you ask of your children, they'll do, and your children will always listen to you because they're very powerful words. Very spiritual words, when you say that. Today we don't say that as much as we should. And that's why our children don't listen to us, and talk back to us.

"I do a lot of thinking about these things, how I talk to my sons, when I talk Navajo to them and how they react to it. And when Danielle's around here I say, 'Danielle, can you wash the dishes?' And she says, 'Mom, I just did my nails' or 'My nails are too soft.' Or she'll say, 'I have a lot of homework.' She always has an excuse. But when I say, '*Shiyazhe*, help me do the dishes; can you help me by doing the dishes?,' she'll do it.

"I thought about it when my boys would get in trouble. I used to talk to them in English all the time, and you just don't do that for this reason. I talk Navajo to them now, because my mom says, 'Talk Navajo to them.' And I talk to them now, I call them *shiyazhe, sheewe*, and I say *ayou ninzhnee*, 'I cherish you. You're a part of me.' And that teaching says if you talk to your children that way, they'll listen to you. And that's how we show love.

"Those three words, if you use that with your family, they say it holds you together. Just like the Christians say, 'A family that prays together stays together,' we say these three words are very powerful and spiritual. Keep those words in your family, and you'll always be together."

6

"Our Skin and the Earth
Are the Same Color"

"When we were really small," says Ella, "we lived on the top of Coal Mine Canyon on the other side of where we live now. It's called Howell Mesa. We went here and there with the sheep all the time. My dad was away a lot, working on the railroad."

Ella is the oldest surviving child. The next three children, spaced about two years apart, were girls: Lula, Lenora, and Genny (there would be a total of eleven children, including four boys). As soon as they were able, the girls did chores around the house. They carried wood for the fire, they herded sheep, they tended their younger sisters. They were dressed in tiny versions of the traditional Navajo dress—layered skirts, velvet tops, and, thanks to the government, leather, lace-up ankle-high boots. Bessie made most of their clothing by hand. Sometimes a friend with a sewing machine would make clothes for them. It was years before Bessie would get her own treadle machine. Even the little ones wore turquoise and silver jewelry. The Navajos wear turquoise (and their hair long) so the gods will recognize them as Navajos.

Every morning, the girls took the sheep out of the corral, where they were penned to protect them from predators, and

brought them to water. Then the girls set out for the day with
the sheep and goats in their endless search for grass. With the
help of the reservation dogs, they tried to keep the herd together. Sometimes, Ella and Lula set out with a little bag of
roasted corn to eat, or some roasted bread. Or they'd forage
for themselves, digging up wild potatoes and onions, looking
for seeds and berries. The children found nuts and knew a
special clay that could be dug up and eaten. The root of one
plant provided a substance the girls chewed like gum. Sometimes they grabbed a sheep, wriggled under it, and sprayed
milk into their mouths.

The girls' lives were in close correspondence with the myths
and stories they heard about the first Navajos and the Holy
Ones. One of the foods the girls gathered when they were
herding sheep was cicadas. This is the story Ella knows about
the cicada and how it came to be edible:

"In the emergence story, they say the cicada was the first
one that came out when we were living in the underworld and
were coming to this world. He's the one who decided to come
up first. And with his feelers, he felt his way up to this world.
And I guess he saw the world and he saw it was burning; there
was fire all over the place. And he met with the Spirit People
that lived there. And the Spirit People said he could never make
a life there because of his wings. They would burn.

"And I guess he made his way up again. And he saw that
it was really nice. And he wanted to ask permission to bring
his people up, and he asked the animal people who had already
come up, and they told him, Well, you have to pass these tests
first. And so they gave him an arrow, and they said, 'You have
to put it through your body, crosswise. And when you have
done that, they will know you will be able to survive on this
land.' So they gave him the arrow, and where the part turns
up, right there," Ella gestures to a place under her rib cage, "I
guess he pulled the arrow through there, and he passed the
test and he came up with all the animal people.

"And after the cicada passed the test, he was permitted to live in this world. He led the people, the five-fingered humans, up. And one of the things the cicada was told was that in the future, he would serve as a medicine. And I guess that little bundle right here—they call it his pillow—people will be able to survive on it. There will be hunger, and that thing will give life to the people; they will be able to survive. And he will also serve as medicine for illness in the wintertime. So I guess he was able to heal people too.

"So when we were growing up, when we used to herd sheep, my sisters and I listened for them. Just listened for that sound and followed that sound and came upon those cicadas. We used to have a bag, and we used to put them in the bag or we used to put them in our skirts and tie our skirts to one side; we would bring them home like that. And we would also use them as toys, because some of them are real small, the baby ones; we used to play with those, and my grandmother used to tell us to eat them because it would serve as medicine for the next winter. She said we would not get colds.

"You just pull it apart and then you just eat it. You can get a whole bunch, and we used to wrap them in paper bags and tie it up with string and put it under the ashes and kind of cook it a little bit. And we would unwrap it and eat it like that. I don't remember what kind of taste it had. But we used to bring them home in summertime.

"My dad said that when he was growing up, herding sheep, he used to gather those too. And eat them as he was herding sheep."

So, the cicada not only provides food, but the Navajos know through their myths that their ancestors also ate cicadas, and why that is so. The Navajos have no word for religion. Belief and life are inseparable. As Navajos say, "The white man goes to church once a week, but we follow our beliefs every day." Most Navajos, even those who have been educated in the white world, believe in the traditional explanations of life and death, illness and misfortune. It is a remarkable fact that in spite of repeated and energetic attempts to turn the Navajos away from their traditional beliefs by missionaries, government agents, schoolteachers, and the first health-care workers, the Dine, the People, have held on to their ways with great tenacity.

In the Navajo view, the world is a highly ordered place in which each living thing has its position and significance, from insects to the mountains, from the rocks to the "five-fingered humans." Each plays its role in the orderly working of the cosmos. Good and evil coexist, not as abstract principles, but as complementary parts of the whole. Good can turn into evil and vice versa; it is a matter of balance. Good is what is controlled, orderly, and harmonious. Evil is out of control, disordered, and comes from the disruption of the natural order of the world. All imbalances, all disharmonies, however, can be corrected, brought back into their orderly place in the universe through ceremonies, which are performed by medicine men, who are highly trained and much revered.

Everything has been created by the Divine Ones, and nature is evidence of their creative acts. The religious historian Mircea Eliade has put it this way: "Man . . . forms part of the gods' creation; in other words, he finds in himself the same sanctity that he recognizes in the cosmos. . . . As a divine work, the cosmos becomes the paradigmatic image of human existence." A tree is sacred; a plant is sacred: each is a manifestation of the divine.

However, a tree is also a tree—a plant, a plant. When Bessie makes an offering before she cuts a plant to make dye for her wool, she is thanking the plant and the Holy People for providing her the plant—but she does not believe she is killing a god by cutting the plant. She is not "buried in nature," as Hegel described archaic man—the Navajos know they are also distinct in nature. But their sensitivity to nature and the cosmos makes them open to the world. The world lives in them. They are never alone. "Openness to the world enables religious man to know himself in knowing the world—and this knowledge is precious to him because it is religious, because it pertains to being."

There is a gravity and a sanctity to the accomplishment of daily tasks that elevates life, because the tasks have been ordered and described in detail by the gods. When hoeing a field with Bessie and Jack, a visitor is awed first by the physical beauty and the grand and rejuvenating effects of nature. But also, the Hatathlies' bearing and attitude toward the work make it more than a back-breaking task—it is, in its own humble way, transcendent.

Count Leo Tolstoy described his own crisis of religious faith in *A Confession,* lamenting that "people live . . . on the basis of principles that not only have nothing in common with religious doctrines but are, on the whole, contrary to them; religious doctrine plays no part in life, or in relations between people, neither are we confronted with it in our personal lives. Religious doctrine is professed in some other realm, at a distance from life and independent of it. If we encounter it, it is only as an external phenomenon, disconnected from life."

The Navajo people feel no such disconnection from the world, themselves, or their gods. The cosmos and their everyday lives are infused with meaning. Divinity is ever-present, and a visitor is hard-pressed not to sense the presence of the sacred when with the Navajos. The essence of Navajo belief, as Ella says, is simple. One simply has to live as the gods instructed, and what the gods instructed the people in was how to live what is now the traditional Navajo life: "The Navajo way is just living the good way, the good life, positive life, always having the positive feelings inside you, in your mind and in your heart, and thinking positively and talking positively to people. And always leaving the negative things out. I guess that would be living your religion, your way of life, the Indian way of life. Showing respect for everything around you, for all living things, even, they say, even the mountains have life—

plant life, animal life, anything that has life. Having that feeling inside your heart."

This harmonious, interactive relation to nature exists only within the Navajos' territory, that area in which the gods are within reach. This is why the Navajos cannot imagine leaving the territory bounded by the four sacred mountains. Inside this area is the sacred world, in which nature is responsive. Outside is the unknown. Outside, one is no longer within the care of the gods; outside is full of chaos, foreigners, perhaps even ghosts.

"Here on our homeland, we know every part of the land. We make offerings to the spiritual beings. In return, the land and the spiritual beings know the people," says Jack Hatathlie. Thinking of moving away from this place brings on fear and loneliness.

"You'll always think about your homeland," says Jack. "You'll remember your home, relatives, cornfields, the road you used to travel on, the hills, the valleys, springs, your offering places, and where you used to go when you were sad or happy. When you are not on your homeland, you will only remember what it used to be like. You have known the land since childhood. It is not easy to erase your memories. You will be lonely and homesick for everything that used to be part of you since birth. . . . Here on the land, when you go into a canyon or come upon a cliff, you yell, and the rocks will yell back at you—the echo sound. This is called the talking rocks. A place like this is also an offering place. If we moved to Flagstaff, it would not be the same. It doesn't have talking rocks, but lava rocks. It's not good. Here on the land, there is open space where you can make your offerings or hold a squaw dance or Yei-bi-chei dance. These are community ceremonies. If we [moved] to another place, it would be different in every way, and we wouldn't be able to have the community ceremonies. We have been here for a long time. There were many generations before us."

In their own land are buried the bones of their ancestors. In their own land are also buried their umbilical cords, around which the soul is believed to wander at night. Jack says that his children, since they have learned the white man's ways, may succeed in living in the outside world. But he cannot: "For us older people, we will not survive if we leave our homeland. We were taught from the beginning that the earth is our Mother and the universe is our Father Sky. Our skin and the earth are the same color. From Mother Earth, that's where we emerged. The first breath we take, when we are born, is from Father Sky. Between our Mother Earth and Father Sky, they have given us life. Even after a person dies and passes back into the spirit world, the person's body is put back into Mother Earth and the spirit has gone back to Father Sky. We are taken back by our spiritual parents. We are connected to Mother Earth and Father Sky in spiritual ways. We cannot sell any of our Mother Earth. If we did, then where would we go? No place to go, since we have sold her. We are part of her, as much as she is part of us."

Sometimes, moving outside of Dinetah is unavoidable, for example, when men are drafted into the armed services. The Navajos have a ceremony designed to rid a person of the effects of foreigners—it is called Enemyway, more commonly known as the squaw dance. (The suffix *way* is a translation of the Navajo word for ceremonial rites or chants. It is appended to the English names of all the Navajo ceremonies, such as Beautyway, Blessingway.)

The Enemyway is performed for, among others, soldiers returning from battle. After exposure to the profane, the warrior must again be brought into a sacred place and reanimated by the presence of familiar gods. Sanctification of a place (like the curing of a patient) involves a symbolic re-creation. To organize a space or heal a person one must "repeat the paradigmatic work of the gods." Making everything right is to return the world to its original condition after Creation.

The idea of a sacred place has parallels in all traditions. "Moses, Moses," cried out Yahweh as Moses turned toward the burning bush, "Do not come near; put off your shoes from your feet, for the place on which you are standing is holy ground" (Exodus 3:5). Eliade explains that the sacred point in space provides the foundation for a start, a beginning. The center of the world becomes the consecrated ground, around which all else is defined.

Although modern society has been desacralized to a great extent, we still cling to customs with ancient roots that reveal the importance of the experience of the sacred. The doors of synagogues, churches, and temples mark boundaries between the sacred and the profane, and their majesty and grandeur can affect even the non-religious. But even more modest demarcations are important—for example, the doorways of homes or other buildings signify, if not by imposing architecture, then by gargoyles or by signs, the boundary and the protection of the divine. There are also behaviors characteristic of passing across thresholds—a bow, a touch or shake of a hand, a prostration—that reveal the notice paid to spirit guardians of the door. Our celebrations connected with the laying of the cornerstone of a new building are related to ancient rites of blood sacrifice made to animate and protect new constructions. "Every construction and every inauguration of a new dwelling are in some measure equivalent to a new beginning, a new life. And every beginning repeats the primordial beginning, when the universe first saw the light of day."

Jack Hatathlie explains how the building of a hogan represents the creation of the universe: "The hogan is very valuable to the Dine people. It was placed a long time ago by the spiritual beings. Before the Dine came into existence, the hogan was the home of the winded beings. That's why it has a dome shape. In the beginning of time, the spiritual beings were like humans. Year to year, winter to summer, month to month, different times of the moon, the dawn, the evenings, and the dark-

ness—all these things were also created and placed in the hogan. All these things can be discussed in the hogan. Everything
was created with songs and prayers. The hogan is very sacred,
and it has its own sacred songs and prayers."

The hogan exists in two forms: a male, or conical, form and
the more prevalent female, or round, shape. The male hogan
is the older version, and its supporting beams and doorposts
represent the four sacred mountains and two additional mountain ranges that are mentioned in myth. Says Jack, "The sacred
mountains are our home, we were placed in it, when things
were created. Within our sacred mountains, that's where our
teachings are and our songs and prayers." The hogan is a
symbolic representation of the Navajo world.

Before a hogan is entered for the first time, it is blessed with
prayer and corn pollen. "Then the hogan is blessed and you
can live there," says Jack. If something should happen to the
hogan, say, if a log breaks, "It's a sign from the spiritual beings
that something bad is going to happen," says Jack. Before anything indeed does happen, the hogan must be fixed and a
Blessingway ceremony held.

The Blessingway is the central chant of the Navajos. It tells
the story of the Creation of the universe by the Holy People.
The Navajo origin myth exists in many versions, with many
elaborations, but in broad outline, the Navajos believe that they
have ascended through various worlds, each of which was destroyed when their ancestors failed to live in peace and happiness. They fell victim to jealousy and quarrelsomeness, incest,
and adultery and were wiped out by fire or flood. Humans of
some form then emerged into the next world, where they tried
again. At one point, men and women were separated because
they couldn't get along or understand one another. After many
trials and abominations, they realized they needed each other,
and were reunited with better understanding.

Emergence to the earth represented the beginning of life.
The ancestors of the People climbed out of a watery mass—so

common to Creation stories—through a reed, following the insects and animals. The animals that played important roles in that exodus have become part of the Navajo pantheon. The Holy People created the moon and the stars and the dawn and the twilight. And they created First Man and First Woman and gave them medicine bundles, which they used, with the aid of thought, to make all the forms of the Navajo world—plants and animals, the mountains and lakes, the hogan, as well as rules about marriage, the calendar and time. The medicine bundles were placed inside the hogan by the Holy People, along with fire, fire poker, water, food, and bedding. The gods taught the People the rules of proper personal and business conduct, and how to maintain harmony among the forces of nature.

The deity Changing Woman, a most important figure for the Navajos, was found on a mountaintop and raised by First Man and First Woman. She gave birth to twins, fathered by the sun, who killed off the monsters that then peopled the earth. Then Changing Woman made corn and the first four pairs of Navajos, from whom all the Navajo clans originate.

The Holy People gave humans the ceremonies and ritual knowledge they needed to live here on earth. After they completed their work, they departed for the Four Corners of the World. The Blessingway tells of all these things. It is not a healing rite, but rather a protective or precautionary one. Jack had a Blessingway in October 1992 to celebrate his sixty-fifth birthday, and also because one of his sheep had delivered triplets—considered a bad omen. The purpose of the Blessingway is to set everything right, to reintroduce the patient to the sacred space and time of Creation.

The Navajo deity Changing Woman is intimately connected with this rite, and her character is emblematic of the chant's purpose: renewal.

> Changing Woman, so named because she renews her youth
> as the seasons progress, was created and trained to bring forth

twin sons, who freed the earth from the monsters. Old, gray-haired, wrinkled, and bent in the winter, she gradually transforms herself to a young and beautiful woman. Restoration to youth is the pattern of the earth, something for which the Navaho lives, for he reasons that what happens to the earth may also happen to him. Regaining strength after disease due to contact with strangers, attack by evil or offended powers, or loss of ritualistic purity is interpreted as rejuvenation like that of Mother Earth.

The Blessingway is a happy chant. Family and relatives travel from all over to attend ceremonies for friends and relatives, but they particularly like Blessingway. One could argue that Blessingway and Navajo life and religion are of a piece. Blessingway is a ceremony of "growth, adaptation, and re-animation." The Navajo word for Blessingway is *hozhooji*, whose root is *hozho*, "beauty."

Tolstoy has written that we tend to confuse beauty with goodness, but for the Navajos, there is little distinction. What is beautiful, what has *hozho*, is what is in its proper place, functioning harmoniously with everything else, normal, blessed, perfect, ideal. Navajo life, with plentiful sheep, plentiful corn and rainfall, large families and good health, on the beloved Navajo land, is beautiful.

Blessingway is "the song of songs, a chant of many parts that contains 'all things out of which man is made.' " Recitation of Blessingway has the power to restore all to beauty.

7

"I Idolized White People. They Were So Clean and So Smart"

Although history tells us that it was the Spaniards who introduced sheep into the Southwest in the sixteenth century, so important are the animals to the Navajos that legend explains them as gifts from the Holy People at the time of Creation. Care of the sheep therefore became a sacred activity, and preparation of wool for weaving, at least something that should be done the right way. Ella continues the story of her childhood and its chores and responsibilities with a memory of carding wool:

"I guess when I started getting a little bit older, Lula and I would card wool in the evening. After we did our chores and after we ate, my mom would bring out her bag of wool and we would sit there and card, and sometimes we would get so tired we would just fall asleep right there by the wool." A wool carder is like a metal animal brush, with short, close metal bristles with which to comb out the knots in wool.

"And sometimes my mom would tell us to hold the card tight, put pressure on it to card it. She would say, 'What's wrong with you girls; don't you have any muscles? Look at your wool,' because when you card it really tight, it comes out really smooth when you roll it. But if you card it really loose, you get those little balls in there, and it's hard to spin. But we did that a lot in the evenings."

The old-style hogans are beautiful inside, their ceilings layered like conch shells, logs in a swirl, one beside the other, walls made of silvery juniper branches, stacked vertically, like bodies swaying in song or in the wind. There was little furniture; in the center was a stove, along the walls bureaus or trunks. The family sat on Pendleton blankets on the floor.

"In the evening," Ella goes on, "if we weren't carding the wool, we would lie on the ground, and we would draw in the sand and talk about different things, Lula and I. And then sometimes in the evening, in those days, we visited people. We visited one another a lot, and now you don't do that anymore. I don't see it being done. When I was growing up, we would visit our neighbors, like my aunt; we would go off in the evening, after we put the sheep in the corral and ate our meal, then we would start walking over to my aunt's—about a mile or a mile and a half away—and we would go over there and spend the night. We did that, I guess, for social reasons: just to talk, catch up on the news, what was happening. And sometimes my mom would carry somebody piggyback and sleep over there, and then the next morning we would walk back to our house and let out the sheep.

"I remember, sometimes at night, I would be sleeping and my mom would be weaving, There was always that sound— like a thumping sound, when she was weaving, pushing down the yarn, and she would be weaving by kerosene lamps, and I would look up from my sheepskins on the floor, and I would look out through the hole in the hogan, the smoke hole, and I remember seeing that blue, blue sky.

"Sometimes my mother would tell us in the evening, 'Bring in the wood before you go to sleep so you won't have to do it in the morning.' But sometimes we would end up playing or something, and we would not bring in the wood. So in the morning, she would tell us to get up and build a fire, and sometimes it was cold in the hogan, and we didn't want to get up. And she would tell us, call us by name, me or Lula, and tell us to build a fire. And sometimes if we didn't bring in the wood, we had to get up and go outside where the wood was, to the woodpile, to gather the wood so we could build a fire. And after that, my mom would take us out to do our offerings—sprinkle cornmeal to the rising sun, and sometimes she would tell us to run—it was supposed to make us strong —to run a quarter of a mile and yell. And my mom would get up, and she would start making her dough. And then she would tell us to roll our bedding, our sheepskin, roll it up and stack it, roll our blankets and stack them.

"Some mornings I dreaded getting up in the cold and I would just lie on my sheepskin and snuggle up and didn't want to get up. We slept in our clothes. We wore them for several days. I guess when they got really dirty, we would take them off. My mom did all her washing by hand, then." For water, the Navajos drove to a nearby school or other facility with public faucets, from which they filled large barrels attached to the backs of their wagons or pickup trucks. At home, the water was carried from the barrels in buckets for washing and drinking. Baths were taken in iron oil barrels, filled with water heated over the fire. Later, shower bags were used.

"In the morning, my mom would fix tortillas. I don't know what we ate with tortillas, probably corn mush, ground corn boiled up with milk. When it was wintertime, she used to feed the lambs, and we would take the bottles over there to the corral. I don't know where she got the milk from. But she used to boil the milk—powdered milk—we used to boil it because if you just gave it to them straight, they would get diarrhea. So we used to boil the milk and carry the bottles to the corral with my mom and feed the lambs.

"We had to feed the lambs because sometimes, because of not enough grass, the sheep don't always have milk, and sometimes they have twins. So we used to take the bottles over there and run around with the lambs, and roll around in the sheep manure—you know, that stinks! When I go home now, I go to the corral with my mom and she'll tell me to feed the goats, and it really stinks. Now I think about it, how I used to chase these goats, and lie on top of the sheep and ride them, and chase them and roll around with the little lambs in the sheep manure.

"I guess it would get in my hair and my clothes, but it didn't bother me then. You know, I would not change my clothes just because I smelled like manure. Now if I went into the corral, I would probably change clothes, but it didn't bother me then. Now when I get home, I wipe the manure off my shoes with a rag or clean it off in the snow."

Ella's earliest memories include images of the white man. There were tourists who drove past the house and took pictures of the girls in return for a few coins. Ella's mother didn't like this, and she signaled the girls home with a mirror she used to catch a ray of sun. The first white person Ella saw was the man who ran the trading post in Tuba City. He scared her— his face was covered with hair, something she had never seen. Once he tried to tickle her, and it made her cry. Later, she got used to the man, and she discovered the treasures that were displayed in his store. As her parents bought food and material, sometimes paying with bags of wool shorn from their sheep, Ella looked over the candy and the soda pop. Later, after she was in boarding school, on the weekends the children walked to the trading post with a few coins to buy peppermint sticks and chocolate bars like Babe Ruth and Big Hunk. The trader had a game then—he'd throw handfuls of pennies in the air for children who had no spending money, so they too, like the others, could buy candy and pop.

Ella also remembers airplanes. In the earliest days, Ella's mother used to wake the children when the engines roared overhead, to show them the strange metal birds in the sky.

"My mom would say, 'Those are the airplanes,' but she never told me that there were people in the airplanes. And I always thought it was just an instrument in the air making that sound. I guess later, way later, I found out there were actually people that flew those things. And after I found that out, I thought a lot about the airplanes, how they could fly in the sky, where they came from. I thought the airplane brought people to earth from the sky. Even though I saw my mother having babies, I didn't think that was how you got people. I thought, 'They brought people down in the airplanes, from the sky.' "

"They," of course, are white people. In addition to traders, Indians became accustomed to the missionaries who passed through, wave after wave, to convert the Navajos and Hopis. Ella and her sisters were very impressed by the people with the light complexions; she and Lula played games in which they acted out the roles of white people—for example, at the store, imitating the sounds that came out of their mouths. "We used to talk English, but it wasn't English, we would just make sounds, like *malemalemale*—just a sound that we made." Later, after they started school, they acted out the Dick and Jane stories.

"I idolized white people," says Ella. "They were so clean and so smart, and they spoke the English language so well."

Did she have any idea that they spoke English well because English was the only language they knew?

Ella says with surprise, "I didn't know that then. We were always told we were dumb Indians. We didn't know anything. The teachers, the white teachers, told us that. We were dumb Indians and that's why we were in school to learn. I didn't realize that the reason they knew all those things was that they had gone to school too."

8

"The Missionaries Got Jobs for My Parents, Working in the Carrot and Potato Fields"

Ella is sitting at her kitchen table surrounded by plastic containers of lustrous cut-glass beads. She is making earrings and bracelets. Sometimes she sells her beadwork to a trader in Flagstaff, or she sets up a table at powwows or the swap meet in Tuba City and sells her work herself. As she works, she explains that while Bessie took care of the children and the sheep, her father, Jack, was away earning wages. Like many Navajos, he worked for the Santa Fe–Union Pacific railroad as a track maintenance man. When he worked in Barstow, California, he brought his family with him. Later, Jack worked at the Navajo Army Depot in Bellemont, near Flagstaff, and the family followed for a time and lived in town, on Flagstaff's south side with other Indian and Mexican people. The family also worked a stint picking carrots and potatoes in Utah. After that, Jack worked as a laborer and landscaper at the Moqui Lodge, a hotel at the edge of the Grand Canyon. Moqui is the name the Spaniards called the Hopis—the Hopi don't like it and consider it pejorative, because it means "those with the runny noses." Jack also drove a school bus for preschoolers in Coal Mine Mesa. His last job was for the Navajo Power Plant in Page, by the edge of Lake Powell, north of Tuba City. When he held this job, he lived in Page during the week and returned home on the weekends. To stave off loneliness, he had a horse with him, and also whiled away some hours playing cards with other Navajo workers. For a few years, Ella's eldest son, Kimo, lived with him. Jack says he never got used to being in town and waited all week to return home.

The way Ella remembers things, life was hard but happy at home with her mom, who sang while she was herding sheep. Bessie's nickname was Singing Lady, and when Ella was anxious about her mother's return in the evening, she would climb up to the roof of the house and listen for her mother's voice, as she rode her horse back with the sheep, sometimes with one of the youngest children tied in a cradleboard to the saddle.

Suddenly Ella looks up from her work, says, "Oh!" and stands up. She opens a drawer and lugs out a large cardboard box of photographs. She rummages around in it for a few minutes before making an exclamation of satisfaction and removing an old black-and white photo.

It shows her mother, young, with a vulnerable openness in her face, sitting on the floor of an old wooden hogan. Pendleton blankets cover the floor and hang on a wall as a backdrop for the photo. Her first four children sit snuggled up against her. There are Ella, Lenora, Lula (asleep) and Genny in traditional skirts and assorted shoes, looking intently toward a chart held up by a middle-aged white couple. The chart, hand-drawn with a diagram of the heavens ("Telestial [sic] world," "Outer darkness," "Paradise," "First Judgement [sic]"), seems also to include pictures of Jesus Christ. The woman is holding up what appears to be a drawing of Jesus with native people. Ella starts laughing.

"I have no idea how they communicated with my mother," she says, "because she speaks no English."

The couple were Mormon missionaries. "They were an older couple, maybe in their sixties," says Ella. "They used to come and visit my folks when they used to live in Howell Mesa. And then, after we lived across the canyon to Coal Mine, they used to visit us there. I guess they used to teach the gospel to my folks, I don't know how they understood it because I wasn't in school yet.

"They used to come over, and somehow they got jobs for my parents in Utah, working in the carrot and potato fields. And then pretty soon there was a big truck that came to pick up people, families, and take them out there. And I think they had like a boardinghouse or something where people lived. Because I remember living in a place where there was a lot of people, a lot of kids, all Navajo. And every morning, they would take us out to the field. And my job was to take care of my sisters. And I remember always sitting against a burlap bag. I used to sit against a burlap bag, and I was always taking care of somebody, one of my sisters, and there was this big truck that used to come, and this big truck used to bring I think sandwiches and candy and pop.

"My mom used to always buy me an Oh! Henry candy bar. I don't remember drinking pop, but I've always remembered that Oh! Henry. And I used to eat tons and tons of carrots, because that's all there was to eat when I was sitting in the field. And I remember sitting in the potato field too. And there was a big truck that used to go through the fields, turning the ground, and the potatoes would come out of it. And people used to drag burlap sacks and put the potatoes in the bag and gather them. I remember that, but I don't remember the truck rides going over there and coming back. I remember my mother's sister being there too.

"I remember living in Barstow, too, by a train track. And I remember a lady who was our next-door neighbor, and she came over and she gave me and my sister a perm, and [we wound up looking like] Orphan Annie. My mom, she tried to keep it down, tried to brush it down, but it was all wild-looking. The perm made it really wild. And my mom tried to wet it down for us too, but it wouldn't go down, and then she started braiding our curls. Sometimes I remember at night, hearing the train, and I couldn't sleep. Then I remembered little things here and there, like my mom used to do beadwork. At that time, ladies used to wear armbands on their sleeves. On their Navajo blouses, they wore beaded armbands. I remember my mom beading. I don't remember what else she made, but I remember the armbands. And then one time, Genny went and got into her beads. And she ate a lot of beads, and my mom was really scared, she didn't know what to do, and I remember her talking to the lady next door. She was also a Navajo. And the lady was telling her nothing's going to happen to her, she'll just pass it in her stool. And that's what happened. I remember that. And I remember my mom washing that diaper, and all these beads were in the sink. I remember that.

"I think we lived in boardinghouses for people who worked the railroad. I remember living in a boxcar too. And all these families, they were living in boxcars. I remember living in a boxcar. I don't really remember a lot about it, but I remember that train that we lived in. And then I remember living in Flagstaff too, when my dad worked on the railroad. But I don't remember living in Bellemont, though."

9

"I Don't Trust Those Doctors; They Might Use Dead People's Teeth"

In the winter, Ella and her parents and sisters and animals moved from the top of Howell Mesa down to the bottom of Coal Mine Canyon. The canyon is a great winding gorge of rainbow-colored rock that divides Coal Mine Mesa. Down at the bottom of the canyon, Ella's father had made two dugouts—two square caves, each the size of a single small room, cut into the earth on the side of a hill and covered with a roof. Ella remembers there were small cubbies in the walls, where the children stored their belongings. Recently, Ella went down to look at the caves with her own children, who were surprised at how small they were. When Ella looked, it was hard for her to figure out how her parents and four girls could all have fit together in the dugout to sleep. The second dugout was used by an aunt. Each cave had half an oil barrel that served as a stove, with a pipe leading the smoke out the roof.

It was warmer in the canyon in winter, and the Hatathlies lost fewer lambs if their sheep gave birth down there. Dennis's aunt Annie Begay also lived in the canyon, not as far down as the dugouts, but on one of the higher, grassy ledges. Annie, affectionately called Annie Oakley by her relatives, is a colorful woman in her sixties, fiercely independent, who lives by herself with her mules and sheep and fowl. She was once married, but her husband left or was asked to leave years ago. Although she's been wooed by men over the years, none has won her hand. Ella says, "She's got all her chickens and her roosters and her turkeys, and she says they all talk to her. She doesn't need to stay with anybody or live with anybody."

Her best-known skill is as an auto mechanic; she has scandalized relatives by donning jeans to work on her cars. Eight years ago, she had a white Ford F-150 pickup whose transmission was broken; the truck only ran backward. This didn't slow her down, however; Annie careened up and down the narrow paths that hug the walls of Coal Mine Canyon—a heart-stopping exercise even in regular gear—in reverse. But when she got the parts she needed for the repair, she not only fixed the transmission, she changed it from automatic to manual. "It was easy," she said. "I just followed the pictures in the repair book." She also changed the valves on the engine, which she called "changing the truck's bracelets."

Annie is a small, muscular woman who wastes time for no one. She bustles about, watering her animals, hauling wood, getting food. Like other people who spend a great deal of time alone, she tends to speak aloud whatever's on her mind.

Ella visited her recently, and Annie happened to be thinking about people whose houses have large windows. Ella says, "She was saying, 'I don't know how people can have houses with big windows. Anybody could see you.' Ella laughs. Annie's corner of the world is one of the most sparsely inhabited on the planet. The Hopi Rangers don't even come down to check on her livestock levels, her place is so remote and hard to reach.

Nevertheless, she is concerned lest anyone should see her in her hogan. "She's got really tiny windows in her house," says Ella. Even so, Annie had just made a new set of curtains which she wanted to show her guest.

"They look real wild," says Ella. One set is bright orange,

with a fluorescent green edging at the border. The others are fluorescent pink with a black border. Annie added an appliqué of a black mountain range in the middle. One can see right away that Annie has re-created on her curtains brilliant orange and pink sunsets, bordered with green grass and marked by the sacred mountains. Annie apparently saw one of Ella's sisters at the flea market with the bright-colored material in hand, knew right away what she wanted to do with it, and asked if she could have it. It's hard to say no to Annie. Ella says she tries to buy her material whenever she gets a chance, particularly when Wal-Mart has sales of odd pieces. Annie also finds pieces in remnant boxes at churches.

Most of Annie's creations are very original. One apron she made for Ella had a waistband tie made of denim, with a matching denim Levi's-jeans pocket in the front. Another apron is black, decorated with a pocket from a shirt. I ask Ella if she thinks Annie wears aprons—something hard to imagine.

"Oh, yeah, she does; she's got a lot of handmade aprons. She always shows them to me when I go down there. I ask her, What did you make? Then she starts taking things out.

Annie does all her sewing by hand, and she does it while she herds sheep. She also makes skirts and blouses for herself, but she adds a different look by making the sleeves of her blouses with unmatching material.

Annie tells Ella she has lately been thinking about getting false teeth. She only has a few of her own left. But after thinking about it, she decided not to go ahead. Says Ella, "She noticed that people who have false teeth make a funny noise. They sit there and the plate makes a noise in their mouth; maybe it's too big in their mouth. And she said she thought about that, and she says it's real annoying when somebody wears that and you can really hear it."

Further, sharing Ella's mother's skepticism about doctors, "She said, 'Oh, I don't trust those doctors, because they might use dead people's teeth.' "

Ella says, "I told her they're porcelain. And she said, 'Well, they probably use dead people's teeth and pour something over it.' So she says, 'I'm not going to do it.' "

Annie has already figured out what she'll do if she loses all her teeth. "She says she'll just live on Vienna sausage. She likes them, so when we go down there, we bring her some; that's her treat."

10

Relocation: "I Want to Go Home"

A few minutes from Ella's trailer is a tract of suburban-type houses built on parallel streets with a similar gentle curve. The buildings are new, one-story ranch homes, painted different colors and with slightly different configurations. There is scant landscaping and few trees to soften the harsh edges of the buildings, which sit on raw earth that still appears recently excavated.

Ella pulls up to a new house with a large protruding bay window. It is perched somewhat awkwardly on top of a hilly lot that rises steeply from the street. Bits of grass have been planted in the sandy soil but seem overwhelmed by the dust. Ella passes through an aluminum screen door into a large living room. In one corner is a wood-burning stove that seems never to have been used; it is set on a platform of red brick, with a brick mantel behind it.

In the center of the room are two gray plush sofas set at right angles to each other, and a huge television set. Two teen-age girls sit on the couches, beading, sewing, and watching television. Ella's grandma, Rena Williams, sits with her feet propped up on a footrest that is built into the sofa. She appears shrunken, almost lost in the expansive, velvety sofa. Ella walks over, kneels in front of her, takes up her hands gently and speaks to her. The old lady's watery eyes brighten, and she greets Ella in a wavering voice. Rena begins to talk in the soothing monotone of the Navajo language, and Ella remains seated before her on the floor; as she listens, she scrapes spots off her grandma's blouse, straightens her skirt. Small children run in and out of the room.

Along the wall near the fireplace is a single bed covered with a patchwork quilt. Rena doesn't like the separate bedrooms of this house, but prefers to have her bed in the central room —near the fire, near the activity, in an arrangement more similar to her hogan.

After several minutes of listening silently, with only occasional exclamations of "Oh," which in Navajo means "I'm listening," Ella gets up. "Okay, we'll see you then," she says, and walks out of the house.

The late-summer night is still warm; the air smells sweet and soft. The sky is all around us, the stars big. This land has a different feel; it crackles with its own mysteries, holds softly its own secrets. We stand outside for a few minutes, and Ella says that a few days ago she drove by Rena's house to see her, and found her struggling across the street with her walker.

"I parked by her," says Ella, "and I asked, 'Where are you running away to?' She said she was going to go visit a friend, one of her relatives. So I asked her, 'Well, where do you want to go today?' She said, 'I want to go home.' I said okay. So we got in and went back to her old house [in Coal Mine Mesa] near the fairgrounds. And we just sat outside. And she enjoyed sitting outside. And we built a fire and we cooked. We just spent the whole day there, taking it easy. She just told me she wants to go back."

But Rena cannot go back. In an attempt to settle a hundred-year-old boundary dispute between the Navajos and their neighbors the Hopis, the U.S. government authorized the redrawing of the tribes' shared boundaries. When the new lines were finalized in 1977, Rena's house, as well as Jack and Bessie's house, and the homes of ten thousand other Navajos, fell on the Hopi side of the line. They were living on Hopi land, they were told, and would have to move off. The government offered them new houses in town or in Tuba City, but many Navajos refused to move from the land on which their gods have come to know them, from which they harvest crops and medicinal herbs, and in which their umbilical cords are buried.

The origin of the dispute dates back to 1882, when President Chester A. Arthur created, by executive order, a reservation for the Hopis. The lines were hastily and carelessly drawn by an aggrieved Indian agent, who included within the boundaries of the brand-new Hopi reservation hundreds of Navajos— hundreds of Navajos who soon became thousands, the result of a huge population boom after their release from Fort Sumner in 1868. Within fifty years, Navajos outnumbered Hopis on the *Hopi* reservation by three to one.

The Navajo-Hopi land dispute has churned through the courts for thirty-five years. It has spawned three federal statutes, a new federal agency, dozens of federal and state lawsuits, and the largest federal housing program in the country. It constitutes the largest relocation of civilians since the incarceration of Japanese-Americans during World War II. To date, it has cost taxpayers more than $500 million, and will cost hundreds of millions more in indirect costs. The government is still moving people, twenty years after the 1974 Navajo-Hopi Resettlement Act, which authorized the division of the land and the relocation of the displaced people. Figures from the Navajo Nation suggest there are still fifteen hundred Navajos living on the Hopi side of the line. Fewer than fifty Hopi families were affected by the law.

Although the Navajos said they would not move, regulations imposed by the federal government in 1972 that reduced Navajo sheep herds by 90 percent to just a handful and prevented them from repairing their houses forced many to accept the replacement houses. Rena held out for almost fifteen years before relocating in 1992. Bessie and Jack still refuse to move.

When Ella found her grandma crossing the street to find a neighbor, Rena told her she was ashamed to be seen walking out of her house. Ella asked her why. Ella says she responded this way: "My grandma says she feels that if you live in a big house, a nice house like that, you need to dress like a white woman. I told her there's nothing wrong with the way she looks."

The relocation is the central preoccupation—obsession—of the people of Coal Mine Mesa. It affects everyone who lives here—either they have been told to move, or their relatives have, or their family has already moved. These people, who are some of the most traditional Indians left in the United States, are not ready to enter the twentieth century. In the case of Rena, living in a white person's house makes her feel uncomfortable and inadequate.

Many who agreed to relocate in the early days of the program have since lost their homes. One old man, Hosteen Nez, moved into a house in Flagstaff and found he was prohibited from growing corn in his front yard. Then the neighbors tried to keep him from butchering a sheep. The incomprehensible sounds from the television confused and disoriented him. He couldn't pay the water and electric bills and the taxes on his new house because he didn't have a job. One weekend he got a ride back to Coal Mine to visit his old home and regain a sense of peace and belonging. When he arrived, he saw that his hogan had been bulldozed. Hosteen Nez suffered a stroke. He eventually moved into a trailer the tribal government acquired for him in south Tuba City.

Others were just as unlucky. Many Navajos who could not speak English signed for car loans that used their houses as collateral. When they got a few months behind on the payments, they lost both cars and houses. Loan sharks lent money to Navajos at exorbitant interest rates. In the early days of the program, houses built by the federal relocation commission were of such shoddy quality that some literally fell apart. Two years after the first relocation, one-quarter of the relocatees were faring poorly. Five years after the moves began, half the relocatees had either lost their houses or seriously encumbered them. Once they lost their houses, they had nowhere to go. They had sold their old homes to the government. Most moved in with relatives or wound up in public housing. The program effectively moved many Indians from self-supporting lives on their own land to lives of dependence on public welfare in the cities. In 1995 the government is still relocating Navajos.

After observing the fates that befell neighbors and friends, many Navajos decided to resist. Jack Hatathlie sadly observed, "Some of the people who have relocated have suffered a lot. A lot of our elders, men, women, and children have passed on. They died of heartaches, loneliness and unhappiness, always not knowing what was going to happen next. Some have also just returned home and are living with relatives."

Those who lost their houses and returned to live with relatives on the reservation suffer the humiliation of their failure, and also a deeper shame at having gambled with Navajo ways and lost. Ella explains: "We get everything from our land. We get food from our land; we get teachings—all related to the land. If you're brought up in a traditional family, you're taught that the land is going to be your Mother for life, that she provides for you, she takes care of you, she's the one that lays out the lesson plan daily so you can learn from her. When you accept money for your land—it's like accepting money for your own mother. Relocating is like selling out on your people—giving up."

Many refused to go. But they live with severely reduced sheep herds and with homes in need of repair. Two of the three hogans on the Hatathlies' property are unlivable because of leaks and rot. And the livestock have been reduced so dramatically that Bessie can't even bring a sheep to a relative's ceremony to butcher.

Ella says the loss of the sheep has a profound effect on the Navajos, an effect akin to going bankrupt, with all the associated psychological and emotional consequences.

"Navajo life was based on sheep. You were considered wealthy if you had sheep. You'd be able to help other people when they had their ceremonies. Around this time of year there are a lot of squaw dances that involve feeding hundreds of people. You would take a sheep over there and help that family cook, and you would meet people. And I know my mom feels bad because when a relative is having a squaw dance, she can't take anything over there. In fall she feels bad because then she used to sell her sheep and with the money buy school clothes for the kids—and give them money to put in the bank when they went back to school. And now she can't do that."

Further, Bessie has nothing to pass on to her daughter and heir, Ella. She has nothing to show for her sixty years of work—no land, no sheep.

*

Rena is still disturbed about her dreams of her late husband. But her full ceremony has been postponed because her daughter, Agnes, is gravely ill. Rena wants the family's energy and resources to be directed now toward helping her daughter get better.

Ella continues to visit Rena. "We talked about the old man. She's been crying a lot, like every time someone visits her, like my mom or my dad, or when I go visit her, she will just start crying. And I guess my dad tells her not to be crying like that. He says it makes you feel bad when you cry.

"When I leave, she cries. We talk about things, and then I noticed inside her house: there's furniture inside the house, but there's nothing that really belongs to her, that she used to have in her other house, like her grinding stone, her stirring sticks, and her hairbrushes and her sheepskin. Things that she's always had, always had in the house. And I asked her granddaughter where they are, and she said, 'Over there at her hogan.' So when we went over there again, we brought most of it back, and I put it inside the [relocation] house for her. Some of her dishes she still had over at the hogan, and her granddaughter said they were too old, and they didn't want them at the house. But I told her, I said, 'Well, but these are the things that belong to her. She had them all this time, and some of them her husband bought for her.' I said, 'You shouldn't be saying these kinds of things about them. That's why she feels like that. When she has things familiar around her, she won't be feeling like that.'

"I brought a lot of stuff from her hogan and put it inside her house. And then my dad had a prayer done for her. Now she's okay." Having a prayer said over someone by a medicine man may be all that is necessary to solve a minor problem, like tension over school or a job. But for Rena, it was a temporary measure to soothe her until she gets her full ceremony.

A few days later, when Ella was with her, she started crying again.

"She was crying about the old man," Ella says. "I don't know why you're crying about him," Ella says she told her grandma. "I told her, 'He's probably not even thinking about you, Grandma.' " Ella giggles. Rena's husband was a famous womanizer.

"Oh, she started laughing. She was crying, and then she started laughing. I said, 'We'll go to the swap meet, and we'll look for a man for you.' " Ella laughs merrily.

"I told her I'm going to be back over there Tuesday. I'll make her corn mush and bread, and I got her piki bread [a flaky phyllo-like bread made from blue cornmeal by Hopi women]. And I'm getting her this really sweet cornmeal [the Hopis] grind up that you drink with coffee. My Hopi friend Rita is making some for me. I told her I'll take it to her on Tuesday. So I'm going to take her over to the old house and talk with her some more over there."

11

"Did I Tell You That My Dad Wasn't Raised by His Real Mother?"

"Did I tell you that my dad wasn't raised by his real mother?" asks Ella. "Rena Williams gave birth to him, but didn't raise him. He was raised by Lilac Tacheenie, a relative by clan."

Jack didn't tell Ella the story of his upbringing until she was a teenager. It has troubled her, occupied her thoughts, for years. Ella wants to know more about her father's youth; she wants to try to find clues to explain why he became the strong, faithful, hardworking man he did, when his blood brothers fought a mostly losing battle with alcohol. So now, with the license afforded her by her role as an interviewer for the book, and armed with a tape recorder, she is posing questions she never before asked.

As a teenager, Ella had been told the outlines of the story. When her father, Jack, was born, Lilac Tacheenie was old, in her fifties, and past childbearing age, but she was poor in the Navajo way because she had only one surviving child, a daughter named Sally. One morning she said to her husband, "Drive the wagon over to my clan sister's house, she has a lot of kids, and I need someone to help me with the sheep and around the house. Go bring me one of the children who can help me." Rena Williams was the clan sister she meant.

Later that day, Lilac's husband returned home from gathering wood with his horse and wagon. He stopped the horses and began unloading firewood. Lilac was watching him stack the cedar branches when she saw a small child in the wagon.

She started to shriek and ran out of the house toward him.

"What are you doing? Why did you bring a baby? What good is he going to be?"

Her husband looked at her and said, "You told me to get a child. This is what they gave me. If you want me to take it back, I will."

But Lilac kept Jack and raised him as her own. Lilac died in 1983, at the age of 106. Lilac was the woman Ella had always known as her grandmother, in fact her only grandmother, since Bessie's mother died of tuberculosis when Bessie was just a girl. Lilac was the one Ella called "my old grandmother," and who had lived as long as she could remember in her own hogan very close to the Hatathlies. Lilac didn't see well, and always felt the arriving kids to determine which was which. She invariably thought they were too skinny, and searched among her things until she found crackers and canned peaches for them to eat. She was known to carry some peaches, crackers, and a can opener with her wherever she went, just in case someone got hungry.

One day when Ella was about fourteen, Jack brought her over to Rena Williams's house and said, "This is your grandmother." It took a while for Ella to understand what he meant. She *had* a grandma, and it was Lilac.

During the time they spent together sitting by her old hogan, Rena Williams told Ella many things, and Ella recorded her words. Rena told her granddaughter that she gave birth to her first child when she was thirteen years old, and delivered four more in quick succession, all boys. Jack was the youngest boy, less than two years old, and when her clan brother came calling, asking for a child, she had just given birth to a girl, Agnes. In part to help out her clan sister, and in part because she was overwhelmed with two babies, she gave over her son Jack. In the next years, she had four more daughters, to make a total of five boys and five girls. Her husband, Hatathlie Nez, who also had three other wives, died when she still had children at home. But then Rena met and married Joe Williams, who already had a wife, but who cared well for her and her children.

Rena Williams:

I thought about my baby a lot, wondered if he was taken care of in a proper way, if he had enough to eat, if his aunt loved him, or if he was treated hurshly. I missed him a lot and wanted to bring him back home, but my husband said he had more love and care than I could ever give him. He said we had enough kids and my clan sister didn't. She would raise him like her own. Sometimes I argued with him, but later I just let it go since I wasn't getting anywhere. I just kept busy with the five children I had at home then.

But sometimes if I saw a kid that was the same age as Jack, I would wonder about him. What he looked like, how big he was. Wondered what he did.

I saw Jack for the first time when he was only six or seven years old. His aunt and her husband were herding sheep nearby, and they came over to where we lived. I asked about my son and they told me, "He's behind the hill watching the sheep." I took my girls over to where he was. I saw him and started running to him. I grabbed him, cried and held him. He just looked at me and didn't know who I was. I told my daughters to shake his hand; this was their brother. I held his hand and walked him back to the hogan. I cooked and fed him. After he was done eating, I went to my trunk and got a brand-new pair of Levi's out for him to wear. He was wearing a white flour-sack pants his aunt had put together. I asked him if he wanted to stay with us. I wanted him to stay, but after he ate, he just got up and left to go back to the sheep. I felt real sad to see him go. I told myself that one day he would come back to live with us.

Jack is very different from my other children. My [clan] sister did a good job of raising him. She was very poor but she instilled in him some life teachings that he has patterned his life after. He's very stable and content in his life and family.

He's very kind and generous, always smiling and joking, always willing to help. He has a good life and a good family. Sure, I feel bad about not raising him, but if I had, maybe he would be different. Maybe he would have a drinking problem and not care for his family. His aunt raised him well. I owe a lot to her.

My first husband, Hatathlie Nez [Jack's father], was a well-known medicine man. He was tall and skinny. He always wore a wide-brimmed black hat with a silver hatband, and his hair was always tied in a knot. He wore Levi's and moccasins. He was a Five-night-way chanter and a Beautyway singer. He brought us material back from ceremonies, which I made into clothes for my five girls. He provided for us very well. We were considered rich Navajos because we had lots of sheep, horses and two big wagons, and a big hogan. He was always gone singing and visiting his other wives and children.

I didn't have time to be jealous of my husband. I had children to take care of and sheep and horses to take care of.

Jack Hatathlie finishes up some errands in Tuba City and drives over to Ella's house. He steps out of his pickup and climbs the wooden steps to Ella's trailer. He sits down at her kitchen table and remarks on the shamrock plant that grows in the light of the large picture window. He calls it the "Catholic plant," because it opens and closes its leaves according to the light, and when its leaves are folded, it looks like it is praying. Ella fries him up some onions and zucchini from their field, and serves him some coffee.

Jack was a bit hesitant when Ella first told him of her idea to collect the stories of his youth. Ella says, "I think before, he was kind of reluctant, and then after a while, we talked about a lot of things, how I felt that it was important that his grand-children know about these things. And how even if he was going to tell Danielle something about his past, Danielle won't be able to understand fully what he's talking about. And I told

him, 'Your grandchildren really need to know the feeling of
how you were raised, because they don't know. And why a
lot of these teachings are important and why they should understand a lot of these things. I really had to talk to him about
it, and after that, he kind of like picked it up. He was telling
me, 'You should talk to so-and-so. And you should talk to so-
and-so.'

"Now," Ella says, "he's really into it," coming by her house
and saying, " 'Do you have that recorder? I'm ready to talk.' "

After Jack finishes eating, Ella turns on the tape recorder
and he speaks with a warm, mellifluous voice, using his hands
to draw rolling shapes in the air, then pointing here and there,
referring to areas around and about Tuba and Coal Mine, areas
he knows as well as he knows the curves of his own children's
faces.

This is how he started the story of his boyhood, parts of
which had clearly been told to him many times in his life:

*My aunt was very disappointed with her husband for bringing me
home. To her, since I was barely two, I would be just another burden
to her. With much disappointment, she got me out of the wagon, scolded
her husband for not bringing an older child home. She carried me back
to the hogan and started supper. When her husband was done with
unloading the wood, he unhitched the team, hobbled them, and chased
them away so they could nibble on what grass was available since it
had been a dry summer.*

*Sitting cross-legged on the ground inside the hogan, he started to
eat the meal prepared for him. Boiled coffee, blue corn mush, and wild
onion soup. My aunt was especially quiet that evening, thinking about
the extra work that would be involved in caring for me and feeding me.
After I was fed, my aunt threw a sheepskin down for me and that was
the only comfort I knew for many years to come.*

*My aunt's husband, Shinali, "paternal grandfather," finished his
meal, rubbed his hands together and down to his moccasins, rubbing
and praying for a good life and giving thanks for his meal. He looked*

up to his wife and said, "I did what you asked me to do. I asked your brother for one of his older children, one that would help bring in wood, herd sheep, and help us around here. He told me to tell you this: 'There's no place in this world where you can get a free handout without having to work hard for it. If you want something in your life, you have to be willing to work and sacrifice. There's not a place anywhere where you can go where everything's prepared for you. Take this child to her. She can take care of him and raise him. He's still not able to walk well, but in time he'll be able to bring wood in.' "

They say the first years of my life I had a hard time. I was always tripping, not very strong. It seems like I was always falling and very unstable. When I was around five, I started getting strong.

I never knew what a mother or father was. One day, after returning from herding sheep, I was told my father was visiting another hogan. My aunt sent me to visit him. I was anxious to know what a father looked like. When I arrived at the other hogan, I was introduced to him. He asked me over to where he was sitting, he cried and hugged me, saying, "You're my baby; I've come to take you home." Today, I don't think he meant it. I slept by him that night. I woke up in the morning, went back to my aunt's place, and took the sheep out, satisfied that I met somebody named Father. I couldn't understand the concept of "father." After that I would sometimes think about him.

One day, while herding sheep with my shinali, he took me up on a ridge somewhere near Gap. He pointed toward the east and said, "Look way over there. See the long dark ridge? At the end of the ridge is where your mother and father live. I brought you back from there when you were just a baby. You have relatives over there." I thought of my parents sometimes, wondered what my mother looked like. I barely remembered the man that was called Father.

We moved around a lot with the sheep. [My aunt and I] moved around Marble Canyon, Page, Gap, Cedar Ridge, Moenave, and around Coal Mine Mesa. My younger years were spent herding sheep every day, sometime sleeping wherever the sheep slept. My playmates were the sheepdogs, the lambs, and goats. Sometimes I played with rocks, imagining them to be horses. I made corrals with the Mormon tea that

"Did I Tell You That My Dad Wasn't Raised by His Real Mother?"

I gathered. I ate whatever I found along the way. Wild carrots, wild onions, wild potatoes. I sucked milk from milkweed; I ate the fruit that grew out of yucca plants. Sometimes I found berries to eat too. For water I sometimes would find a water hole. Find an old can and dip water out of the water hole. Sometimes I think back to it. The water would contain all kinds of flies and bugs. It was muddy, and horses and sheep and cattle would go and stand around in it, sometimes peeing in it. But people drank it.

When I hauled water, I would just pull the wagon into the middle of the watering hole and load water into the container I had. While I was loading water, my team of horses would pee and shit in the water, but we used the water that way. They didn't have water tanks then, so we depended on natural springs and whenever it rained. Sometimes people even brought their laundry there.

My clothing in my early years was made out of flour sacks sewed together for a shirt and pants. I wore them until they fell apart. I saw other boys wear Levi's, but it didn't bother me that I wore flour sacks until I got to be a teenager. I went barefooted or wore moccasins.

When it was still dark, my aunt would get me up. She would say, "Get up, my little one, run toward the Dawn and meet the Holy People. Get to know them. If you just lie there on your sheepskin looking pitiful, you'll never get anywhere in this life. You'll always be a victim to hardship. Make your body strong physically and mentally. You have a long life ahead of you."

I can still hear her now. I would want to sleep some more, but I would manage to get up and run. I would breathe that fresh air, fill up my lungs, and yell at the top of my voice, to make my lungs strong, as she would say. I would run back to the hogan, grab my rope, and look for the horses. Sometimes I would just run to the sheep corral and take out the sheep. I wanted to take them to the watering hole before it got hot. I didn't think about breakfast. I would eat whatever plants I found on the way. Sometimes my aunt's daughter, Sally, would meet me on the way back with a piece of bread that I would eat. I gathered pieces of wood that would make the evening fire.

I was young—maybe six—when I herded sheep by myself. My aunt had a big herd. Sometimes the sheep would just start wandering away from me. I couldn't round them up by myself. Sometimes I came home late at night without the sheep. I would get a scolding and was chased out of my warm sheepskin to look for the sheep. Sometimes I couldn't get the sheep to start home. Maybe they were not afraid of me because I was small, so they would just keep going in the direction they wanted to go. Sometimes I slept with the dogs and sheep wherever they stopped. I would use the dogs for my pillow and keep warm from their body heat. When they jumped up and started barking at something in the dark, I would just find me a warm sheep to lay by. I don't remember ever fearing anything in the dark or any strange noise.

Ever since I knew what life was about, I have always been around sheep. Somehow, since I was taken from my family, the sheep I took care of became my family. I knew every one of my sheep. I had names for them.

My aunt used to tell me, "Take care of those sheep. When I'm gone, they will become your mom and dad. They will provide for you, give you meat. The skin will keep you warm at night and your feet dry. Lambing season will put change in your pockets. They will take care of you." Today I can still hear her as she was sitting by me. I know her words spoke the truth. These same words I use to teach my children about sheep.

Emboldened by her success gathering stories, Ella visited Sally Williams, Lilac Tacheenie's daughter, who was a teenager when Jack was brought into her parents' house. This is what she recalled about Jack's youth:

Sally Williams:

I know I was still at home many years ago when Jack's parents came for him. I'm glad he decided to stay with us. I know Jack never blamed his mom for giving him away. He's not that kind of a person to hold bad feelings against anyone.

I know Jack many times felt confused about who his real parents *were when he was very young. One day while we were herding sheep he told me that he was going to show me a place where his mother and father lived.*

He took me on a hill, pointed east toward Howell Mesa over the blue ridge and said, "I heard, way off in that direction, I was born there. I have what is called a mother and a father." We sat there in silence for a long time just looking that way. I could tell Jack was thinking, trying to figure out what that meant. I knew he was thinking about how he ended up with us. After a while, we both got up and Jack said, "Let's go pick some firewood to take home along with the sheep. It's almost sundown, and Mom is probably wondering where we went. She's going to get worried if we don't get home before sundown." That's what he called her, Mom.

Harry Williams, Sally Williams's son:

Jack Hatathlie's father was my grandmother's [clan] brother. They made an agreement because my grandmother only had my mother, no other children. So that's how my grandmother picked up Jack. My mom was getting to be a teenager, I guess. So he was raised sort of like a brother to my mother, really. And so that's how I remember it.

When my parents were working around Flagstaff, near the Army Depot in Bellemont, I was raised by my grandmother, and Jack Hatathlie was there, and my oldest sister, Susie, also was there. We were raised together, all up in the Coal Mine area.

Jack was really a person who had a lot of determination. He's more of a person thinking about survival all the time. Nowadays people always depend on somebody, but it was never like that. I guess my grandmother and my family, we always looked up to him. And I guess, a lot of teaching he got from my grandmother, because my grandfather died in the late forties, so ever since then, he was the head of the house. People looked up to him.

I believe he was asked to go to school. But he would always say, "I will see what my mother has to say." And my grandmother was one of those people who would say, "He's the only person who's around here." I almost did the same thing, not go away to school, because of my grandmother, who would have liked me to stay and take care of the flocks. My grandmother was always saying, "The sheep are your number one concern. All those other things come second." Because of my grandmother, Jack never went to school.

I was pretty much in the same boat, but I had a grandfather named Tillman Hadley, and he's the one who took me to school. I was about eleven years old. He was a police officer at the time. Later on, he was a judge.

Jack used to make toys for me. He used to make horses for me out of clay. And he used to carve small wagons for me out of wood. Then he'd take the sole off a shoe and cut it up into rounds for the wheels. And then heat up a wire and burn it through the leather wheels, for the axle. That's what he used to make me. He used to make toys for me. We called him Bayzhe—"the One with the Knife." The way you say it is, the person who has a knife all the time. The handyman.

The other thing is, like when he was going to the store, he'd always bring candy back. Right now, from the store to here, a chocolate will all melt, but he used to carry the chocolate all the way to Coal Mine [without it melting]. I don't know how he did it.

I looked up to Jack. He was his own person. He was the person he wanted to be. Like one year, he had a watch, a pocket watch, and I always wanted to have one. I don't know how he got a hold of it. Little things like that; I always looked up to him for things like that. He was one of the first people in Coal Mine to get a truck, a red truck. At that time, most people had wagons with wood or metal wheels.

To me, he was always perfect. What I mean is, like right now, he doesn't really depend on anybody. But I really depended on him, it seemed he was always there when you needed him. He would always help when you needed it. When there was nothing to eat, he would get up to get it. He would take off about this time of the night, in the snow, and by midnight, you'd hear him outside: he'd have ended up killing a [Hopi] horse or something. Or, if there was nothing to eat, he'd walk all the way from Coal Mine to the store, the trading post in town— about thirty miles—and he would take coffee, sugar, baking powder, salt, and a twenty-five-pound flour, on his shoulder, all the way back to Coal Mine. In those days, people would look up to you if you did that. If you did that now, people would think you're crazy.

I always wanted to be the kind of person who would do that, but I never did. I ended up going to school and going to the military, and so that's about all I can tell you right now.

Glenabah Williams, Sally Williams's daughter,
Harry Williams's sister:

I have known Jack all my life. I just thought he was my grand-mother's son until I asked my mom. I went away to school and married and had children. During those years, I would come back and Jack was always there helping my grandmother or my folks. In fact, I accepted him as part of the family, so I never even asked who his parents were.

My grandmother was well taken care of when she was living by Jack and his wife. Bessie was very devoted to [Lilac]. Bessie was a hardworking mother, always busy with the children, livestock, and weaving at night. Sometimes, I think Grandmother favored Bessie over my own mother because of her weaving. Bessie had a lot of children, so Grandmother was never alone. She always had one staying with her. Sometimes when Jack didn't come over to visit, Grandma would pack her flour sack with canned fruit and crackers and walk three miles to Jack's residence. She was always welcomed there. I don't think the children even knew she was not a blood grandmother.

Growing up, Jack was always alone a lot. I thought he was always thinking about everything. He always had a question for his clan mom. She would always try to answer him. Jack was very gentle with animals. Gentle manner about him, always happy and always joking.

His clan mother didn't give him a lot in material goods, but she raised him to be the person he is today. Different from his natural brothers and sisters.

I think the Creator chose him to be raised this way so he could be an example to his family.

His natural parents then were very well off in terms of how many hogans they had, wagons, sheep, horses, and cattle. His mother was a very dressy lady with loads of jewelry. His father was a medicine man and had three wives and was able to take care of all of them. I used to see his sisters off and on. They dressed nice and always wore lots of jewelry. He was considered a very wealthy medicine man.

My grandparents were very poor. We just had our sheep, which we moved around with all the time searching for green pastures. My grandmother I never saw dressed up with loads of turquoise. She only wore two strands of coral beads and sometimes a bracelet. She was a hard worker, always working with wool or in the cornfield, so she could feed her family. She harvested corn, used corn more than a hundred ways, and lived completely off the land. She gathered seeds and roots, herbs, to eat with their meals. I know Jack many times did not eat, except for one meal a day; maybe sometimes he didn't eat at all. My grandmother always had him busy, always talking to him. She would make clothes out of flour sacks for him, made his moccasins, and in the winter he wore goatskins wrapped around his feet for warmth. His hands sometimes he wrapped with goatskin to keep warm.

I am saddened to remember today how he was raised. But he overcame all that hardship. And I think my grandmother raised him that way for a reason.

Bessie's childhood was not so dissimilar from Jack's. Livestock dominated her attention, and she had few, if any, physical comforts. Her mother died of tuberculosis when Bessie was three. She and her older sister moved in with their grandfather and lived with him for several years until he died. When Bessie was eight, she and her sister moved out on their own, following the sheep, ever in search of greener pastures, from Badger Spring to Blue Canyon and back and forth over Coal Mine Mesa, staying with relatives as they found them. The sheep became their parents; the sheep tended the girls, providing them with meat and wool and lambs, as the girls tended the sheep. Bessie and her sister learned where all the wild foods could be found; they learned every turn of the land and murmur of the wind.

"Did I Tell You That My Dad Wasn't Raised by His Real Mother?"

She caught the eye of Jack Hatathlie around Coal Mine Mesa when the two found themselves at the same squaw dances, or at the sheep dip, where the animals were treated for parasites.

"In 1950, we met at the Flagstaff powwow," says Jack, "and decided to make a life together. We didn't have a wedding because Bessie didn't have parents or grandparents to speak for her, so we just decided to make a life together." Bessie was twenty years old, and Jack was twenty-two.

✳

Harry Williams remembers when his beloved Bayzhe started to spend more and more time away from home and more and more time with Bessie at her relatives' place:

At this time, we were living right near where Jack and Bessie live now. I guess this was the very, very beginning of Jack and Bessie getting together. He was just then starting to go back and forth to see her. And one evening, he and this other relative killed a horse and skinned it. I think it was only the second or third time he met Bessie, and he wanted to take some meat over there, one side of a rib and a leg.

She lived right over the ridge from the rodeo ground. So he wanted me to ride over there with him on horseback. We took one horse over there, we took the meat, and he was sitting ahead of me and we went to Bessie's place and it was kind of the evening. And he unloaded the meat, and I had to take the horse back to my grandmother. That was something I always remembered. I guess it was kind of strange: he was always around the house, and then, all of a sudden, he was going somewhere else.

He was very good at getting Hopi horses. Probably, there was a trick to it; I don't know what it was. In the winter, Navajos don't eat cattle. They don't taste right. So we depend on horsemeat. It was survival. What they'd do, when it started snowing, when the snow started accumulating, they'd go up there to Hopi on horseback or running. They'd chase out a horse, kill it, skin it, butcher it. Jack and Sam

Begay, who were closely related, they'd get together and do these things. That was the main source of meat in those days. We never had any confrontation with the Hopis. You couldn't take a horse from a Navajo, because everybody knows everybody. That was a problem. I remember a couple of times, they even killed two horses in one night.

At this time, goods from the white world were starting to make more of an appearance on the reservation. The iron-wheeled wagons were seeing some competition from motor vehicles, and, as Harry recalled, Jack was one of the first to get a truck. Levi's were the rage on the reservation, and the style was to buy them long and roll the cuffs up about a foot—just one fold—and the tops would reach almost to the wearer's knees. Men wore boots, neckerchiefs, and cowboy hats. There wasn't much drinking yet; later the Navajos and Hopis would make home-brewed alcohol to drink and sell. Card games were a popular pastime, and although gambling in excess was and is thought to be a sign of imbalance, many Navajos enjoy gambling. "I remember the old men used to play cards," says Harry Williams. "They would play for matches or pennies. And pretty soon the fight breaks out; they used to fight. I'd always see a lot of hair the next day. They used to fight at night." The men's hair, neatly pulled up in a *tsiyeel*, apparently came down to the shoulders in the melees, and quite a bit of the long black locks would come out in other people's fists.

✳

Jack Hatathlie:

That same year we got married, we had a son who only lived a few weeks. He died of some illness. The doctors said he had water between his skull and his brain. In 1952 we had a baby daughter who we named Ella, and, in Navajo, Dasbah, same as her mother, meaning "Going to War."

"Did I Tell You That My Dad Wasn't Raised by His Real Mother?"

In Navajo, we say that children are your teachers. They teach you about what true love and sacrifice is. So Ella was our first teacher.

She was chubby with lots of curly hair. I had never been around babies, so I was always afraid to hold her, afraid she would roll out of my hand. Her mother put her in a cradleboard, and I would hold her and sing for her, and she would laugh and giggle. Her mother used to stand her up in a cradleboard against the hogan while she carried on her chores and her weaving.

We weren't sure how to take care of a baby, but we learned fast. Today we have seven daughters and four sons. We lost a son and a daughter. Each child is different with different personalities. They are unique in their own way, with some of my characteristics and some of Bessie's.

My wife was always a hard worker. When our children were arriving, we supported them with what work I could find. My wife wove all the time. During the day, she took care of the kids, cooking, cleaning, and washing all the time. She took care of the sheep and horses and also cattle. At night, she wove her rugs with just a kerosene lamp. She would weave late into the night and still was able to get up at the crack of dawn. She would start the fire, make roasted tortillas and fried potatoes; sometimes she made stew if we had mutton. They didn't have welfare or general assistance then, but we managed to raise our little ones. We always had something to eat.

I managed to put a wagon together and a team to hitch to it. This was our transportation, I hauled wood, coal, and water with it. When I was away working, my wife and the girls used it. I taught Ella and Lula how to hitch the horses. They were young, but they learned.

Sometimes they would hitch the wagon and go to my aunt's place to spend the night. That time, people visited each other a lot. You would go and spend the night with your relatives just to visit and share news.

We learned early on in our marriage that we wanted to have a good life. Most of my wife's relatives had passed on. The others had their own lives to lead, so there really was no one to help or give her direction. I was raised by my aunt and was just getting acquainted with my relatives. So, in a way, we both really felt like we didn't have a family *to fall back on. We became each other's family and decided to take care of one another.*

She's been a good relative and a good mother to my children. She made me a wealthy person because wealth is counted on how many children you have, in the Navajo way. We both learned something new with each child. We're richer now because of all the grandkids we have.

If you want a good life, you have to trust one another, take care of one another, even through hard times, always being positive and thinking good thoughts. Rise each day with prayer, and always walk with a prayer in your heart. Train your mind to be strong, to resist temptations. Learn to talk to one another and to respect each other.

Your children will watch you, and by observing you, your children will pattern themselves after you. It's hard to be positive, think and talk positively, but you can train yourself, and things are always brighter and happier for you. I want my children to learn this because it's an important part of life.

＊

Ella says that her father was surprised by how easily he spoke about the old days.

Ella says, "He said, 'I never talk about these things.' And when I ask him questions, we laugh about it, and he says that when he was young, the way he was brought up, he never thought about abuse or anything like that. He said, 'I just thought it was normal,' the way he had to work really hard, and I told him maybe today these kids are different. They know a lot or they're real smart, but he says it's really different. He never thought about those kinds of things growing up—the things we think about, the things we do. And it's—he says today's life is so free; you can do just about anything—he says it catches up with you because whatever you're not supposed to do, you end up doing. It's going to catch up with you later in life. He said he was raised with a lot of, you might say, taboos. He says today, people do it and it's nothing to them;

they know they're not supposed to do it, but he says it's much freer, and it's a much easier way of life. It's not a harsh life like the way he was raised."

✳

Jack understood that to provide for his family, he would have to earn wages. He also realized as a young man that alcohol was something he had to stay away from. Ella remembers an episode that took place when she was very small and Jack and Bessie had only two children. They were returning to the reservation from Flagstaff, where her father had been drinking, and the cops stopped him. "He got caught for DUI, so they took all of us to jail. And we had a little goat. And we stayed in a cell with the goat, and my dad stayed in another cell. That's the only time I remember my dad getting a DUI. Our relatives brought us some evaporated milk for the goat. But they couldn't bring the goat anywhere, so the goat stayed in the cell with us. I think we [my mother and sister and I] were free to go in and out, because they didn't lock us up or anything. I remember that goat staying in there on the bed and the cement floor. It was cold. It was in Tuba City."

Earlier in life, Jack had got drunk at a squaw dance and fallen asleep by a campfire. During the night, he rolled toward the fire and burned his back. Ella says he showed the scars to his children and shows them to his grandchildren, calling the burns the "stains of wine."

Part Two

12

School: "We Were Made to Feel Ashamed of Our Language and Our Culture"

Ella was born on May 5, 1952, at the Tuba City Hospital, weighing eight pounds, eight ounces. Records at the hospital show that she was sent home on May 8 with three dozen diapers, two shirts, one pair of socks, and a "white bag." Ella thinks the bag must have been a flour sack, an item Bessie used for years as a handbag.

According to records, Ella was back in the hospital six days later with an ear infection. When she was readmitted, the hospital records noted that her possessions included one shirt, one velvet skirt, one blanket, no shoes, one diaper and one diaper pin, a cradleboard, and, again, a white bag.

Bessie dressed her daughter in tiny skirts and placed her in a cradleboard, the traditional carrier Navajos use for their babies. The cradleboard holds them tightly like swaddling but also has a wooden backboard and a crown around the head for protection. It can be placed flat to make a bed or propped up, for example, to allow the baby to observe the goings-on in a room. In this position, they are at eye level with the adults and other children. Cradleboards can also be tied to a saddle so that the mother can herd sheep while her baby is safely secured.

Navajos traditionally keep their babies in the cradleboards until they start walking. One can sometimes see little ones toddling around while still tied in the cradleboard—a sure sign it's time to graduate. Ella points out that quite a few Navajos have flat areas on the backs of their heads as a result of the cradleboards. Nowadays, thicker padding is placed behind the baby's head to prevent this.

The cradleboard is a practical item, but like most objects the Navajos use in their daily lives, it is imbued with sacred significance. The two boards making up the back represent earth and sky. The arch over the top to protect the baby's head represents the rainbow, and the ties up the front that close the swaddling represent sunbeams. These natural phenomena, in addition to representing the most powerful forces of nature, are laden with symbolic significances that are elaborated in Navajo myth and in the ceremonial system. The cradleboard design was given to the Navajos by the Holy People, and the wrapping of the child in the sacred gift of the gods bestows divine protection on the child and the family. ". . . The children were wrapped in clouds and covered with Skies—Darkness, Dawn, Blue Sky, Yellow-evening-light, Sunbeam. A rainstreamer was the fringe of the top cover; there were carrying straps of sunbeam, pillows of Mirage and Heat."

Cradleboards are passed through a family, one baby after another. If and when they are no longer needed, they are placed as an offering in the tree from whose wood they were originally made. One might say there are very practical advantages to objects of daily life bearing spiritual significance—a child wrapped in the representations of the Holy People and the awesome forces of nature will be treated with matching reverence. Navajos love their children, but the fact that the baby lies wrapped in the sacred cradleboard—tied with symbolic sunbeams—may in a moment of a caregiver's panic or frustration protect it. Further, work done with sacred grinding stones and stirring sticks is more than a chore—it is part of a divine system, sanctioned and handed down by the gods. These kinds of sacred reminders help give meaning to life and to daily struggles.

Ella laughed when she saw, from the records, that her mother closed her diaper with a single pin.

Baby goats and lambs and sheepdog pups were the children's toys. Later, Ella remembers having a little bag of sheep bones—bleached white bones from the feet of sheep and goats—that she imagined to be different members of the family. Her grandmother would get a lift over to the Hopi mesas to trade or visit with friends, and Ella remembers accompanying her and bringing along her little bag of bones—sometimes playing with Hopi children and their own bone dolls.

She learned about planting in the cornfields; she attended the countless ceremonies for her relatives and neighbors. She danced by the bonfires in the summer evenings during the social part of the squaw dances, when couples wrapped in Pendleton shawls stepped rhythmically, sedately, in a large circle around the fire, as if imitating promenading couples in an Old West town. There was carding wool and staying up late as her mother told her Creation stories about the "animal people." There was hauling water and wood and watching her mom make bread and butcher sheep.

The hard but happy life at home ended for Ella, however, when she was six. She remembers the arrival one day of Jimmy Begay, an uncle who worked for the school district. He brought some socks and panties and two little dresses, each of the same design but one red, one blue. "They had sparkly designs on them, and they were a floral print," says Ella. "I always remember those dresses."

Not long after Begay's visit, a yellow bus pulled up in front of the hogan, and the driver came in and said something to Bessie. "My mom went in, and I remember her folding my dresses. She laid them on top of this cloth and she tied it, tied it in a knot. And then she went to this one jar. It had a whole bunch of change in it. And she took out some change and gave it to me."

Bessie led Ella out to the bus. "I was crying and fighting

when I found out she was putting me on the bus. And all I remember her saying was that I was going to school, I'll be back, but the bus was here for me. I was the first one; Lula wasn't old enough. And I don't remember exactly what happened, but I remember there were a lot of kids, girls, on the bus, and this bigger girl that knew me, I guess a relative from Howell Mesa, she came over and told me not to cry. I guess she'd seen me with my family. She gave me some candy. She said, 'Oh, your mom and dad, they'll come see you and check on you.' I didn't know what it was all about."

As soon as the children arrived at school, they were herded into a large room. White powder was sprinkled in their hair, and their heads were wrapped in towels. It wasn't until later that Ella had any idea they were treating the children for lice (whether or not they had any). Of course, she spoke no English. Ella remembers that her scalp burned and the fumes from the powder made her already teary and irritated eyes run and run.

"Then I remember lying on this bed. Metal beds, metal army beds. It was the first time I'd slept in a bed. At home, we slept on sheepskins. But [the dorm] smelled really strange, and [the bed] was hard, hard, hard. They had these army blankets, and they were so harsh. I guess I must have been allergic or something because I was scratching and scratching myself. And that army blanket was just like straw. And I remember, some time after that, a lady putting salve all over me and scolding me for the rash I got from that blanket."

Many more incomprehensible things happened. Ella remembers fire drills in the middle of the night. The children had to grab their army blankets and run outside, even when it was wintertime. "We would get in line [by height], even though it was freezing. I remember that."

Then there were astonishing developments, like water running out of faucets and electric lights that went on and stayed on. But the wonder of these discoveries was dimmed by the activities they allowed. The girls were required to wash out their socks and panties by hand every night. The clothes were inspected, and if they were not clean enough, the girls were ordered back to the sinks to try again. Once the cleaning met inspection standards, the children hung their laundry on the edges of the metal beds to dry overnight. Once a week the clothes would be gathered up and sent to a laundry in Flagstaff for a good cleaning. Why were the children forced to hand-wash their socks and underwear if they were sent to the cleaners every week? Ella has no idea.

On Saturdays, the children shined their shoes. All the shoes, which the tribe provided, were black or brown. If, after polishing, they were not shiny enough, the kids polished them again. She remembers being punished for speaking Navajo—which was forbidden, even for very small children who knew not a word of English. No comfort was offered by the dorm aides —the women who had the closest daily contact with the children, and who were known for their punishments. Usually it was hitting, on the hands, with sticks or rulers; otherwise, the children were told to stand in the corner. Ella remembers that on Fridays, the children were served ice cream and vanilla wafers. "If we were on restriction, we stood in the corner while all the children ate their ice cream and vanilla wafers," she says.

She stops as she remembers these scenes, overcome by the memories. When she resumes, she says, "The tactics they used really damaged the emotions of a lot of the students." Although Navajos themselves, the dorm aides ferociously maintained the BIA rules. They distinguished themselves by their cruelty and sadism and determination to beat or scrub every bit of Indian-ness out of the children.

To this day, Percy Deal, a longtime tribal official who also attended Tuba City Boarding School, remembers the smell of the eggs and bacon that were served to the white school officials and teachers, who sat behind a separation in the same room as the Indian boys, who were served gruel. They were little boys, many of whom had just been taken from home for the first time. As Deal recalls watching and smelling the plates heaped with aromatic food carried by, the pain of the experience still contorts his face. The cruelty of the deprivation of food cuts deep. In the Navajo way, food is divided among all the members of a family. This is a fundamental tenet of life: food is shared. "One of the worst things to be said about a person is 'She refused to share her food,' or 'He acts as if he had no kinsmen'—meaning about the same thing." One anthropologist tells a story about the importance of sharing food among the Navajos:

> Once while I was principal teacher of a preschool operation, I had a parent come to me to ask that one of the teacher aides be fired. The parent said that she had been at the aide's home while the aide and her husband were butchering a beef and that they refused to give her any of the meat. The parent said that any person who acted like that should not be teaching the younger children, and the community nearly dismissed the aide over the incident. The aide saved her job by explaining that the beef belonged to her husband who was Anglo, and that he did not want to share it and did not understand the Navajo attitudes toward sharing food.

Ella says that the cruel treatment of the Indian children at boarding schools caused serious damage to the little ones. "A lot of the students who went through boarding school showed no interest in self-improvement or direction," she says. "Only a few people were able to get out of boarding schools and to off-reservation towns to get training or go to the universities. A lot of them just got stuck in one place."

Some of these people, Ella says, seem to have taken to heart the lesson they learned at boarding school: that their Navajo heritage has no worth or value. And now they don't want their children to learn anything about being Navajo—even the language. "In my generation, they say they don't want their children to speak Navajo in the classroom, or even write Navajo. And I ask them, 'Why do you think that way? Why don't you want your children to learn to speak Navajo?' and the first thing they say is, 'I don't want my child to be held back. I don't want my child to have difficulties at school because of Navajo.' I think it's just what the BIA schools did to students, where we were made to feel ashamed of our language and our culture and by the way we pronounced certain words and by the way we acted.

"Like handshakes. Shaking hands with somebody, that wasn't accepted at boarding school. When you shake hands with somebody, that's how you show kinship to one another. The right hand represents compassion; it represents the woman's side of yourself. And when you shake hands with somebody, you say, 'I want to be your friend.' 'I acknowledge you as my relative.' In a way you're showing friendship, kinship, and love to somebody else by doing that. In other cultures, people hug one another. And I think about it; in our way, the Navajo way, we show affection to one another, deep feelings for one another, by shaking hands. I acknowledge my son when he comes home; I shake his hand. And I acknowledge him not by calling him his name, but his relation to me. I say *shewee*, my baby, or *shiyazhe*, my little one.

"Even little children, even babies—when I was growing up, older people would come over and shake a little baby's hand, even if he's in a cradleboard. They will acknowledge the baby in this way. Usually they'll greet him with his kinship relation, like, Hello, my son, or my uncle, or Hello, my grandfather. And that shows right away what their relation is and, too, some of what their responsibilities are toward one another. Then when that baby is a toddler, I can tell he's probably going to have a good upbringing because that little boy, he'll come up to you, that little girl, and extend his or her hand. That's a handshake. And they'll do that throughout their lives. I feel they probably have some good teachings."

The children were punished at boarding school for offering their hands to one another in greeting.

＊

In boarding school, the matrons seldom referred to the children by name—but not because they offered diminutives or Navajo terms of kinship instead. Rather, the children were most often referred to by number, which was determined by the child's seat in class, which was determined by her height. For example, if she was in Row 1, Seat 5, she would have that number all year, and respond to it if it was called out. All of her clothes were marked with the number, as was her toothbrush, and the tiny cubbyhole in which she stored her possessions. If a child was missing from her seat, the dorm aides would call out the number of the empty seat, and they'd begin a search. Children often ran away, or tried to run away.

After they were disinfected, forbidden to speak their language, scrubbed, taught to wash their clothes and shine shoes, they were taught table manners. Ella laughs, saying, "We learned what they called a 'family-style setting.' Nowadays I don't see it anymore. But I guess in a way they were trying to civilize us, all these—this bunch of wild Indians coming in." She laughs again.

"They showed us how to use a fork, how to hold a fork, how to cut your meat, and also how to use your butter knife. How to hold your bread when you spread your butter on your bread and then the proper way to eat it: you break it in half, and then you eat one side and then you eat the other side, instead of eating the whole bread at one time. How not to use your fingers: that was bad manners. How to take your napkin and fold it in your lap, not up here [at the neck] but in your lap. And then how to use just one side of your finger to hold

*Ella's first view of the white man: the young son of
visiting Mormon missionaries.*

Jack Hatathlie and daughters
Lula, Lenora, and Ella.

Mormon missionaries
explain salvation to Bessie
Hatathlie and Genevieve,
Leonora, Lula, and (behind)
Ella.

Ella and her puppy.

Bessie Hatathlie
with Lula and Ella
beside a mud hogan.

Ella and her foster sister Nancy Carter.

Ella and her foster family: Melvin, Mildred, and Nancy Carter.

Ella as movie star.

Ella in Navajo clothes before a Mormon church awards evening.

Dennis Bedonie

Newlyweds Dennis and Ella and their new Dodge Charger.

Dennis, Kimo, and Ella in Phoenix.

Danielle

Buzz

Ella and Kimo

Danielle

Danielle and her grandfather, Jack Hatathlie.

Danielle dancing in a jingle dress at a powwow.

Ella

Dennis

Ella and her grandmother, Rena Williams.

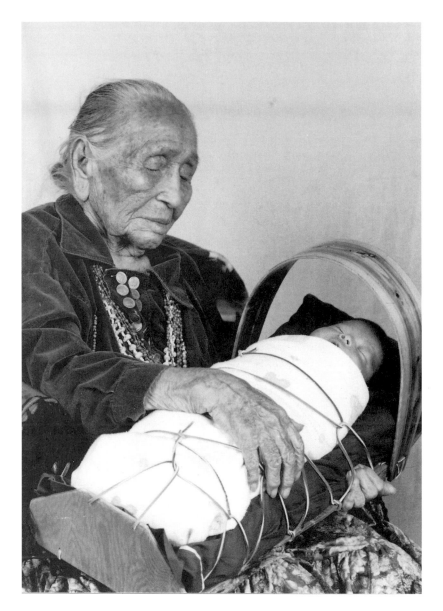

Rena Williams and her great-great-grandson.

your fork, the proper way to hold your fork, the proper way to hold your spoon, and you always had to have one hand under the table. You said, 'Thank you, please pass the potatoes' and 'Thank you, please pass this.' And you always had to pass it this way, in a circle.

"I guess at the beginning I was kind of shy, and I never used salt if the salt was over there; I was too shy to say, 'Please pass the salt,' you know. And we had to sit, like, boy, girl, boy, girl, and the way they did it, we would be coming in a line and the boys would be in a line and we would pair off. Every day we sat with somebody different during mealtimes.

"And when we had our tray in the food line, you had to say, 'May I have a small amount?'—never 'May I have a large amount?' I never understood why. Even though you said a small amount, I guess the food servers always knew how much to give you. And they just went ahead and gave you a portion. And we had to say thank you for every portion.

"Then when we got to the table, we put our trays down and we had to stand and wait for the boy [who sat next to us]. We had to all stand and wait until everybody got to the table, and then the guy would hold the . . . there was a proper way of holding the chair. He put both hands on the side and he pulled it out, and you sat down and he pushed it in. And a lot of boys got in trouble because I guess somehow they would bend their knee to push you in, maybe you were too heavy or something, and they would push it in and they would get in trouble and they would get their knees whacked. And then you would sit down and eat like that."

One of the dorm aides, a woman named Carmelita, took a particular interest in punishing her.

"I told myself that whenever I got big or got old enough," says Ella, her voice calm, "I would really, really get even with her. Because she was so mean to me. She was very strict, she always stuck the soap in my mouth for talking Navajo at boarding school. And she made me and my sister stand in the corner, because Lula would never shut up, and she always said something to me and I had to respond, or she said something to me and *she* would see us and I would be looking at Lula and she would think I also was talking, so she would make me stand in the corner.

"And on Saturdays, we used to take a walk to the trading post, and this guy [at school] started a banking system where even if we had 50 cents, he'd put it in a little envelope with our names on it and on Saturdays, after we did our duties we would go in there and he would call our names one by one, and we would get in line there and we would check out some money. I would check out a quarter, maybe, and then that afternoon, maybe about two o'clock, we'd walk to the trading post and buy candy, as usual.

"But if one of us had nits, bugs, lice, we had to stay, and we used to sit on the stairway, and we used to pick each other's lice. Or Carmelita put kerosene on our heads, or that lye stuff. She was just really mean to me. One time, I don't know what happened; it had something to do with peyote. I don't think anybody brought it to the school; it was just, I think, somebody was heard talking about it, and I was brought in there. I think I defended peyote or something, and I was brought to the office, and she told me, 'I heard you said this about'—they call it 'the medicine that you chew' in Navajo—and I said, 'Yeah, my parents use it.' And she said something like 'You guys are like rabbits, you just eat anything, any grass that's growing, that's what a rabbit does. It's bad for you.' She just kind of carried on like that."

Peyote is a cactus that is ingested by participants in services of the Native American Church. Although it contains alkaloids, the best known of which is mescaline, it is generally not considered to be addictive. Most often it produces nausea, though in some people it can produce visual or auditory hallucinations. There is indeed a physical reaction to peyote, one that is believed by adherents to augment the spiritual effect of the ceremony. Navajos say, "The medicine is working on me." Peyote is considered by Navajos to be a holy substance, a sacrament, a tool with which to communicate with the divine. Although many Navajos and government officials opposed the peyote religion after its introduction to the reservation in the 1930s, it has now been widely embraced, even by the traditional medicine people, who seem to view it as another weapon in the arsenal against bad health and misfortune.

"Carmelita punished me for a long time, and she wouldn't let me go home when my dad came. And she wouldn't let me participate in going for walks. Anytime there were walks or anything happening, I had to stay and clean; I had to stay in the dorm and clean. So I really developed that feeling inside me. And I told myself that when I ever, ever [got out], I'm going to really get even with her for what she did. And I would see her [after I left the boarding school] whenever I came back [home]; I would see her around. She never acknowledged me or anything. She's from Coal Mine. I always thought, well, one of these days I'm going to really, really get even with her.

"She was very, very much against [Navajo] culture. I guess because of the BIA then—she was working for the BIA. She was very, very strict. I really resent a lot of the things the BIA did, the way they treated us. Then there are some things that through the years I thought about, even lately, now, I think about it all the time. Maybe I've resolved a lot of those bad feelings; I've let go of a lot of those things.

"I look at some of the positive things that came out of my experience being in boarding school. Maybe that's where I gained some independence. And I—they teach a lot of crafts. And I learned how to sew, I learned to bead. I learned to do leather crafts. There are many different ways to sew. Like we used to make tablecloths using embroidery using fancy stitches on the borders, like cross-stitching. I learned that back in boarding school."

She also has at least one memory of a kind person at school.

"I remember a lady. She was a really nice Anglo lady, her name was Miss Desmond. And she was from New Jersey. I always remember that. She was from New Jersey. She was a real skinny lady. And she taught us how to pray. She would go to each room, and she would tell us, 'Go like this with our fingers and stand like this on our knees.' And I would kneel on my bed straight up like this with my hands. And I learned how to say the Lord's Prayer. And she was really nice, that lady. I remember her really well. There were some Anglo teachers who were really nice. They were affectionate; they would put their arms around you or talk to you in a nice way—rather than just yelling at you or just scolding you."

But then there were the relentless attempts to break the children's spirits: brushing teeth with salt—if the tooth powder was all gone. Getting the older girls to scrub the bodies of the younger girls in the gang showers. Rubbing their bodies with Lava soap until they were sore and bright red, as if the dorm aides wanted to scrub the very color off them. Cleaning the dorms with toothbrushes as punishment.

The older girls had to take care of their younger sisters, a task that seemed to get Ella in trouble. "I learned how to braid hair in boarding school. I guess it came to the point where, I don't know why, I guess maybe I started really hating braiding my sister Lula's hair. Maybe I wanted to do something else; I always had to take care of her. If she wet the bed, I had to go and wash the sheet for her. And I guess at one point I got really tired of it or something; somehow I took a pair of scissors from the classroom and I cut her hair. I cut her braids. She had real short hair, like this. Yeah, I got in trouble for it. But they always found ways to make me do things."

Ella had her own considerable resources. The expression one sees in early photographs of her is a dark distrust, sometimes softening to wary skepticism, an expression that these days appears on her face only in small flickers. She met a formidable adversary in Mr. Tucker, a black man, who was a guidance counselor. She thinks it was second grade, and Mr. Tucker wouldn't let Ella go home to visit her parents.

"He made this new law that you could go home only once a month. Before, you could go home anytime. And only if you had good behavior, you could go home once a month. And I remember I really wanted to go home; I was so lonesome and I don't know why I was getting punished all the time. And I wasn't allowed to go home. And I wanted to go home, and my dad came for me.

"I guess the parents really had no voice then; they weren't part of the school system. They just put us there to go to school because we were told we had to go to school. So my dad came. He wanted to take me home, but I was on restriction, and I hadn't been home for a long time, so my uncle Jimmy Begay came with him and he talked to Mr. Tucker. And that black guy wouldn't let me go home. And I don't know what Jimmy said, but he finally let me go home and I went home. I think Jimmy Begay was with, like, supplies or maintenance with the school.

"I always remember that incident there, when they had to talk to him so I could go home. But then I remember on the way home, Jimmy was talking to me: 'If you don't do as you're told, this is what happens. They won't let you go home because there's something wrong. You should always try to do what they say. You should do what they ask you to do right away; that way you get to go home once a month and you'll have all these privileges.' He was telling me that.

"See, my parents had no way of getting me. All they had was a wagon, and it's twenty miles or so. And my dad was always working somewhere. And my mom couldn't just leave her other kids and the livestock and get in the wagon for the long ride down. And so I guess it was a long time before my parents came to see me. But when school let out, they came for me and I went home.

"Other girls there, sometimes they had a chance to go home,

and when they went home, they would bring back mutton, boiled mutton, and fry bread, and we used to share it. And then later on, they used to bring back watermelons. Or my parents, they would have somebody who was going this way bring some watermelons to me. My uncle would give me watermelons, and they would mark my name on it. But I guess sometimes the matrons, they would eat it themselves. My uncle Jimmy would buy me a bag of candy and they would put my name on it. I would take out maybe one sucker and one bubble gum every so often when I asked for it. But I think a lot of times they took it too.

"I've talked to a lot of people that went to boarding school, and they have those feelings, the feelings I had toward those instructional aides, bad feelings. And I guess one time I read in a study that people who were raised in dorms had a hard time raising their own families. They turned to alcoholism and other things. And it was really hard for them to get themselves going after they got away from boarding school.

"It's just, I think, what they went through, all the abuse that they got. I guess later on it affected them, like, right around my age. They neglect their children, they drink, their family's not stable.

"When the boarding schools came, culture and tradition were thrown out—that was bad. You were forced to learn English, Christianity came in, you were assigned to churches. I think back then, if [Navajo] culture had had a role in BIA schools, maybe it would have been different. I don't remember ever reading a book on Indians other than the history books where the Indians were portrayed as the raiders—killing people—savages, being the dumb Indians. That was what I read in history books. Today, it's different. We're trying to teach our children to have pride in their culture. And we have a lot of materials now available. But we never had that kind of education. And so my generation, a lot of my generation, they kind of put a mental block in their heads toward raising their children in the old ways.

"And maybe they see themselves stuck in one place, never going anywhere, because they were brought up speaking Navajo. Maybe because of that they had problems in school, with comprehension or reading. I remember it was hard for me to pronounce the *r*s and the *th*s. We don't have an *r* or a *q* in our language. And we don't have a *u*.

"They think that speaking your language sets your child back—that learning two languages, it's hard for the kids to comprehend. Navajo is phonetic and it's very descriptive. But whatever we name, we describe whatever it is. It seems when you try to describe something in English, it's very short and very simple. But in Navajo it takes more to describe it. Like a pencil sharpener. I can say 'pencil sharpener.' But in Navajo I would have to say, 'The one you sharpen your pencil with.' If I was going to talk about a boy named Billy—say Billy has an emotional problem—I would have to really get into detail about it. There's no term for 'emotional problem,' so you'd really have to get into the details of whatever emotional problem he has. Sometimes I think back; maybe I've blocked it. I try to remember how I actually learned English when I first started school, when I was first introduced to Dick and Jane.

"I remember the teacher that we had, in fact all the teachers I had: they tried to read the first two sentences of each page, and we had to read the same thing, but she wanted us to sound just like the way she was talking. And it was really hard for us because in our language, everything is just kind of monotone. There's no exclamation or excitement. And I think that was just really hard for us.

"I had problems learning English at school. A lot of time I felt that maybe I couldn't get some of my ideas across to the teacher, or a lot of times when I was made to do an oral report, I put a lot of my time into it, and when I did my oral report I thought it was to the best of my ability. Maybe because of the way I pronounced my words, I was given a lower grade than I did on my written report. And maybe I didn't show excitement [vocal expression] where I should have. Maybe I should have paused at a certain place. And a lot of times, at boarding school, reading poems, I remember teachers telling us to do poems. And it was really hard for us to do that too. And the teacher would stand up there and read the poem like the way it should sound. Sometimes it was recorded, to where we had to listen to it over and over and over. And we had to recite the same thing over and over until we got it right.

"So I think maybe because of those kinds of experiences, a lot of these parents don't want their children to go through the same thing."

Over and over Ella returns to the beatings and punishments the children received for trying to express themselves in the language they knew. What they had to say was forbidden, and only the new words, the new pronunciation, and the new inflection were acceptable. The truth is that almost no Navajo —except those brought up away from the reservation— pronounces words like an Anglo. Almost every Navajo has a distinctive manner of speech that includes glottal stops on certain consonants, and that has a different inflection and rhythm. So for all the beatings and repetitions, the teachers were unable to tear from the children's ears the sounds on which they had been suckled.

Many children endured the punishments bravely. In fact, their determination not to flinch while being struck probably spurred the worst of the teachers to even greater efforts to break the spirits of their charges. Just about every Navajo between thirty and fifty who went to boarding schools will offer stories remarkably similar to Ella's. Those families who were inclined toward Christianity, or who felt the boarding schools were too far away, sent their kids to the mission schools that popped up on the reservation. For the most part, they were similar to the government-run schools; some were better. Most boarding schools are now closed, and have been replaced by state-run or tribally run day schools, junior high and high schools. Some mission schools remain.

Most children, at one time or another, tried to run away from boarding school, and some even died in the attempt. Ella herself once tried to escape.

"I was very small," she says. "I don't know what grade I was. I tried to run away with some cousins of mine who were from Coal Mine. And they were much older than I was. I think they came to school at an older age.

"I don't remember how we snuck out of the school, but I remember the sand dunes over by Castle Rock. We were there. And I remember walking, and at times, I guess, I would get tired. And they would carry me piggyback. There were three girls. And somewhere, I don't remember where it was, I think they knew where they were going, and we went across that Moencopi wash. I remember them jumping from one rock to the other; there must have been just a little water. And I remember falling and slipping a couple of times, and we managed to get across, and I remember going up a hill, and then I got thirsty and I was really tired and another of the girls started crying too.

"We started back; I started back with her. The sun was going down, and we [had] left real early in the morning. So the [other] girls went on and we turned back and we got on the highway, and we were just walking on the highway. And I guess they were looking for us, because we saw this pickup truck come by and the man came out; he just really yelled at us. I don't remember what he said but it was to where we were both crying. We were really crying and he got us into the truck and we got back to the dorm and I remember they hit us with ruler sticks, yardsticks, on the bottom, on the back. We were standing. Because when they were doing that to her, the yardstick broke. I was crying. I don't remember feeling the pain, but I remember being hit, and I was really crying.

"And then they put us under the dorm—it was a real black—I guess it was the basement and it had dirt floors. They put us in there and they closed the door and it was dark in there. And we stayed in there for I don't know how long. Every once in a while, I could feel bugs crawling on me. And we cried. I don't know how old she was; she was older than me. She came over and she was feeling around and she found me and she put her arm around me and she was talking to me and telling me not to cry, that we'll get out; they'll let us out. And if I kept crying, they would hear us and they [were] not going to let us out. I guess I stopped crying. We just stayed there, I don't know how long we stayed there.

"Then after we got out, I guess at one point, when they brought us out they asked us, where did those girls go? And we kept saying we didn't know. 'They were just walking that way, and we just decided to turn back.' I guess she was doing the talking. And when they were questioning her, I don't remember what responses she was giving them, but I could hear them hitting her again. And after we got out I wasn't allowed to go home; my parents didn't come by either. I don't think they were ever told that I had tried to run away. Tincer Nez's wife, she ran away [when she was a little girl]. I remember her running away, again, later. I remember hearing there were some boys who ran away and they froze somewhere. Kids used to run away. I remember hearing that kids ran away."

✳

In spite of her treatment, Ella has made peace with her experiences in boarding school. She realized she had put away some of her anger when she began to bump into Carmelita, her dorm aide nemesis, at powwows. Carmelita's granddaughter and Ella's daughter, Nell, became friends, so Ella and Carmelita saw each other now and then and talked. Ella doesn't know if Carmelita knows or remembers that Ella was once one of her charges. Ella has never brought up the subject.

"Today she asks me for help," says Ella. "And I help her. I never talk about my boarding school years with her. And Dennis tells me, 'You should talk to her.' But I haven't."

"She always calls me; she's always happy, which you know [was a side] I never saw. She's an older person. She'll come over and she'll lay on my bed and she'll talk. She'll come over and talk, and she'll ask me, you know, 'How do you make this, can you help me, can you help me write this paper, or can you help interpret this paper for me?' She's from out there [back home in Coal Mine, but] she had a relo house built. But anyway, she always comes around, she's always laughing. She's always in a way encouraging me to keep going the way I am, and she even tells me to do more. And one of the things she tells me: she told me a couple of months ago, to move away from Tuba City. She said, 'You should live someplace like San Francisco or move back East and start something over there with Indian people,' and she said, 'In cities, Indian people are lost. And they don't have somebody to talk to them about their culture.' And she said, 'You should just go somewhere away from Tuba City and work with Indian people over there because they really have a need for someone to bring them their teaching.' "

13

Mormon Placement:
"I Remember My Foster Mom Crying.
She Was Crying and Hugging Me"

Boarding school dramatically changed the lives of Navajo children. It was a real and symbolic stripping down, an abrupt introduction to a new world and a rather violent replacement of the familiar with the new and strange—new clothes, new haircuts, new language, new ways. No explanations.

Ella says the message was plain: the children were good for nothing. She says, "I wish somebody had told me that if I set my mind on something, I could accomplish it. At boarding school, they always put you down a lot. They were never really trying to encourage you."

"What were they preparing you for?" I ask.

"Oh, probably to become a housekeeper. Live with a white family, be a housekeeper for them. A lot of young people, they sent them off to live with white families, that's how they made extra money in the summertime."

The message of the Navajo children's unacceptability was compounded and intensified by its coming not only from the white teachers but also from the Navajo dorm aides—those poor souls who beat the children and stole from them the few possessions they had that connected them with home and the familiar.

Of course, in addition to the brutality and the resounding messages that the children were worthless, there were other, subtler messages that confused the children because they were so different from what they learned at home. In the Navajo home, it is not customary to ask for food: you simply take what you need. In school, the children were instructed to ask for food, though Ella could never bring herself to ask for her favorite treat—salt. And the children were never to ask for the amount of food their bellies demanded—only "a small portion, please."

The boarding school overlooked an essential element that all children need to grow, to know themselves, to learn, and eventually to become productive citizens—the day-to-day experience of being valued and loved. No one provided this. Though the children were taken from their families, no substitutes were offered, save the occasional kind white Christian lady who taught them how to pray to a strange god.

In addition to the lack of love and nurturing, after they were stripped of their Indian identities no accessible substitute system of behavior and ethics was offered. Some of the children became shells, walking automatons. Ella sees them around. Some now belong to "Holy Roller churches," as Ella puts it, but don't really understand what it's all about. Most of the children were taken to churches and baptized—parents weren't consulted; in fact, many have been baptized more than once, by different denominations. Most Navajo kids don't remember much about the churches except which ones offered after-school basketball.

The summer after her first year in school, Ella was sent away in an airplane to a hospital—she doesn't know where but thinks it was Salt Lake City—for an operation to correct her hip. The congenital hip defect comes down through her mother's family—her mother's sister has the problem in both hips —and eventually Ella and three of her sisters would be affected by it. By the time Ella's younger sisters, Theresa and Levon, were born, medical technology had advanced, and the problem was corrected by putting casts on the children when they were babies.

But Ella was sent for an operation. She remembers being escorted by a nurse into an airplane and then taken by car. "I remember when I was leaving, my mom brought me a bag of mutton, and I didn't know what to do with it, and I threw it in the trash, and then when we left on the airplane, I cried for a long time because I wanted to eat some mutton. And she brought me a box, a little jewelry box that had red beads; there was a lot of red beads. Maybe she knew I would be a beader in my future. She bought me a box of beads, and I took that."

She remembers the cribs: "The ones that slide up and down; they look like cages?" This was quite strange for a girl who, before the bunk beds of boarding school, had always slept on the floor. She remembers getting prepped for the operation, and she remembers being in a cast up to her waist, down to her ankle on her left leg, and down to her knee on the right. She remembers lying in bed for a long time, on her belly, using a bedpan, getting turned by the nurses. She thinks that sometime after the operation, she may have been returned to the Tuba City Hospital for her recuperation, because she has one memory of her parents coming to visit.

Ella was sent to Salt Lake City for the operation not once, but twice. The first time, the doctors botched the job. When she went back for it to be redone, Lula went with her, to have her own hip operated on. Although her memory of the time is fragmentary, there are images and moments she remembers vividly. One of them was when the doctors removed the metal wires with which they had pinned her bones: "They stitched our legs with something like wire. I remember digging inside my cast and feeling that wire. And I think there was one wire that went all the way up—because I remember when they would snip one end, and they would get these pliers-like things and they would pull it real fast, and it came out. I don't know how long we had our casts on. We had our casts on for a long time, and then when they took our casts off, that's when they took that wire out of our legs. It was stitched with our legs. I remember it hurt. I was crying really loud and the doctor was mad at me."

Ella has two scars, each a crescent shape, from the back of her waist, forward and around her hip, about twelve inches long, one inside the other. She says a big chunk of skin near her hip is also gone.

In the hospital, she watched TV for the first time. Bugs Bunny and Caspar the Ghost. "Those were the movies I liked." There was also a kindly man.

"I remember the janitor. He was really nice to me. He used to bring me something all the time. I used to listen for his mop bucket. He was mopping the rooms. And I always knew that right after dinner he would come around and mop. And I would ask, 'Can I eat? Can I eat now?' I guess because I was thinking that after I ate, I knew that he would be coming along pretty soon. So I guess to hurry it up I would tell the nurse I wanted to eat. I know he was an Indian; he had black hair. But I don't know if he was a Navajo. And I always remember he had a ring too. A turquoise ring. And he used to let me play with his ring when he was mopping the little room where the kids were. And I would listen for his mop bucket, then he would let me play with his ring. Then one time he brought me a doll. And he would bring me little things to play with. I don't know; maybe I was homesick. At night sometimes I would cry. I guess I was lonesome or something. The second time, I remember Lula too being there. And she would cry. I would tell her not to cry, you know, then I would cry at night, and she would start crying."

Ella graduated from high school when she was nineteen, so she figures she lost a half a year for each operation—including the surgery, the several months in a cast, and learning to walk again. The doctors told the girls they should never ride horses, but they did anyway. Ella still walks with a rather pronounced limp, which she says gets worse after hard work. When she was pregnant, the doctors told her that she might have trouble with it, and that when she was older she might get arthritis in the joint.

✳

In about fourth grade, Ella decided to leave the Tuba City Boarding School. She saw sheets on the bulletin boards informing children of a program called Mormon Placement. She signed up, though she had little idea what it was. She knew just one thing—it would take her away from the Tuba City Boarding School and the Carmelitas of the world. Perhaps this decision saved her from the fate of many of her classmates, the ones she says were unable to find a direction or motivation for the future.

Her decision seemed matter-of-fact, and her parents didn't object. In time, her sisters Lula, Lenora, and Genny would also go on placement. Navajo families considered it a good opportunity for their children to have experience in the white world and a chance for a better education. Also, in those days social services didn't exist, and sending kids off to placement offered a financial relief to families who had many children at home. In addition to her own eleven children, Bessie took in other children over the years whose parents for various reasons couldn't take care of them.

In fifth grade, Ella set off on a new journey, another bus ride, much farther than the twenty-five-mile trip to Tuba City. But this time she didn't greet the bus with screams and tears.

"They just told us to report here at the church on a certain day," she recalls, "and we all just packed up and got on the buses and we left to various places.

"Our bus went to California, to Pomona, to a big church. And there we spent the night. I think they gave us sleeping bags. And the next day they gave us a big breakfast. I don't remember if I knew the other people on the bus. I must have known some of the kids. Some of them had already been on placement, so when they got [to Pomona], their foster parents were already waiting for them. So they went home right there. And those of us that were new, I guess, just waited. And the next day after breakfast, I think they talked to everybody. I remember something happening, and then they just told us to wait, that our families were going to pick us up.

"I don't remember thinking who I was going to be with. I must have thought about it. But I remember being really maybe nervous, kinda like, in a way anxious about my name being called. Every time somebody came, I would wonder if my name would be called.

"And then they called me.

"I went into a little room, and there was my foster mom and foster dad and foster sister. I guess she was the last one at home; she had not left home yet. But everybody else had grown up and left. And they introduced me to the family. Their names were Melvin and Mildred Carter. And Nancy was their daughter. (There were three other grown children: Clarice and Louise, two more foster sisters, and a foster brother named Terry.)

"I remember my foster mom crying. She was crying and hugging me. They were older, and later on I heard they had a hard time being approved for taking in a child because of their age. But he had so much influence in the church, and he was a bishop in the church, and she had so many roles in the church, and I guess that's how they got approved.

"At their home, I had a room. They kind of had a bedroom in the middle of the house, and the next room was her room, my sister's. Then there was a living room. I was kinda way on the other side."

The Carters lived in a predominantly Mexican part of town. Melvin ran a ward—a division of the Mormon church system. He also ran a business that manufactured airplane engines, and taught English to Mexicans at night. Ella felt that her foster parents were good and kind, always "helping people," a virtue that was valued by Navajos. Ella was discouraged, however, from socializing with the Mexicans, and after a brief tenure at the neighborhood schools, she was sent to school in a more affluent part of town, the same school that her foster sister Nancy attended.

Her foster parents were very protective of her. Her best friend was a Mexican girl from the neighborhood, but, according to Ella, "[my foster parents] wanted my friends to be people from the church. The church that I went to wasn't Mexican either. It was just white people, [though] we had some Hawaiians. There was another Mormon church that was for Mexican people, and it was taught in the Spanish language too. But for some reason, they didn't want me to get mixed up with those people, I guess. I got to know a lot of my neighbors, my friends who lived in the neighborhood. I couldn't spend the night at their house. But I could spend the night way over here, three miles away, in Montebello. I could go over there for a pajama party. But it had to be a Mormon family too; it couldn't be just anybody. It had to be somebody from the church.

"I did everything that they did. I was just part of the family. I was never made to feel different from them. Everything was equal. I got to be real close to my sister who was at home, the last one to leave. I was included in everything. During the wintertime, we traveled. Anytime that we were off, on vacation, we were always going someplace. I had a chance to go across the United States to Virginia—Norfolk, Virginia. They had a son-in-law who made a career in the navy. I never really got to know that sister, because she lived all over. [She was] a navy wife.

"I think when I first got there, I was lonely. I was lonesome for my family. I remember crying sometimes. I guess sometimes I was quiet, I got too quiet or something, I guess they worried I was lonesome or something. They would try to take me places

to get me out of that. And my foster mom, she was really—
she was really a warm person, a loving person. She would talk
to me, you know. And then when I came home, I guess through
the years I looked forward to going back. And it didn't bother
me after that. I don't think I was homesick after that, after
going home for the summer.

"I saw in other students that went—when they went back
home, they didn't want to sit on the floor to eat. They wanted
to wash all the time. At that time, you couldn't use water like
[I was used to]. It was mostly for washing the hands and face
and for cooking. I had cousins that went [on placement]. Later
on, when I got to high school, I found out that every time they
came back during the summer, they would say they didn't
understand Navajo. And people were interpreting for them. Or
they would talk real funny in Navajo. To me that was stupid.
I knew darn well they could speak Navajo as well as I did.

"I don't think I ever said that I forgot the language of Navajo.
I knew what was expected of me when I got home, and I just
went right back into that role. When I got back on placement, I was able to make the transition back into that role. And
today, I think about it, and I think I acted different when I was
home. I acted the way I would act being around my family,
taking part in everything; that was a natural part of me. And
then when I went back [to California], I made that transition
back to the white world. I had to work hard at it. Just, I guess,
just like in the white world, my family, they kissed a lot. I
guess after I got older, I didn't like it. Every morning, my mom
kissed me before I went to school. And later on, I guess, I
didn't like it. I told my foster dad that I preferred shaking
hands." Ella laughs. In the Navajo way, "little children are
hugged and babies are kissed, if they're babies, but not when
you get older.

"But I didn't really have a problem going back and forth in
those worlds. [When I was with my foster parents] I guess I
acted like them, talked like them, showed excitement. I don't

know. I just become a part of the way they were. I don't have any regrets about going on placement. I think about it: maybe that's where I saw that it's important to go to school, because they really stressed it. They stressed education."

Ella excelled in school and in church. In an article for a Mormon newspaper, she wrote: "The time that I've spent here has really gone by fast. I can't believe how or where time could creep by that fast. In this year and a half that I've spent here on my mission, I've learned more than I could have learned from seminary. The gospel must be lived all day long to really get the meaning of it. It's a great challenge but a wonderful goal we are aiming for."

In the same issue of the local paper, Ella's foster mother writes of her pride in Ella's accomplishments at the Regional Indian Conference for the Indian placement students. She noted that Ella won an "excellent" for her speech and an "excellent" for her handicrafts. She remarked that all the students mentioned their gratitude to the Mormon church for its high standards, and also the love of their foster parents. She exhorted more families to take in Indian students "so they can become leaders and be able to help their own people."

The Mormons have special feelings for Indian people.

"They say that the Indian people were the first people," says Ella. "And the prophecies say the Indian people will save the world, that Indian people are really the direct descendants of the person up there. They call us Lamanites. There's a scripture in the Book of Mormon that they always brought out, and it says that in the Latter Days the Lamanites will blossom as a rose, that they're the ones who are going to save the country, and stuff like that. They were, in a way, helping the process of that scripture. They felt that they were helping one of the Lamanites to maybe be one of the leaders in the church. They really put a lot of emphasis on that one scripture. The whole Mormon church is based on that, the Book of Mormon. It talks a lot about different things that happened."

Indians are believed to be a lost tribe of Israel whose skin turned dark "after they had dwindled in unbelief." When they return to the Mormon fold, "their scales of darkness shall begin to fall from their eyes," and they shall become "a white and delightsome people." A leader of the Mormon church told the Los Angeles *Times* that the complexions of Indian children did in fact lighten when they were on placement—owing to the fact that they played piano and flute and were exposed to higher culture. Navajos drily point out that the children's skin lightened because they were away from the hot Arizona sun.

Not all of Ella's life in California was devoted to religious work. Her foster family seemed to run in some interesting social circles. "We went to see Paul Newman," says Ella. "He had a real short haircut. Yeah, Paul Newman had something to do with my foster father's company. I remember going to see him. I remember going to see, what's her name, Sally Field, when she was a really young girl. We went to visit Sally Field's grandmother, I think, an old lady, and Sally Field was there, she was going to acting school. She was a model or something like that. She was already doing shows. *Gidget*. Well, at home, everybody called her Gidget too. I didn't like her. She just ignored me. I don't know, maybe [because] I was different. I wasn't the same color as they were. We just sat out at the pool while they did their thing. I remember going over there to visit. I remember going through a locked gate.

"They were up there in the Beverly Hills area. They had something to do with my foster dad. It was a business-type thing. And my foster mom, she went to a lot of social events. Because I remember meeting these people also at plays, theater. They were boring people to me. It was so boring to go to those sort of things. The plays, the parties, the open houses. The operas.

"They were trying to, I think they were trying to . . . how do you say it? They were trying to acculturate me. But I never cared for those things. And I remember my foster mother saying, 'We spent so much money for that seat and you didn't even enjoy it.' I remember her quoting me once a price of $75 to see a play called *Seaside*—no, *West Side Story*.

"I didn't understand it, maybe that's why I didn't like it. We went to see *Funny Girl*. She really liked Barbra Streisand, so we went to all the Barbra Streisand movies. Anyway, it was all these plays—*Fiddler on the Roof*. Maybe I didn't understand it."

Ella still feels left out by the chatter of white people. "They talk about things that are in the headlines," she says, "like what's happening in Afghanistan, Africa, or Guatemala. You know, I really don't know that much [about those] things, so when they talk about it, I can't relate to them. And then they talk about certain sports, like some of them play hockey, the men, and I can't relate to that. They talk about vacations that they go on with their families. They talk about things like that, and it's just totally different from my life.

"They talk about different foods. I think I asked somebody what an hors d'oeuvre was. Okay, they talk about things like that. I didn't know what that was, and I asked somebody about it. I think a lot of Indians are like that. They don't feel right in talking to white people, because they've been, all their lives, they've been looked down upon, I guess, by white people. They think the way they live might not be accepted by a white person. What they eat might not be accepted by a white person, or the way they eat. They feel like that."

But when it came to the plays and musicals to which her foster parents brought her, part of the trouble may just have been her age. Her foster sister seemed to be as bored as Ella was. "She felt the same way as I did—didn't understand it."

Ella encountered new foods with her foster family, foods that are now common in her own home. "Every Friday we ate out. I was in high school, actually, maybe junior high, when I first ate pizza. And I didn't like it. So when we went to a pizza house, I would get something else, maybe like spaghetti or something. I didn't know what spaghetti was. And my first impression was that it was some kind of worms. I didn't know how to eat spaghetti either."

For nine years, Ella went back and forth between the reservation in the summer and her foster parents in California for the rest of the year. In summertime, she butchered sheep, hauled water, participated in the ceremonies, caught up on family news, gossiped, laughed, went to the swap meet, visited her relatives, wove, and did bead work. In winter she followed the ways of the Mormons, went to school, traveled, attended theater and saw movies. She played the role that was required of her in each world, though she found it a strain.

"I was able to go back to this life, when my parents did ceremonies. When you come from a traditional family, particularly in the summertime, the whole family's involved in sharing and helping. If there's a ceremony, you go over there and help over there, if you believe in these things. [But in California] your whole world revolved around the church. Everybody that you met, communicated with or related to, they were all Mormon people.

"I guess at one time, I believed I would leave [home] behind and just become totally Mormon."

✸

Ella did not make plans to go to college after she graduated from high school in California. It is hard for her now to remember how or why she made some of these decisions. As she speaks about it, it has the quality of a dream, as if she were not quite a full participant. Her memories are sketchy. Ella says she didn't go to college, because "I think my main thing was doing work for the church. I was trying to get recommended for temple work."

In the temple, she says, "there are rooms, celestial rooms, these rooms represented the different phases of where you go to when you go on [in Mormonism]. With the Mormon people, they don't preach [that] you're going to go to hell, burn in hell. I heard it there, but it wasn't, like, pounded into your head. It was always teachings about the afterlife, how to earn the right to get into the next world. And there was always this, [even if] you didn't live the word of God to the fullest, you still have the chance to go up to the highest kingdom."

Perhaps this aspect of Mormonism appealed to Ella because of its similarity to the Creation stories of the Navajos, in which the people ascended through three worlds before finding this, the fourth world. She was also fascinated by the concept of sealing—a married couple could be sealed—and they would therefore be reunited as husband and wife in the afterworld. One could also be sealed with one's children, which guaranteed everyone would be together in the afterlife. "And they say if you didn't have a temple marriage, or if you didn't get sealed in the church, then when you'd go into the next world, you would just be by yourself; your family wouldn't be with you," she recalls. "And if you had a temple marriage and were sealed together in the temple and your spouse died, but you remarried later in life, when you died and went to the afterworld, you would be with your first wife."

Ella says Navajos have a concept of an afterlife: "[It's] a place where your body is put back to the natural state. There's life again. You meet all your relatives, your kids, the people who have passed on. And you continue to live again. It's just another step in life. They say [the people in the north] see us."

Navajo myths and stories do not offer detailed pictures of what this place would be like, unlike elaborate descriptions of the afterlife in other Native American cultures. Leading scholars argue about whether the Navajos have any concept of individual immortality. The focus of Navajo life is most definitely on this world, in maximizing the time and quality of life here. One Navajo scholar has written, "Christianity strives for future personal survival and resurrection by trial on earth; Navajo religion, accepting the body and all personal shortcomings, emphasizes the opportunities of the present and tries to amalgamate them into a unity of experience and being with the past and future."

Perhaps in her teenage years, Ella found the highly detailed theology of the Mormons appealing, along with their concept of ensuring one's place in the afterlife. Ella pauses for a moment, then says, "I don't know. I guess I really wanted to be a Mormon. I wanted to live that life. A life that was comfortable."

Nevertheless, in her own way, Ella managed to defy her foster parents in almost the worst way imaginable. Again, it all seems to have happened to her. When she speaks of it, she does so in a low voice, with little expression, as if she'd rather not remember too much.

14

Robert Ortiz

"He was my best friend's brother. [His name was] Robert Ortiz. I knew him since I was in junior high. He was way older. He was ten years older than me. I married him when I was like eighteen. He would have been how old? Twenty-eight."

Though her foster parents encouraged Ella to make friends with the Mormon children in the more affluent parts of town, Ella's closest friends were the Mexicans who lived in the neighborhood in which the Carters lived. Although she had been indoctrinated in the Mormon faith and professed to want to work in the church, she married a Catholic. Ella can't explain any of this. When I ask her if she loved Robert Ortiz, her best friend's older brother, she answers, "I don't know."

"How did it happen?"

"I don't know. I don't remember. That's been a long time. I knew him way, way back when I was in junior high. Maybe even before. He was just like—I would take my dolls over there [to play with her best friend]. And he was in the service and often on leave. He always had military clothes on. And we would be playing in her room. And he would come. I guess I was maybe like Danielle [who is twelve now]. Maybe he was like Kimo [who is twenty]. He would take us to the movies, for ice cream, take us to Long Beach, the carnival rides. Things like that in that time.

"Sometimes in the summer my friend would write to me and tell me her brother was home again on leave. And then after that, I heard he was in Vietnam. I don't know what happened in Vietnam the first time he went. I never asked him. But he was in the hospital. I think he was two years in the army, and then he went into the Marines. Special Forces.

"His family, they were very strong Catholics. And they spoke nothing but Spanish. Even around me, they all spoke Spanish. The mother didn't speak English at all. And the grandfather spoke English, but he rarely came to visit. Maybe I saw him less than ten times. Because he would fly in from Madrid and come to visit his kids. She was Mexican, from Guadalajara, and he was from Madrid."

Robert's uncle became involved in the Mormon church, and brought Robert with him a few times.

"I don't think his mom really liked that. I remember her saying, 'We're going to always be Catholics.' And I remember going to the Catholic Church a couple of times. And my foster parents knew I went to the Catholic Church. They didn't say anything about it. And then [Robert] started coming to our church. Maybe I invited him to something at our church. That's when he started coming to church. I'm not saying he really had an interest in it, but . . ."

"Did your foster parents approve?"

"Well, it was something I guess I did."

✳

Ella and Robert married and moved into a small apartment, but Robert spent most of his time at Camp Roberts near Monterey. He soon left for another tour of duty in Vietnam.

Mildred Carter suggested that Ella move back with them

while Robert was away. They set her up in the guest house. Ella's foster sister Nancy had proposed that Ella come live with her, because she had an apartment of her own across town. But Ella's foster mother said she didn't think that was a good idea—so Ella stayed with her foster parents.

Most of this period remains a blur to Ella, except the day when Robert's brother and three servicemen arrived unexpectedly at the house. She was with her foster sister inside when her foster father came to tell her that some men from the military wanted to see her. He suggested they pray together first.

"I didn't know what was going on," says Ella. "And so we prayed; we prayed. And then he took me out there and I saw these men. I didn't know what they were there for. They gave me a letter, one that said his helicopter had been shot down, but there were no bodies found. So it said he was missing in action. That's all they told me."

Ella was five months pregnant. She discovered that she was not listed as a beneficiary on Robert's insurance policy. His mother was the beneficiary, and Mrs. Ortiz did not offer Ella any financial help.

Ella's life had very quickly turned dark. She had precipitately married out of her own and her foster parents' faith, to a family that did not accept her. She was pregnant and her mate was missing in action in Vietnam and presumed dead. Neither she nor her unborn child received any financial help from Robert Ortiz's life insurance.

The one bright spot in her life was a Hawaiian man from her church named Kimo. When she was younger, Ella had babysat for Kimo's brother. Through the years, Kimo had spent a lot of time with Ella and her foster family. "He was like my big brother. He was the one who took me to my prom. He was the one who took me to all my school functions, even though he wasn't my boyfriend. I called him my brother, he called me his sister."

He also took Ella and Nancy on a forbidden trip to, of all

places, Sunset Strip. "Sunset Strip was a bad place to go," recalls Ella. "I mean, I didn't see anything bad about it—I was too young. Maybe bad people hung out there, prostitutes. Even to look at one was a sin. You didn't talk to those kind of people. And he used to drive us down there to Sunset Strip, and it was new to me. I lived in this glass world, and I guess I was so naïve about all these things, and I would watch TV about all these things that were happening in the world, but, I don't know, I never really thought about it. He was really, really strong with the church too. But he drove us to Sunset Strip. I didn't know what was bad about Sunset Strip. I'd never gone down there."

Kimo spent much of his spare time with Ella. "Kimo was there. He knew that I didn't have anybody around, so he would come. He spent a lot of time with me. He would talk with me, going to church and praying in church. We did a lot of praying." Ella laughs softly. "He just told me to forget about [Robert]. He just encouraged me to get more into the church and not sit at home all the time, but to do things—like they had young marrieds, young people's meetings, activities, religious societies for older ladies who would get together."

"Were you scared about what would happen to you?"

"No."

"Did you miss Robert?"

"I guess at the beginning I did; that's why Kimo used to take me to the church a lot. He would pray with me. He would tell me I had to start thinking about what I was going to do now. I remember going to some kind of night class. I think I enrolled in a night class for something."

"Was Kimo in love with you?"

Ella shakes her head, dismisses this question out of hand. "No. He was like a brother. I don't know. We went everywhere, my sister, me, and him. Even after I was pregnant, we just went everywhere together. He was helping me get over it."

At this time, Ella's father, Jack, called her repeatedly, asking her to come home. Her sister Lula called; her uncle called. "You need to come back," they told her.

About a month after the death, Kimo told her that perhaps it would be the best thing to do. "Kimo said maybe it would be better if I went back to my people, have my baby around my own people. Up here, everybody's kind of like grabbing. 'You need to be with your own family,' he said. So we got on a plane to Phoenix. I came with Kimo. We came to Phoenix, and then we caught the bus to Flagstaff. My dad was there waiting. He brought us back to Coal Mine. The next day, my uncle took Kimo back to Flagstaff and he went to Phoenix."

"The week that I was supposed to be due—they told me I was due the last week of August—Kimo came back. They [thought I'd give birth] on August 29. He was here for the weekend. I still didn't have my baby, so he went back [to California] because he had to work."

A week later, Ella gave birth to a boy, whom her father named Arnold, after a medicine man named Wilson Arnold, a man who also taught Navajo culture at Navajo Community College, and was a leader of the Native American Church. He was also known for composing peyote songs.

Arnold was the boy's official name, Arnold Ray Ortiz Hatathlie.

A month after the birth, Kimo came to visit. He had decided to go on a Mormon mission, and was trying to get assigned to the reservation. "And the next thing I knew, he was here," says Ella. As a missionary he was not allowed to spend much time with any single person, however, but was required to work the population, missionizing. Ella explains, without a hint of resentment, "You're supposed to talk about the word of God, nothing else, if you're a missionary, no interest in anybody. Your only purpose is to pray for people. So when he was on a mission here—I understood that part—whenever we got together it was only at church; even though I was no longer a member of the church, I would go to the church. We would talk there. Outside the church, we only talked when his, they call it 'brother'—you have two people who are together all the time. I guess the reason is to make sure that you don't do anything wrong."

Kimo stayed about six months and then moved to New Mexico for a year and a half. Then he went off to Brigham Young University, where he met and married a Navajo woman. They had eight children. His wife eventually left him and returned to the reservation, and he moved back to Los Angeles with the six youngest children. Although Ella has not seen him recently, she hears news of him from her foster sister.

"Ella, don't you think Kimo was in love with you?"

This time, Ella laughs. "I don't know. I never felt that way toward him. He was like a brother to me. I didn't get goose pimples when he was around or anything. He was a person I could talk to about anything."

But he did ask her to do something for him. "Kimo said to me, 'When you have your baby, if it's boy, name him Kimo.' That's how Kimo got his name."

When Ella returned to the reservation, the appeal of the Mormon church vanished. She was back home, in the bosom of her family, with the people who loved her and would support her no matter what happened. The sting of her experience with Robert's family remained with her, and although Robert's uncle occasionally wrote, informing her of family matters, she never wrote back. Her mother-in-law made an effort, when Kimo was ten years old, to contact Ella and inquire about meeting her grandson. Ella did not answer her letter either.

Ella discussed her feelings about the Mormon church with her friend Kimo, and she was immensely relieved when he told her he understood her decision to abandon it. However, he urged her to talk about her decision with her foster family, who had nurtured her for nine years and who had had such high hopes for her within their community.

"Kimo said to me, 'You need to understand how your foster

family is feeling too.' He's the one that made me talk to my foster family about leaving the church—because I was scared to tell them about it—why I wanted to just go home."

And once she was home, it was hard to imagine how she could have thought of living in any other world. Her father was overjoyed to have her back, and very excited about being a grandfather.

Years later, Jack told Ella how he felt about the day of Kimo's birth:

My first grandchild. I kept thinking about it. It was a very weird feeling. I wondered what it would feel like to be called a grandfather. I got used to being called Daddy after eleven children, but now I was going to be a grandfather.

When I first heard from my daughter I was going to be a grandfather, I kept thinking about it. I wondered if it was going to be a boy or a girl and wondered what it would look like since it was going to be part Spanish. As I got closer to the birth of my first grandchild, I worried about my daughter. I wanted her to come home from L.A. So I called her and told her I wanted her home to give birth here.

On the evening of September 7, 1971, I took my daughter to the Indian Health Service hospital. I burned cedar for her and left her at the hospital. She was in labor all night, and the next day, September 8 at 1:42 p.m., she gave birth to a son, nine pounds, four ounces. I saw him when he was only a few minutes old.

I looked through the glass window at the newborns. All the babies had dark black hair and chubby brown skins. I looked at all of them and picked out one that had dark black hair, and lots of it too. I said, That's my grandson. I asked the nurse to confirm it. She pointed to one that was all red-skinned and bald. She told me because he was a half-breed; he lost out on the hair. I stumbled to my daughter's room and told her my grandson was bald and there was a mistake. She told me that he was my grandson. My wife was so excited too. She was also expecting again; within the month Levon was born.

Before my grandson was born, I said that I would carry him in my pocket all the time if it was a boy. Well, he sure stuck to me. He followed me everywhere. I took him everywhere with me. He didn't want his mom, so he slept with me, and when she was at work and, later, school, he stayed with us. When I lived in Page, he lived with me too. Kimo and I are very close. We named him "the Light One of the Bitter Water Clan." Our relatives knew him by that name too. He's got some of my character, always acknowledging his relatives, smiling and very generous. I spoiled him a lot, and even today he's special because he added to my wisdom.

15

A Real Navajo Wedding

Soon after Kimo's birth, Ella's grandmother, Lilac Tacheenie, decided Ella needed a man to help raise her son. Ella had no inkling of Lilac's activities until one day when she was informed that her wedding clothes had been made.

She would be marrying Dennis Bedonie, whose relatives lived down in the canyon and had a lot of sheep.

Ella's first thought was that she would run away.

※

Dennis and Ella are sitting in their living room. Ella is on the couch, repairing one of Nell's powwow outfits. It is covered with hundreds of metal cones that make a pleasant jangling noise when Nell moves. I look at one of the cones to see what material it is, and I see, on turning over the rolled-up circle, that it is the metal top of a snuff can. Ella laughs, and says that it is getting harder and harder to make jingle dresses because snuff cans are increasingly made out of plastic. Dennis pulls over a footrest covered with a shaggy goatskin. Nell sits quietly on the floor, very interested in the stories her parents are telling about their early years, some of which she's heard before, some of which are new.

Ella says that she had formerly received marriage proposals from other relatives of Dennis's down in the canyon, but her family had refused them. "This family gambled a lot," she says, and her grandmother didn't approve. But Dennis's close relatives were not gamblers, and although they lived in Flagstaff and Dennis's parents were Christians, her grandma thought it a good match.

"Your parents were willing for you to marry a man who didn't speak Navajo?"

Ella: "My grandma said, 'Oh, he'll learn. He'll learn.' "

Ella had even met Dennis a couple of times. One of her friends in Flagstaff was Dennis's cousin, and Ella had accompanied her friend to dinner at the Bedonies' on a few occasions. All Ella remembered about Dennis was that he had recently returned from the service, usually ate silently, then retreated to his room after dinner.

Dennis didn't balk when he heard of the plans for him, because he had already refused to be married once before. A year or so before the announcement of his marriage to Ella, his parents had talked about marrying him off to some relatives in Red Lake. Remembering it, Dennis's eyes get big and his face takes on an expression of disbelief.

"They were going to give me away!" he says. "And I told my mom, I said, 'You do that and I'm gone. I don't want any part of that.'

"And she said, 'Well, you don't have any say-so.'

"I said, 'I don't even know who that lady is!'

"Then she was telling me, 'Well, this is the way it's done!' And I thought, God, they're going to give me away to some strange girl? Some strange family?

"I was in the military and I was home for a couple days' leave time, and they sprung it on me. I said, 'Man, you can see me in court; I'm going to take off.' It was a real funny feeling, like, wow, gee, you're just going to give me to these people? What about me? I have rights as a person!'

Ella laughs, saying, "See, he was thinking like a white person."

That betrothal never took place. Dennis doesn't remember when he was informed of his impending marriage to Ella, but he didn't fight it.

Ella remembers her grandmother's announcement.

"I came home from Flagstaff, and I had a boyfriend, and he was Sioux."

Nell interrupts here. "Mom!" she says.

Ella starts to laugh.

"You never told me that!" says Nell. "Here I am asking you all kinds of questions, and you don't say nothing to me!" Nell mimics her mother: " 'I never had a boyfriend,' I'm never going to ask you anything again." Ella is practically falling out of her chair, she is laughing so hard. She puts her hand up to her mouth.

"*Unsolved Mysteries,* Nell. See, I had a boyfriend and he was Sioux, and my grandmother used to tell me, 'We have invested too much in you for you to go somewhere else.' She said, 'It's not going to work out between you and him. You're just going to end up like these other women who get kicked around and abused. You would be too far away from us. And you're not going to have any family around who can be of help. And all these upbringings, all these things we taught you, it's not going to amount to anything. You're going to raise your children like the way [the Sioux] raise their children,' and she said that 'even if you come back, it's going to be really hard. You're here in Navajoland; you're going to be trying to raise your kids and saying they have to learn these things, and he's going to feel left out. And your belief system is not going to be the same; he's going to have his own values, from the way he was raised. And there are certain things you don't do in the Navajo way that will probably be okay from his view.'

"She told me that and she said, 'You're better off marrying someone from the Navajo tradition. Any other tribe is alien. If that person dies, his spirit will always come back and try to find you.' That's what she told me. 'We're just going to lose you if you go over there. With people from different tribes it's difficult, because they have a different set of values.'

"So she talked to me like that and my mom said, 'Your wedding clothes are already made.' Harry [Williams]'s sister made that dress.

"It was purple, light purple, kind of like a lilac color. I never liked that color. To this day, I don't think I own anything that's that color. I have one picture. We still have the recordings of [the wedding]. [Dennis's] dad recorded it. My grandfather, clanwise on my mom's side, he came and officiated.

"I think I called my foster parents and my foster parents said, 'That's not right; that's against the law.' They said, 'Why don't you go to Western Union and we'll send you money for a ticket to fly out.' "

Dennis laughs.

"I had no transportation to run away," says Ella. "So, I guess I thought about it: it was already planned. It was decided. There was no way for me to run away."

"Do you remember how you felt?"

"I was kind of confused. I guess I was raised where I had a lot of respect for my parents and I always listened to them. And just like I was always told: as long as you were living, your mom and your dad still make the decisions in your life. Today it's still like that. If something's bothering me about the kids, or if something's not right with me, I'll talk to my dad about it. And they'll tell me, well, maybe you should have done this a certain way, or I'll tell them I try to talk to my boys, and it's like this. And they'll say, maybe you need to say it this way, or maybe you need to have a prayer said for them. And it's still like that."

The wedding took place on a Saturday in the log hogan

where Dennis and Ella would later live. Ella and her relatives gathered on Pendleton blankets, waiting for the groom's party to arrive. But something appeared to be amiss.

"I remember two or three times a vehicle came and my grandma and my mom and dad were all out there talking," says Ella.

It seems there was a problem with the cow, the traditional bride price. The groom's family brings a cow, which is butchered after the ceremony by the bride's female relatives and distributed among them. "I guess it's kind of like a rejuvenation of those elders' own weddings, and they all wanted to take part in it. They all brought their knives.

"You know, before you get to our house, there's that big hill? [Dennis's family] were way over there. And I remember somebody; I remember [Dennis's] mom coming the second time. I guess the first time was to tell them that they couldn't find the cow. The cow had run away. And then I guess they wanted to tell them, 'Well, we're going to bring it on another day.' I guess my grandma said, 'No. No cow, no marriage.' "

"Was there an additional bride price too?"

"I don't think so. I don't remember. Just the cow. I remember that car leaving again. Pretty soon, I saw the second time Dennis's mom came, and his dad and his uncle and I think his aunt from Red Lake. They came, and everybody was out there talking again, really talking. Then I saw my grandmother leave the crowd, and she comes in [and says,] 'They don't have no cow, so I don't see why they wanted to have a wedding.' I didn't say anything.

"Then one of my aunts came in and I said, 'What's happening?' And she started laughing, and she said, 'Well, the cow they were supposed to bring, the one they were supposed to butcher, they can't find it.' She said, 'That lady brought a concho belt; she wanted to give that to the family in place of the cow. And I guess they told her, well, you can't eat a concho belt. If you give a concho belt, that concho belt can only go to one person. And I don't think anybody would want to have a piece of that one concho belt. We asked for a cow; we want that cow. If you don't bring that cow, go home.' "

Ella laughs. "I guess they left again, and pretty soon the sun was starting to go down, and pretty soon there was another vehicle that came again. Dennis's uncle from Red Lake, his mom's brother, came. I guess his mom gave that concho belt to him, and he went all the way back to Kayenta [to get a cow].

"And all this time, [Dennis and his family] were waiting way behind that hill."

Dennis says, "Well, my mom and I don't know who else, they were the negotiating party. We couldn't go [to the hogan] until all the logistics were figured out." All this time, Dennis was sitting in a vehicle with his dad, waiting for the women to broker the deal.

Ella says, "They had to come all at one time, with the cow, the grand marshal." She laughs. And finally the cow was there.

"And I guess whoever brings the cow puts it in the corral, and they park all around the hogan on one side. And then they all walk in and sit all on one side, the left side. That's when my side of the family comes in."

As the family entered the hogan and took their places on the floor, Ella's grandmother was making the last preparations in another dwelling, where Ella was waiting with her.

"And my grandma, I remember watching her, she was making the mush, and all the time she was telling me about the wedding prayer. 'You should do like this, or you shouldn't do like this.'

"She said, 'I know how you're feeling. You probably don't want to be involved in what's happening,' but she said, 'we already made the decision and you have no say-so. If you just take off and go away from here, leave the wedding, you're going to bring shame on the relatives, on the whole clan. So just try to make the best of it, and talk to one another about certain things if you have problems—like when you start having children—if things are wrong between you, you'll notice your children are going to be different,' stuff like that. She was telling me all these things.

"Anyway, she got all the mush ready, and I got dressed, and they put all this jewelry on me and I followed my dad. My dad had a basket made. I remember we had the basket and the pottery. My dad had a traditional wicker water jug. You make it out of—the kind you make with a basket? It coils, and they kind of wrap yucca plant all the way around, and they kind of make it into a basket.

"Then they put pitch on it, pine pitch; they put it all around it to seal it and put water in it. And my dad carried the water in front of me, and I carried the mush [in the wedding basket], the corn mush in the basket. And I followed him in. Dennis was already sitting over there in his place, and I sat by him and I put the [basket] down, and my dad sat in front of us. And my grandfather was there, and he was telling us in what direction to push the mush, because he had already put the pollen in."

The water jug is used to pour water over the hands of the bride and groom, who sit along the far wall of the hogan, between their respective families and next to the medicine man. Ella was dressed in her wedding clothes and jewelry. As Ella says, "They dress you in the image of the Holy People," which is basically the traditional Navajo costume. And the family put on their finest, just to dress up. Legends maintain that turquoise was one of the precious stones given to the deity Changing Woman. Wherever a Navajo goes, he or she should wear turquoise. "It's a sign to the Holy People that you are a part of them, that you will be protected," says Ella.

The core of the Navajo wedding ceremony is the eating of blue cornmeal mixed with pollen by the bride and groom and their families. Ella's family was concerned that the Bedonies, Christian converts, might object to the corn pollen, since Navajos pray with it. But they quickly decided they wouldn't worry about it. Ella says, "My side of the family said, 'Well, that pollen is for fertility and for us to have grandchildren.' Then my grandmother or maybe one of my aunts said, 'We're the ones who are running the show; they have no say-so. If they didn't want one of us, then they shouldn't have bothered.'

"Well, first, we had to wash each other's hands with the water that they brought in," says Dennis.

Ella: "And it was my dad who poured the water on us, huh?"

"Yeah," says Dennis.

"Do you remember what you felt like?"

Ella says no and laughs.

Dennis says, "My feelings at the time were 'Gee, what, what's this? What's going on?' "

"Half the time we were interpreting for him," says Ella.

Dennis: "And it was, like, okay, you wash your hands, and then you take the corn mush out and put a piece in your mouth, and then the other does the same. At the same time I was kinda, uh—"

Ella interrupts: "Did I put it in your mouth? I don't remember. Or did I just do mine?"

Dennis: "You put it in mine, and then I took out some [from the basket] and put it in yours. Like your dad goes with the four directions, through the center." (Jack had sprinkled corn pollen, which is food for the gods, and also a fertility symbol, in lines across the basket, first east-west and then north-south, dividing it into quadrants representing the four directions. Ella and Dennis then scooped mush up from the four quadrants.)

Dennis: "The feelings that I had at the time were, God, a little confused, a little kind of questioning all these things that were happening. A little foreign—wow."

Ella: "And his mom was on the side telling him in English how to go about it."

Dennis: "I could only understand bits and pieces. But to me it was the first time I'd done anything, seen anything, like this. Wow, you know, all these people; what if I goof up?"

Ella: "That basket, then after we eat, that basket is handed over to his mom, and they share that mush, they eat it all up, and she keeps the basket. It's kind of a security thing. As long as she has the basket, her son is always going to be taken care of. And that basket is right here. That was our wedding basket." Ella points to a Navajo basket in her corner cabinet. "She gave it back to us."

Dennis: "She said, 'I'm getting to the age when I don't want anything to happen, so I'm going to give it back to you guys to take care of it.' "

✳

Jack Hatathlie explains the significance of the wedding basket, which is not only used to hold the corn mush in weddings, but is also used in almost every curing ceremony. Although after a wedding the basket is retained by the family, after a healing ceremony it is usually given to the medicine man as part of his payment. The Navajos believe the basket was given to the Navajos by the Holy People at the time of Creation, with all the other necessities of life. The design of the basket is repeated in many Navajo crafts—crocheted pillows, pottery, and paintings—which decorate most Navajo homes.

Jack Hatathlie:

Our grandparents say the basket was used when the earth was created. People used it in ceremonies. Today we still use it as we did long ago. Baskets are woven from the center out, counterclockwise. They are made in different sizes. The basket has three colors: red, white, and black. There are only three colors used on the basket. The design and the colors of the basket have significant representation. We still make the same design that was given to us long ago. They are woven in one direction. Baskets are still made out of sumac.

The designs of the basket all have meaning and names. The white part represents dawn; the opening of the basket is the doorway. It is also the doorway of your thoughts. The center white designs are the sacred mountains. Some have four white points, and some have six in the center of the basket. The sacred mountains are placed in the east, south, west, and north. If there are six points, Mount Huerfano, which is the doorway, Gobernador Knob, which is the sunlight opening, are added to the other four mountains. Navajos have songs and prayers for the sacred mountains, and we are all known by them.

The red part of the design on the basket is the sun's rays. The sun shines on us every day, and the plants and people use it for growth. The black parts of the design are darkness and clouds. We have clouds for rain and snow. We have darkness for night. The lace around the edge of the basket is our roots. You tie the edge of the basket with your thoughts and values and prayers. These are the reasons why the Navajo people regard the basket as being sacred. It is used in almost all ceremonies. The basket holds life, livestock, and thoughts of our people. It is important to our people.

The basket is also used to hold the soil bundles that some Navajos have. I keep mine in a basket that my wife has had for many years. This basket is used only in special ceremonies and is never used as a payment for services from the medicine man. You can have a basket to hold your jewelry too.

✳

Ella continues, "I gave him the corn mush, and they [his family] shared all that corn mush. My side of the family prepared all of the meal. After we got married, they brought all the food in and they put it on the side where his side of the family was, and they all ate. And then my family brought, I think my parents butchered, about eight sheep, and those were boiled and put in boxes with flour and salt and sugar, in boxes to give to his side of the family." The bride's family not only provides a feast for the groom's family to eat in the hogan after the ceremony, they also prepare packages of food for the groom's extended family to take home with them.

Dennis: "And what we did on our side—"

Ella: "They gave a cow."

Dennis: "They drove up with that big truck and a big huge cow, and all the women, whew, they had their knives. They divided it up among themselves. I remember they used a sledgehammer." The cow is usually killed with a blow to the head with a sledgehammer. Sometimes it requires several blows to kill the cow. Sometimes the cow is just stunned and doesn't die until its throat is cut. The butchering takes place on the ground. Children run around, trying to get a better look. The women have developed their own unique ways of butchering to keep the dust out of the meat. For the women, this is serious business. They each go about their appointed tasks in a very determined fashion and divide the meat among the family—a leg here, a rib cage there. Everything is saved, including blood for blood sausage and intestines and brains and skin.

Ella: "We didn't have any cake or nothing."

Dennis: "You couldn't believe all those people."

Ella: "Nowadays, traditional weddings, you see cakes."

"Did you get presents?"

Ella: "Yeah, we got presents."

Dennis: "They kind of mixed it—they gave some blankets, something to start out with."

Ella: "Pots and pans. I still have my wedding cards."

"And what happened at the end?"

Ella: "His side of the family went home."

Dennis: "Everybody kind of dissipated, and they were gone. We were just sitting there."

Ella: "They just talked to us. My side of the family talked; they talked. I guess the purpose was to establish relations, cooperation, helping one another, [introducing] new relations, expressing the strength of those clan ties. The lectures, I think, went on for a long time. There were people thanking each other for their new in-laws, and talking about grandchildren. Something way beyond us—God, they're talking about kids for us?"

Dennis: " 'They're going to be good, and we expect to see you around. We wish you well.' "

Ella: " 'Don't be jealous, and don't be like this.' "

Dennis: "All these words of encouragement, all these words. . . ."

Ella: " 'Take care of one another.' "

Dennis: " 'Have good prosperity.' "

Ella: " 'Take care of your in-laws'—just like that." And, speaking to Dennis, "Your mom stayed, huh? And then we left for Phoenix the next day. His mom and his sisters, I think they stayed. They had come up from Phoenix. So they stayed the night in the hogan."

"So did you two spend your wedding night in the hogan with all of them?"

"Uh-huh."

Ella: "He had his own bedroll; I had my own mattress. I wrapped myself up in my blanket." She laughs, making a motion showing that she rolled herself up alone in her own blanket.

Dennis: "It was kind of busy all day."

Ella: "I just went to sleep; I was so tired."

Dennis: "I was tired; we were still kind of talking. 'Do you remember what's-her-name saying this?' 'Do you remember so-and-so?' There were so many people talking to us, shaking our hands. 'Oh, oh, oh, you're related this way' and 'Oh, well, we'll see you.' And a lot of lectures. We were both just sitting there, thinking, 'Boy, a lot went on today. We're exhausted.' We just kind of laughed about some things."

16

Married Life in Phoenix

Ella: "The next day we left for Phoenix. I guess they already had plans that he would go to Phoenix and get a job. Somebody, his brother-in-law, got a job for him already."

Dennis: "I started working at a place where they do assembling of starters for vehicles—stripped them down, washed them, sandblasted them. But I had to wait on that job. Ella [actually] started before I did."

Ella: "I got a job teaching preschool. We went to live in a tiny house. For about three months we lived with Dennis's sister. Then we got our own place. We had nothing."

Dennis: "All we had was one suitcase and a blanket. And then some little trinkets. That was it. Sometimes we reminisce and think about this."

Ella: "Our building manager, he knew, I guess, we were newlyweds, and he kind of was sorry for us. He lived right next door. He gave us a table, and then he gave me an ironing board. I guess he saw me ironing on the table. Then he gave us a bed. This was on Indian School Road and Third Street."

Indian School Road is a main east-west thoroughfare in Phoenix, so named for the federal boarding school for Indians whose campus stretched over one hundred acres in the heart of the city. The school is now closed, and the federal government swapped the land for some Everglades land that it wanted to preserve. The developer who handed over the Everglades land planned to build a mixed-use development on the Indian school site, but the real estate slump in Arizona that descended in the late 1980s has kept the project from moving forward. Members of the Indian community, including Navajos and Hopis, Pimas and Tohono O'odham, White Mountain Apaches, among others, wondered why they would not benefit from the sale, since so many Indians either attended the school or had relatives who did, and many still bear searing memories of their time there. Indian children who tried to run away from the school were forced to cut the grass of the campus with scissors while wearing signs around their necks bearing the words "I ran away." Boys who were unruly and repeatedly tried to escape from the military-style school had their heads shaved and were forced to wear dresses. Whippings with a harness belt provided the regular form of discipline. Children were taught to read and write, but it was basically a vocational school.

Dennis: "Actually, [our house was a couple blocks over on] Clarendon and Third Street. Now, if you go down there, that whole place is gone. But there was a little house that my sister used to live in. We were sharing it! It was kind of a house-apartment. It was all these little houses. We lived there for about three weeks, then we managed to get an apartment [of our own]; it was about a block from there, it was upstairs. That was our first apartment. We still have a picture [of] Buzz standing there." Buzz, Ella and Dennis's first child together, was born in 1974. His full name is Dennis Bedonie, Jr.

"When you're married as strangers, do you wait until you've had a chance to get to know one another a little bit before becoming romantically attached? Before sleeping together? Or do you just go ahead and do it?"

Ella: "I guess . . ."

Dennis: "We were trying to adjust to one another."

Ella: "When we got to Phoenix, you know, I guess, we had to instantly plan how we were going to make a living. Where are we going to get some money? So I was out looking for a job all the time, and he already had a job—well, I got my job first. And then he got a job, and we [Dennis and Ella and Dennis's sister and her husband] were all living there in one little place."

Dennis: "We were sharing expenses."

Ella: "And there were just two rooms."

Dennis: "We shared the living room portion."

Ella: "So I guess during that time, we got to know each other."

Dennis: "A little more."

Ella: "Yeah, a little more. I guess, ever since we got married, we've had somebody living with us. We're never alone. We always had one of my sisters, and, well, Freddie lived with us."

"Are you trying to tell me you never had sex?"

Ella, laughing: "We never had time! And my sister, Theresa, whom we call Budge, came to live with us when she was really small, she went to school there. And my brother came. Budge started kindergarten there. My mom just had a lot of kids, too many mouths to feed. She was always busy. So I took Budge with me, and then later on [my brother] Freddie came; he went to the high school down there. He liked it; it was a good opportunity for him. When we moved back, he stayed down there, he stayed with a friend of mine and graduated.

"After Budge went home, one day I was sitting there. I just came back from work, and I was really tired and somebody drove up. There was a window, and [I looked out and] there was a guy that got out of the car. And there was a knock on the door, and he goes, 'Does Dennis live here?' And I said, 'Yeah.' And he says, 'So I'm here to stay with him.' I didn't know who that guy was." Ella laughs.

"He just brought his bags in. I guess he was kind of drunk, he was drinking a little bit, and he brought his bags in, put his bags down, and says, 'I'm moving in with you. I'm Dennis's cousin.' I didn't know who he was. But he lived with us too, off and on. And even up until after we got a new house, and he moved in with his wife and his kids—he lived with us for several months."

Dennis: "If there was somebody who was kind of down on their luck, or couldn't find a place, or they just needed time to get their financial bearings, or whatever they wanted to do, we helped them out. Genny came down."

Ella: "Genny came down."

Dennis: "She stayed for about a month."

"Did you ever get tired of this?"

Dennis: "We were just helping."

Ella: "I never felt like that. I never expected anything out of them. After we had kids, we always had somebody living with us. And to me, I was trying to help them out. I always thought that one of these days if my kids ever come to a situation like that, I hope somebody would be there to help them out. I always felt like that. It never bothered me to have somebody else stay. I don't think any of them ever helped moneywise. At NAU [Northern Arizona University], we always had somebody with us. We were always feeding people. We never had very much money, but we always shared whatever we had."

"Do they come and say, Can I stay with you?"

Dennis: "No, they kind of just show up at the door. With us, it's not polite to say, 'What are you here for? Are you going to stay the night?' Or 'How long are you going to stay?' To us, it's, well, they're here. Let's accommodate them."

Clan obligations require Navajos to try to provide their relatives with whatever they need, no questions asked. If a family member needs a new transmission for her car, she may ask her brothers and sisters to help with money. If they refuse, they will be considered ungenerous, uncooperative in the profound-est way. This convention provides a sense of security, a knowl-edge that your relatives will try to help you out. But the custom of giving to whoever asks serves as a leveler. If anyone should get a bit more of something—anything—a higher wage, a par-ticularly big harvest, a new truck, a musical instrument, the rest of the family will inquire about borrowing money or using the new item, until parity is reestablished.

What enforces the system is gossip. Navajos grow up know-ing what is expected of them, and they also know that should they refuse a plea or keep riches to themselves, the outrage will be expressed fast and furiously. This kind of gossip can get vicious and out of hand. This is the way control is exerted over the group—everyone must conform or be subject to wilting public criticism and whispering campaigns.

*

There were some things in the city Ella began to see that she wasn't prepared for: Drinking.

Ella: "His brother-in-law used to come over and they would go out and party."

Dennis: "Oh yeah."

Ella: "I used to just stay home. And one time, I barely heard Dennis coming up the stairs, and then I saw him coming, and I kind of looked down and he was crawling. He crawled to the bathroom, and I thought, where did he go? I didn't hear him anymore, and he was sleeping in the bathroom. And I just went in there and covered him with a blanket, and left him there." She laughs.

Dennis: "Those were some of the embarrassing times of my life."

"What did you think when Dennis started coming home drunk when you were newlyweds?"

Ella: "I don't know. I guess, he would come home drunk

and just go to sleep. Or he would buy beer and stay home and drink and drink with his brother-in-law, or his cousin who was staying with us. It wasn't like he came back and yelled—"

Dennis: "Or running with somebody I never knew before."

Ella didn't know how to react to Dennis's drinking. She had been taught that drinking was wrong, but she had had no firsthand experience with drunks. No one in her immediate family had a drinking problem.

Dennis and Ella lived in Phoenix for about six years. Ella taught, Dennis worked, Buzz went to school. And Ella was exposed to a kind of life she had never experienced before. There is a picture of Dennis and Ella standing beside their new car, a Dodge Charger, low slung, with wide wheels. Dennis's shirt is open several buttons from the top, and Ella, though her arms are crossed protectively across her chest, smiles broadly, like a young woman ready for adventure.

But her upbringing had been too strict, and she had learned the lessons too well to travel too far down the path of Anglo life. She quietly watched Dennis drink with his friends and observed with reserved concern when he returned home drunk. It did infuriate her when he failed to return one night—the night her mother-in-law was visiting!

Ella recalls, "His mom came down one weekend, and he didn't come home. Everybody wanted to know where he was, and she came over and said, 'Oh, you must have done something to him because he didn't come home.' Well, his brother-in-law didn't come home [either], but he came home later, and Dennis didn't come home all weekend. She kinda like blamed me for him not coming home. I guess that was the only time I was that upset about it, but I didn't make a big issue about it. I just thought, well, it's really his business.

"And then later on, I guess it started bothering me. We used to go grocery shopping and he would want to buy a case [of beer], and it was like $1.25 a six-pack. If it was on sale, it was like 99 cents or something like that. It was pretty cheap, but to me, it was quite a bit. We could have used that money for something, you know. And I would tell him that, and he would say, 'Well, you know, I need it to relax. I work all day. And I need something to relax when I get home.' And then pretty soon, he would tell me to go buy it when I went grocery shopping. And I would buy it for him and his brother. I guess it really never bothered me when we were down in Phoenix, because everybody else did it. People drank down there.

"But when we moved back this way, 1977 or 1978, and they were talking about the land dispute and my dad was saying that they were making a big issue of the livestock, we need to control our cows. . . ."

Dennis: "I was drinking real heavy, now that I think about it, right about then."

Ella: "He was drinking hard stuff, Jack Daniel's; what's that other one, the one you mixed with Coke?"

Dennis: "I think it got really severe, because [while in Phoenix] first we were living with my sister, and my brother-in-law was drinking; you know, he was available [to drink with]. Then when we got our apartment, they moved to a new apartment, not too far from us, just a block away. And they would come see us; we were close, and they still partied."

Ella: "Yeah, some of Dennis's relatives, they drink and party."

Dennis: "Then we moved from the upstairs down to where the manager lived, and he drank."

Ella: "They would invite Dennis over and he drank."

Ella decided one day early on in her marriage that she would try a drink to see what it was all about.

Ella: "When we first got married, when we first moved there, he used to go to an Indian bar down the street. His sisters, everybody, went. [One time] I went with his sisters over there. What was that drink that I tried? That weird one?"

Dennis: "Strawberry. . . ."

Ella: "These guys were drinking, [and his sister said,] 'Well, why don't you come along? Might as well join him.' So I went over there with his sisters. They were all there. I think they ordered me something. It tasted real sweet. They called it slow screw. I don't remember who bought it for me.

"I didn't like it when she brought it for me. I didn't like it. I mean, just that one drink. There was nothing wrong with me. I was sitting there and it was time to leave and I got up and I felt that something was coming over me, like it's all the way down, this real funny sensation. And we got home and I just went to bed. I mean, I was starting to get sick. I couldn't figure out what was wrong with me; [I was] going like this, What's wrong with me? And I got really bad diarrhea from it. And the next day, I had this really bad headache. I didn't know what was wrong with me, and I sat in the bathtub and had the toilet bowl by me and was vomiting, and I went to the doctor, because I was just really sick.

"These guys never told me what it was like. I didn't know what a hangover was—I mean, my head was this big, and my ears were ringing really bad." Dennis laughs. "Just that one drink.

"I thought I was going to die. I got so scared. I didn't know what to do, I kept moving around, I was so uncomfortable. Just the thought of food, just thinking about food made me throw up, even though there was nothing there to throw up. Even for a long time, remembering that feeling, I would get nauseated.

"And when I talked to the doctor, I said this is what I'm feeling, and he took all these tests, and then he asked me, 'Well, what did you do yesterday? What did you eat? Was there something unusual that you did, that you ate?' Then I said, 'Yeah, I drank.'

"And he asked, 'What did you drink? How much alcohol was it?'

"I said, 'I don't know. All I know is I drank a glass; that's all I had.' And then he says, 'Well, where did you go after that?' And I said I just went home.

"And then he just laughed and he said, 'You have a hang-over, honey.' "

Dennis and Ella laugh.

"I was so sick. For a long time, just thinking about it, how I felt that time, my head, you know, I would get sick from it. And I thought, God, these guys, they do it all the time."

Ella hasn't touched a drop since.

"Dennis, why did you stop?"

Dennis: "There was a choice. There were two choices."

Ella: "I said, 'We have kids.' "

"Did she give you an ultimatum?"

Dennis: "No. She mentioned it. Then it was up to me. She gave me the other option: it was party your butt off, do what you want. But . . ."

Ella: "It never bothered me in Phoenix when everybody did that. When we came back to my place, you know, my family, they don't drink."

Dennis: "Yeah."

Ella: "I've never really known anybody that drank. And my parents would go places, and sometimes they'd say, 'Oh, so-and-so was drunk.' But I had actually never been with a relative that was drunk. I saw people at a distance, but that was about it. When we came back and we used to go to Flagstaff, he used to buy beer, and he used to have an ice chest in the hogan, where he kept his beer and he would drink it."

Alcohol had to be smuggled onto the reservation because tribal law prohibits its sale or possession. Some Navajos believe the prohibition only increases problem drinking. If someone is going to drink, they tend to drink a lot. And since it must be gotten off-reservation, to get home means to drive drunk, which leads to many traffic deaths. Some Navajos, particularly those in tribal government, who have gone to college or lived around whites, often drink socially without problems. Some Navajos believe that the strict prohibition against alcohol precludes the opportunity to learn social drinking. However, the ravages of alcohol on the reservation can cut so deep that most people prefer to see the ban in place. Most Navajos believe that Indians have a susceptibility to alcohol abuse that is genetically determined and related to the relative newness of alcohol in the culture.

Bootlegging is a lucrative business on the reservation. Just bringing in liquor from the border towns for private use is tricky. Ella remembers, "One time we were coming back with a whole bunch of beer, and there was a roadblock over here. And the kids were small. And Dennis started throwing out beer. And Buzz was small and Buzz started throwing out beer. We threw all the beer out on the side of the road. By the time we got back to the roadblock, that guy just waved us on." Ella and Dennis laugh.

Ella continues, "Talking about my family—again, it really bothered me, him doing that. My dad would every so often say, 'This is the house you were married in, this is a ceremonial house, and a lot of people, our relatives, got together and bought the lumber, and put the covering on the house and put it together. Your aunt put the covering on the roof. And it's the ceremonial hogan.' And he said, 'Why don't you talk to him and tell him he shouldn't be doing that. He can go somewhere else and do it, but not here.' And he said, 'You have brothers who are impressionable. And you have a fireplace too [meaning that Ella has embraced the Native American Church, which is strictly opposed to alcohol]. Maybe it's good if you talk to him about these things and you can pray together. If he's going to keep on doing that, it's not going to do any good. You have little kids, you have to think about your kids, you have to talk to him.' So we would talk, and I would try to talk to him."

Life on the reservation is very difficult. To keep the family going requires almost nonstop work from all members from sunup to sundown. If a family member is drunk, he or she is not available to work. If a worker is drunk, he may do the job wrong—which could have profound effects on the family: ruining a tractor or wasting water or seed. The traditional clan group exerts significant pressure on members to conform. Once the men began taking wage jobs, however, and freed themselves financially from the sheep herds and the communal work arrangements based on the home, the clan lost some of its influence.

Dennis, as it turns out, didn't stop drinking until he and Ella moved back to Coal Mine Mesa and rejoined a communal order that was centered on Jack and Bessie's house. Jack spoke to Dennis, sharing his thoughts on alcohol, and at the same time Dennis began attending healing ceremonies, as relatives are expected to do. He started to learn Navajo, which he now speaks fluently. Ella believes that the teachings offered and represented by her father are successful at keeping people on the right track because they are not punitive, but embracing. The ways are clear and simple—live the good life, live in beauty, follow the traditional path, think of yourself in nature, respect all things, respect your relatives. The Navajo way encourages positive thinking, good thoughts. The Navajo way, the sacredness of daily tasks, makes one feel part of a whole that is bigger and grander than the individual, a state of affairs that can be immensely comforting. And the Navajo way offers redemption to anyone who chooses to return.

Ella says, "It seems like the white world to me is based on negative things; like even with the Ten Commandments, it's all based on negative things, like do not commit adultery, do not bear false witness. Whereas with the Navajo way of life it's always positive things. *N'zhonie*, the beauty of things. You attain these things, positiveness, doing good things for other people; you're brought into this world to do these things; and everything is laid out for you. In the white man's world, it's different. It's all the negative side of things. There's no such thing as

'Develop good thoughts, develop your mind.' That stuff isn't there."

But to let Dennis know she was serious about living the Navajo way without alcohol, she had to let him know the consequences of his continued drinking.

"I guess it came down to the point," says Ella, "where, if he does this in front of my kids, then my kids are going to start doing it, so he had that choice, you know: either stop or go home to his mom."

Dennis: "That was what, 1978? That's how long I've been dry."

Ella: "And that's when he first went to the meeting, huh? Peyote meeting. Who was it ran that first meeting for us? Howard. He spoke English. That's why my dad asked him: because he spoke English, so he could talk to [Dennis] and explain what the fireplace meant.

"One other time when we were in Flagstaff, we really needed money. I think it was during the summer. I was working for the school district. And during the summer I was off. He was in school, but the money they gave us wasn't enough. And that time, I wove a lot. We would go down to Sedona and sell our rugs. That was before I got into beading. I was always weaving. And then one time we decided to bootleg. We bought a case of that cheap wine; we bought that. It only cost us like $5 [a case] and we were going to sell it for $2 [a bottle]. And we brought it back.

"And all this time we were quiet; I was thinking about it, I was thinking, 'Gosh, is this the right thing to do?' All these things were coming in my mind. 'What if somebody gets really drunk? They get in an accident, and they bought it from us.' All the time I was thinking about it, and [Dennis] was doing the same thing.

"There was a squaw dance here. We were going to go to the squaw dance, and we were coming up on the road, and I guess it really bothered Dennis; he goes past a couple of winos that we saw, and Dennis told them to go over and we gave them the whole case."

Dennis: "I said, 'You guys want some wine?' One of them said, 'Yeah, but we don't got no money.' "

Dennis replied, "I'm not asking you for money. Do you want wine?"

"Yeah," they said.

Dennis opened the back of the truck and took out the case and handed it to the two men. "I'll always remember that," says Dennis, "because of the expression on that guy's face."

＊

Jack Hatathlie wanted to tell Ella his thoughts on marriage. He came to her house and sat down and asked her to turn on the tape recorder. This is what he said:

I believe marriage is the foundation of life, or at least it is to me. I believe it is also true for other cultures. Through my years, I never went to school, but I have learned through my observations.

In today's times, many young people are facing a confusing and difficult world in which past values and guideposts are changed or ignored. The teachings of the traditional Navajos with regard to marriage and family life are as true and important today as they were hundreds of years ago.

Some of my feelings and thoughts have come from watching my children and relatives. They have been my greatest teachers, and with eleven children I feel I deserve a Ph.D.

In a traditional home, married life is important, with a feeling of happiness and responsibility between husband and wife. Each has his or her own important job to perform, but each should feel close to and respectful of the other.

The beginning of a married couple's life involves the extended family and clan, as well as other community members. In the minds of those relatives, the newlyweds reflect the beginning of a new life, just as one would feel at birth. Advice is given at the time of marriage by those attending and participating so that the young people have the benefit of the experience and wisdom of men and women who have been married for years. They are told of the possible problems and probable solutions in terms of the road of life on which they are starting. The Navajo way of life is reinforced by the marriage ceremony itself.

Today many young Navajos get married in such a way, whether in a church or in a Navajo wedding ceremony, that they lack the feeling and understanding of what married life is all about. Sometimes the traditional role of each partner is not understood.

In the past, marriages were arranged by the parents of the boy, who selected a girl and her family for its ability and for its strength.

Today many young people choose one another often without regard for clan or for kinship and related restrictions and prohibitions. Although the foundation of Navajo society still is marriage, it is now on thin ice, like the white people say. A Navajo wedding is not only a social occasion involving two people. It is also a deeply meaningful and spiritual experience involving two families and their clans.

Marriage was an important and sacred time for a couple. Today many young people live together for years before they have a Navajo, church, or civil wedding. This weakens the strength that our young people can and must receive from their culture and traditions. In the Navajo way, turquoise represents the man, and the white shell represents the woman. This concept should continue with married couples so that getting married is something that directly ties the young couple to the Holy People and to the traditions and power that are evident in Navajo culture.

Today many young people either do not know or they don't believe it. If one cannot relate to one's own tradition and the beauty and strength of one's religion, then one is considered poor and weak.

Today among Navajos, in their desire to acquire status, one will buy a new pickup, live in a house with nice furniture, and so forth. In doing so, they lose and neglect those things which make them uniquely Navajo, and which tie them to the Holy People and to the rich and beautiful traditions that are a part of the Navajo way.

If we push our Navajo culture aside and try to be something that we're not, we are like leaves on the tree waiting for the wind to blow us off.

Many young couples come to me for prayers because they have unhappiness in their marriage. I always tell them that love, understanding, communication, and sacrifice are the most important things in a relationship. If one of those is missing, then their relationship will not hold together.

Today many Navajo wives use their children as excuses for not having time to take care of the needs of their husbands. The children come between the husband and wife and are the ones that are placed first in many families by the mother. That is not the way a traditional family operated. The children were important and were loved by not only both parents but by the kinship group which surrounded them. Today where mothers are employed, it has caused tension and insecurities in many families. In a time when money is essential, sometimes both parents have to work. Sometimes the wife has better skills than the husband. The wife's job interferes and comes between the relationship of the mother with her husband and the children. The job becomes the focal point of the family and becomes number one in terms of the working mother. This places strains on the marriage. If the wife gives up her job, the problem is not solved because finances are important. The wife is in and out of the house like the father was when he had a job.

Marriage as the center of life is not important anymore in today's young people.

I have watched our people go to school. They are away at school so much of their young years that they do not understand how a marriage should be; they are not in a home environment where love and security are around. Some of them grow up in boarding schools and do not know how a family should function in a traditional way.

Another problem I see with marriages is jealousy. While at Page, I often confronted this on a daily basis.

I saw wives calling their husbands at work, checking up on them, and they are disturbed their husbands are not available to the telephone. Men whose work often requires them to be away from the office or away *from a particular place of employment are criticized by their wives for running around or seeing another woman. The reverse is true in terms of the husbands, who believe that their wives are looking for opportunities and excuses to get out of the home or at least to meet with another man.*

Today husband and wife are jealous of one another. When they go shopping, the husband stops to shake hands or talk to another woman; the wife will question him, who the lady is, wondering if that's his girlfriend or not. If the husband sees his wife talking to another man, he automatically thinks his wife is running around with him. He starts criticizing and accusing his wife. This is usually the result of no trust in a marriage. I believe jealousy destroys the love and trust that are needed to have a happy home. I stressed this to my children as they were growing up.

In the old days, far more trust existed between the man and woman, husband and wife. At a time when a man had several wives, jealousy was more controlled, and it did not have the devastating power to destroy that it has today. I know that, thinking of my own parents. My father had three wives and children from these women, yet my mother never ceased to love my father and take care of her children. Sometimes she had to help his other wives when they needed help. From talking with my mother and adopted clan mother, they both influenced me so greatly in terms of my respect for the way Navajo women brought love and understanding into the home and into the marriage, even in situations where problems and tensions were great.

Part Three

17

"You Have to Sit There and Think,
'I'm No Greater Than Anybody Else' "

One of the most difficult adjustments that Navajos must make
if they are to succeed in the Anglo world is to think and act
competitively. Navajo children are brought up in a world in
which cooperation and consideration of kin are the paramount
virtues. Cooperation is the basis of the economic and social
security of the group and is reinforced in the healing rites,
in the tending of sheep and cornfields, and in all family
interactions.

Further, humility and an appreciation of their place in nature
are an essential part of the Navajos' view of themselves. As
Ella has said about thinking the Navajo way, "You have to sit
there and think, 'I'm no greater than anybody else, I'm just a
simple person, and I want to be able to get this knowledge,
and I want to be able to relate to everything around me.' Everything can be made simple, and you just talk to whatever's
around."

But in the Anglo world, even before children enter school,
they are taught that competitiveness is a virtue, and once they
reach school age, teachers expect them to be aroused to learn
by competition. Teachers at the Indian day schools, which re-

placed the boarding schools, eventually learned otherwise. They learned that singling a child out by virtue of her top grade or performance caused immense discomfort; she did not like standing out from the group. The Anglo teachers were compelled to adjust their teaching styles.

But in the schools of the towns that border the reservation, no such sensitivity exists, and their Indian students can feel bewildered and trampled in a matter of moments. Being noncompetitive does not mean that an Indian child is not motivated to excel, or that he or she isn't a perfectionist. What is different is what motivates him to learn, what turns him off from learning, and what kinds of rewards and teaching methods are appropriate for him.

Ella says, "Indian students are good observers. They are taught at home to learn from observation. A lot of times [at school], they're asked a question or given instructions that they don't understand. If the teachers showed them what to do, they would get it after looking at it. Indian kids are raised to observe and listen."

They are less likely to learn by rules. Gladys Reichard has written that even when it comes to ethics, the Navajos learn from what they see, as opposed to abstract ideas: "In Navaho life ethics is empirical rather than theoretical or theological; ethics includes actual as well as ideal behavior, etiquette and law, as well as religious restrictions. Since he seldom sees a white man who treats him as a brother, the Navaho does not comprehend the preacher's statement that all men are brothers, though he shares the ideal. Since the whites he knows scheme and cheat him whenever possible, their verbal reiterations that honesty is the best policy leave him unconvinced. He may not know that their belief in rugged individualism admits cutthroat competition while it consigns honesty to religion."

Moreover, it can be argued that, unlike most Jews and Christians, Navajos do not believe in a dualistic, Manichean world in which good and evil are clearly separate and opposed entities forever locked in battle. Rather, good and evil exist, and knowledge, particularly the ritual use of knowledge, can be marshaled to transmute good into evil. Good is what is under control; evil is what is out of control. Sex is good in marriage. Excessive sex is bad. A little gambling is okay; excessive gambling is bad.

Because a Navajo child comes to school with a different frame of reference, it may take additional help for him to make the most of what is taught. If a child is asked to determine whether the following hypothetical situation is "right" or "wrong"—"This man stole some food from a neighbor's cornfield for his family"—the child would likely not answer the same way an Anglo child would. If a Navajo child is asked whether it is more important to save a piece of nature from development or protect a businessman's financial interest in the same property, he will probably answer differently than would most Anglo children. In each case, the Navajo child would likely ask for more information. For the Anglo child, the categories of right and wrong may be more sharply defined according to Anglo-Saxon law.

Once the child reaches adolescence, many of these confusions and misunderstandings may manifest themselves in problems concerning the child's opinion of himself. Does he recognize the person that is reflected back to him in the eyes of the teacher? In the eyes of the other children? If not, if he sees himself as devoted to his family and Navajo teachings, perhaps a good artist and eager to play basketball, yet the teacher looks at him as if he were slow, stubborn, and contrary because his reactions to her words or behavior are not what she expects, how will he see himself at the end of the year? How quickly will he be turned off to her teaching, or any teaching at all?

Ella faced these problems herself as a girl—first in boarding school, and then while on placement in California. But soon, she would have to face the troubles again, this time through her own children, a situation that in many ways was more painful.

Teenage Buzz—Ella's second son and Ella and Dennis's

firstborn—reacts to feeling different, an outsider, by combing his hair like a Mexican gang member and acting like a gangster. He watches kung fu movies and violent adventure shows. He identifies with angry young men of other cultures, but so far has not acted out those wishes too dramatically, though he has experimented with drinking. He affects a blank, inexpressive look on his face and cracks very dry jokes. Ella finds his expressionlessness peculiar. She told him, as he walked out of the trailer dressed in his new dark silk shirt for his portrait sitting with his girlfriend, Sonya, "Smile, son, for your picture, so you won't look like a wooden Indian."

Ella one day noticed Buzz walking along Main Street in Tuba City with a Mexican friend of his who had spent some time in prison. Ella says, "I laughed so hard—we were coming up Main Street—[Buzz] didn't see us. But he's walking with this cool friend of his; he's a Mexican, got married to a Navajo family out here. And I saw Buzz walking down with him, and he had this stretch cap on, he had it pulled way down, and I looked back, and I looked at them and slowed down really slow like this, and I looked at them and I started laughing and laughing.

"I said, 'You guys look funny!' I just laughed and laughed so hard. And then when they came up here [to the trailer], I said, 'I don't know what you guys are trying to prove,' I said. 'Were you guys trying to act like gangsters?' I said, 'That's stupid.' "

In 1985 and 1986, the most popular television show on the reservation was *Miami Vice*. Even young men who lived in hogans with no electricity would rush home on Friday nights to plug an old black-and-white TV set into the car battery to watch the show. One reason may have been the preponderance of ethnic characters on the series, and the elegance of their operations—they weren't two-bit drug dealers, but immensely wealthy ones, with cars and houses and women. And they often held unusual religious beliefs. Lieutenant Castillo, who subscribed to a dignified Far Eastern religious discipline, was an immensely popular character. The protagonist of *The Karate Kid* is very popular among Navajo children as well, his Asian discipline and mysticism quite compatible with Navajo ways.

In their own lives, role models are offered by medicine people—among those families who value traditional teaching —and by the Navajos who have gone on to college and gotten jobs. But children, who spend all day in school, don't see many role models there. Anglo teachers, most of whom do not understand Navajo ways, do not provide images for the children of what they might one day be. Slowly, however, more Navajos are becoming teachers, and gradually classes in Navajo language and culture are being introduced in the schools. Progress is slow, and the BIA bureaucracy is not especially responsive.

Buzz has little interest in schoolwork, and his parents would be pleased but surprised if he goes on to college. He is a gifted artist, however, and earns good money selling his drawings to teachers and friends. He also has a thriving tattoo business. His specialty is roses, which he also draws for Nell as the template for the designs she beads on her moccasins and powwow costumes.

Navajo children who live in border towns must not only adapt to a world with different rules, expectations, and logic, but also one in which space and time themselves are different. On the reservation, the child can wander about for great distances without fear of attack or danger. Ella says, "Out there [on the reservation] it's open, and here [in town] you're so confined to one little spot. I see it in my kids. They get irritable, and they don't like it because they can't do very much and they can't go very far from where they live. And someone's always around watching them, or [someone] says, 'You're not supposed to play here.' When they're home, they go as far as they want and do anything they want."

As space is uncluttered, so is time. Life is not layered with appointments for piano lessons, gymnastics, soccer. More time is spent alone in contemplation. People don't speak fast. Except

in the urban-type areas like Tuba City, telephones don't ring
—contact with the world comes through the mail or by word
of mouth.

The children play with objects that white children would
never play with, like stones and sticks and animals. They play
at beating drums and singing. They play with flowers and
plants that they find as they trek over the land. Their imagi-
nations are different.

Jon Norstog, an Anglo land-use planner, works for the Navajo tribe and lives with his wife and son in Window Rock, the
capital of the Navajo Nation on the far eastern edge of Arizona.
Originally from the Pacific Northwest, he has worked with the
Navajos and lived near or with them for the past eight years.
He says, "One of the things I like about living here is that it's
basically wild and free. And one of the reasons it can be that
way is that people have respect for individuality, but also everybody knows what can and can't be done. And that's a paradox,
I guess. In the outside society, theoretically, there [are] no
checks on individual behavior, but in fact the outside world is
full of people who are trying to bust you for one thing or
another. [There are] deadlines to meet—we're going to cut off
your electricity, we're going to ruin your credit, we're going to
fine you if you don't get those library books back in, we're
going to put a bench warrant out if you don't pay your parking
ticket. It goes on and on and on. There's a lot of pressure that
you don't really realize.

"Law enforcement is really heavy in the dominant society.
It's not here. I don't know how kids can live in the dominant
society anymore. I just don't understand it. Kids need a certain
amount of room to swing. And the society and all its organs
of [social control] are so pervasive out there. They're so ready
to come down on anything. They're throwing kids out of school
if they don't like their tee-shirts.

"Who ever heard of anyone killing someone with a tee-shirt.
Right?"

Norstog lets his own son range far with his Navajo friends, because he knows the boy is safe. "Over here, you don't have the same problems because the society cares a lot more for the individual and there are outlets besides violence. There's not a lot of hugging and kissing. But Navajos show their love and affection in different ways: shaking hands, greeting each other, showing respect."

Norstog thinks that white people could profit from learning about Navajo social life: "I think the most important thing [that we can learn from Navajos] is to rediscover and to reestablish community life. This is something that white people had until pretty recently. European [immigrants] all had extended families, they all lived together and settled nearby and provided mutual support. And they all used to go to churches or synagogues or whatever and get together on a regular basis in that kind of environment. Also there used to be a community culture where people used to meet for political purposes. And this has all been knocked cuckoo in the twentieth century, especially since World War II. The basic unit is the household; you have suburbs full of households and apartment buildings full of households, and nobody's talking to anyone else.

"You go into an American suburb, you can walk all day and never run into anybody on the street. Whereas if you go and walk around in an area, even Coal Mine Mesa, you'll run into somebody and they'll want to talk and they'll find out what's going on with you and you'll find out what's going on with them. You might get invited to eat—things like that. And maybe it's not as efficient economically, but it's a lot more fun.

"Also, people are always together, they always come together for religious things, they're always supporting each other. For example, if you go into a Native American Church service, there's a period during the worship when everybody says something nice about everyone in the place. Sometimes they'll offer guidance, but mostly it's telling you that you're okay, or sympathizing with your problems, or praying for a solution. It's a very supportive culture for individuals. Children come in, and they absorb that very young."

In the Navajo society, it is harder to become isolated, to feel that there is no one looking out for you. Says Norstog: "There's not much in the area of reality-checking available for individuals in the dominant society, that is, you tend to get so isolated, your only feedback is maybe from television or from people inside your house. Maybe you don't talk to your neighbors much, and maybe you don't even know who they are. And there's also a lot of opportunity to exercise dysfunctional behavior, which in Navajo, things like that would be worked out in a constructive way—somebody would let you know that you're not behaving properly, a member of your family, or maybe you'd find out about it when you went to a prayer service. But it would all be done in a very positive way [as] an offer of help. If you confront people in a bad way, it disturbs everything. It doesn't work. In a way, your community can be your mother."

The warmth and coherence and security of the community are striking to Anglos who get to know Navajos. The positive, embracing manner with which this affects the people can be seen in the way Navajos behave. "First of all, people have these impressions of Indians, and especially Navajos," says Norstog, "that they're taciturn and fierce and not very friendly and not very talkative. And when you're up here you realize that people are real open; they love to talk, and they love to tell jokes. They're always laughing and happy; even when times are tough someone's making a joke and trying to get some personal pleasure and enjoyment out of things.

"It's a very positive attitude that people have. It keeps them alive and functioning, and that's one reason that no matter how tough times are, people are always willing to have children and make those steps into the future."

Norstog believes that the source of the community spirit and hopefulness can be summed up in one word: "I think it's prayer. I've come to understand that people regard almost everything they do as a form of prayer. If their lips are moving, they're praying."

✳

Ella began to think about the differences between Navajo and Anglo life with more and more concern as her boys got older. She felt more acutely the conflict between trying to teach her children to be Navajos and helping them succeed in the white world.

Ella once told me that Buzz was a very good runner and liked to compete in track meets. I was very surprised when she told me later that she had told him he shouldn't win all the time, that if someone else really wanted to win, he should let him. I was shocked. I thought that this would have undercut his impulse to run and win—and he eventually did stop racing. But I came to understand how this disapproval of competitiveness is an important element of the culture. It contributes in part to the comfort and security that Navajos (and outsiders) find in occupying a place in it. Also, an individual's awareness of his relation to the spiritual, to nature, to others, is very different when he is not competing with those around him. When intent on winning, an individual may overlook many other aspects of an activity that might be noticed without the pressure to be strongest, fastest, best.

In their speech, in their manner, in their businesses, Navajos are not trying to beat one another. They want all to succeed, and all to be heard. The more affluent help out their relatives who are less well off. Cooperative care of the livestock benefits everyone. Looking after children of relatives, even for extended periods, benefits the whole family. Family members all pitch in to pay for religious ceremonies and bring food to help feed guests.

The traditional economic system held that not only was this

cooperation necessary for survival, but it also ensured success for all. However, the Navajos' economic ideas are rapidly becoming outdated and irrelevant. "The Navajo 'economic theory' assumes that there is a potential abundance of goods, and that through cooperation, the amount of goods will be increased for everyone; in other words, they would deny the basic assumption upon which much of our own economic theory depends, namely the scarcity of goods."

The fortuitous arrival of livestock from the Spanish, and the tremendous increase in the herds from the seventeenth century until the 1930s, reinforced the idea that bounty would increase as long as the Navajos adhered to their religious beliefs. The Navajos believed the increase of their woolly herds was a sign of approbation from the gods. When government scientists told them the range was eroding, the Navajos replied that because they had been forced to reduce their sheep, the gods were holding back the rain, and that's why the grass wasn't growing. In the minds of the traditionals, as long as the Navajos tended their sheep, and the herds grew, the Holy People would send rain to help renew the grassland. Inconceivable was the notion that the sheep might grow too numerous for the fragile desert land.

The deterioration of the range in the late nineteenth century brought families into competition for grazing land, introducing the concept of scarcity in real terms. Sheepherders had to travel farther and farther to find forage for their herds, but they believed that if the rains came, the land would be refreshed and the days of plenty would return. The concept of permanent scarcity was realized only after the government initiated the first of a half-dozen livestock reduction programs in 1933. Within twenty years, the total number of livestock was halved, while the population doubled, causing deprivation, poverty, suspicion of the white man, and despair.

As the population continues to grow robustly, competition for all kinds of resources, from government-sponsored jobs to tribal scholarships, increases. And it is more and more difficult for educated Navajos to believe in the truth of the old economic theory.

But the Navajos' duty to cooperate with relatives is deeply embedded in the culture, and trying to compete in the white way leads to profound conflicts. For example, if a Navajo owns a trading post and a relative comes in with a pressing need, the owner will feel obliged to help. Then another relative may desperately need a new halter for his horse, another some feed, another some flour. And pretty soon, since Navajos have so many relatives, the trader will be out of business. Navajo entrepreneurship has therefore remained somewhat undeveloped. One area that is not so full of conflicts is the sale of handicrafts; it is less likely a relative will claim he needs a necklace or a bracelet. Nevertheless, Ella, who began by selling her own beaded jewelry, ran into problems when she expanded to selling jewelry she bought wholesale from other artists. When Ella's sisters see something they like and ask her for it, her natural impulse is to give it to them. "I know what it's like," she says, "to want something when you don't have the money to pay for it." When she sold her own beadwork, most pieces didn't go for more than $30, so giving away a piece here and there didn't cost her too much. Now she is buying more expensive items. When her sisters eye something, and ask her if they can put it on layaway, Ella has a hard time not simply giving them what they want.

The traditional system held that self-interest and altruism were the same thing. Doing the right thing for yourself was the right thing for your people. But when the Navajos were forced to deal with modern economic reality, that system no longer worked the same way. If a wage-earner does well and wants to save money to send his children to school, it is in his interest to do so, but perhaps not in the interest of a relative who wants to borrow money. Before the Navajos had commerce with the outside world, the accumulation of money was meaningless; it was better given away to needy relatives.

The belief that the world is benevolent (as long as one observes taboos), and that a plea for help will be satisfactorily answered, runs into direct conflict with the mores of the dominant society. It has caused elderly Navajos, particularly those thrust into the outside world by relocation, to fall victim to unscrupulous real estate agents or loan sharks whose operative principle is *caveat emptor*—let the buyer beware. The Navajos, especially the elderly who do not speak English, operate under the belief (or desperate hope) that they will be dealt with fairly. There were examples of older people paying more than 100 percent interest, and putting their house up as collateral on a loan the lender knew they couldn't repay.

Further, the Navajo belief that when a request is made, help is ensured, leads to resentment and disillusionment when dealing with government agencies. Ella explains her mother's blanket distrust of the white man: "The government is always associated with the white people, and every time anything bad goes down, there's always a white man bringing the bad news. Or he's the one in office when she's denied assistance. That's why she has the feeling about them, that they can never be trusted." On several occasions, Bessie has applied for help from the tribe or the BIA—for aid in repairing their house or to get "commodity," cheap food from government surplus. But since her husband earns a good living, she is usually denied help, even though she felt she had demonstrated need. She didn't understand that the aid was given to the less fortunate. All she knew was that the system didn't work as she expected—she asked for help and didn't get it. When her kids unsuccessfully applied for tribal summer jobs, and she saw the white director's son with a job, she felt the system was corrupt.

✳

Indian running offers some insights into competitiveness among Indians. Indians have long been known for their long-distance skills. Popay, from San Juan Pueblo, is perhaps one of the most famous; in the late seventeenth century he organized runners to spread the word among the seventy-odd Pueblos of a planned revolt against the Spaniards. The runners traveled more than three hundred miles, passing knotted cords that determined the date of the attack (1680) and the resulting uprising, known as the Pueblo Revolt, that drove the Spaniards and the hated Catholic Church from the sacred kivas and preserved the religious artifacts that the priests had so energetically attempted to destroy.

For hundreds of years, Indians ran to communicate between far-flung villages, to hunt, and to fight. Courier-runners existed among tribes from Iowa to Peru. They not only ran; they were counted on to remember and repeat, word for word, the messages they carried. These runners were known to cover hundreds of miles, their skills were highly valued in their cultures, and they enjoyed high status. Running was a calling, and there were stories of supernatural performances possible with the aid of "ancient knowledge." The Navajos talk of medicine men who know songs about running and who know how to make a salve of butterfly wings to help runners become fleet of foot. Just as Bessie insisted for her children, Navajos are encouraged by their parents to awaken early every day and run, and in the days when Navajos supplemented their winter food by stealing and butchering Hopi horses, strong runners were highly valued.

Relay races have long been a part of tribal and intertribal life. But the focus is not all on winning. One Hopi, a champion marathon runner trained in the white as well as the Hopi way, explains, "Running was something the elders used to preach to us. Anytime you go somewhere on foot, you should try to run. It is a big part of our life. Even when you are old, as long as you can race or trot, at whatever pace, it makes you feel younger." Hopi men used to run from Oraibi to their farms in Moencopi, a distance of more than forty miles, to tend their crops. This was not considered unusual.

When asked to compare tribal running with marathon running, Hopi runner Bruce Talawema said: "There's no comparison. There [in the competitive world] you're running for yourself. Here it's all tribal. We're running for the people. The other Pueblos are feeling the same thing. It is a matter of getting there and what we're carrying in terms of the message of peace and harmony uniting us as a people. Not to the extent that there might be another revolt, that's pretty much out of the question, but to find each other again. Time is not important to us, it's how we do it."

Indian runners don't revel publicly in their wins, and though there is great excitement during races and plenty of bets laid down, even attempts at witching, the winner is not mobbed at the finish line—he is apt to walk away alone. Sports stars are not made into idols and heroes who are worshipped. Winning is a private matter, a matter between the runner and the Holy People and his beliefs. The runner may believe he is offering strength and pride to his people by his win.

Although there have been Indian standouts in American competitive sports, people like Billy Mills and Jim Thorpe, Indian runners have been less successful in the intensely self-absorbed training required of world-class competitive athletes. One Indian coach told a reporter for *Sports Illustrated* that one reason there were not more Indians on the world competitive scene is that an Indian runner in training would leave to tend to a family matter at home if he or she was needed. This is not how Olympic winners are made. They must be single-mindedly focused on their goals.

In the twenties, the world was excited by the entry of some Tarahumara Indians in long-distance races. Two ran nonstop from San Antonio to Austin, Texas—89.4 miles—and another broke the world record from Kansas City to Lawrence, Kansas—51 miles. But attempts to get the Tarahumaras into a competitive circuit failed. Writes Peter Nabokov, author of *Indian Running*:

It seemed the Tarahumaras, as with other Indians, found it difficult to extract their running prowess from its cultural context and reshape it to fit the white men's criteria for competitive sports . . . their metabolism could not make the adjustment from their normal diet of *koviski*, pinole or corn gruel, to a training program of eggs, milk and beefsteak. At home they shunned the fried foods of their Mexican neighbors, preferring roasted or boiled foods. Nor did they much like meat, sweets or fat. Running in endless circles bored them. These races gave them bad dreams, they said. The cleated leather shoes required at Olympic meets did not conform to their splayed, bark-hard feet. The scrutiny of howling strangers contrasted with the support of backers and friends at home and the winding stretches of quiet mountain trails.

18

"I Can't Believe They'll Really Force People to Move off the Land"

Dennis and Ella returned to the reservation in 1978 and moved into the log hogan at Bessie and Jack's camp. Dennis taught at the Tuba City Elementary School, and Ella taught at Head Start and was a Navajo-culture consultant for the school system. But a sea change had occurred in Coal Mine. The passage of the Navajo-Hopi Resettlement Act of 1974, intended to settle the boundary dispute between the Navajos and Hopis, had thrown the Navajos' lives into turmoil.

Jack and Bessie's entire camp fell on the wrong side of the line drawn to divide the Navajo and Hopi lands in half—including the hogan in which Dennis and Ella were married and into which they moved. Dennis, Ella, Kimo, Buzz, and later Nell, born in 1980, were living in a log hogan that was falling in around them, and which they were forbidden to repair, as a result of the building freeze imposed to encourage them to relocate. Hogans must frequently be repaired, since they are made of logs and mud. When termites and rot set in, the hogans must be moved and their foundations rebuilt.

The new law fundamentally changed the lives and prospects of the Hatathlie children. Ella, who stood to inherit her parents' land, would in fact inherit nothing. She had lost claim to any home on the reservation. The Hatathlies' livestock operations were also destroyed with the stroke of a pen.

After much discussion, Dennis decided to go to college, and he enrolled at Northern Arizona University, from which his father had just retired as a maintenance man. And in 1981 Dennis and Ella moved into student housing in Flagstaff.

Life on the reservation as Ella had known it was over.

✳

The Navajo-Hopi land settlement affected ten thousand Navajos, a tenth of the entire Navajo population in 1994. But its effects are as traumatic on that part of the population as the Long Walk had been for the entire tribe in 1864, when Colonel Kit Carson defeated the Navajos and drove them on foot in the middle of winter to Fort Sumner, on the Pecos River in New Mexico, to stop their raiding of sheep and horses from the New Mexicans, and in turn to protect them from retaliation by the angry New Mexicans. At the time, raiding had become such a well-developed economic activity for the Navajo raiders that they are said to have left several ewes behind so the sheep herd could restock itself before they raided again the next year.

Between 1846 and 1850 "nearly eight hundred thousand sheep and cattle and some twenty thousand horses and mules were reported stolen in northwestern New Mexico." In retribution for the stolen stock, the white New Mexicans captured Navajos as slaves. It is estimated that in 1860 five thousand to six thousand Navajos lived as chattels in New Mexico.

That same year, a war party of one thousand Navajos, led by Manuelito, a powerful headman, and Barboncito, a respected and well-spoken medicine man, attacked Fort Defiance, in an effort to rid their land of the Anglo military presence. The attack prompted the U.S. Army to launch a full-scale campaign to subdue the Navajos. Kit Carson was assigned the job, and four years later, after he had burned their cornfields and fruit trees, destroyed their homes and gardens, and killed hundreds in a final battle in Canyon de Chelly, the Navajos surrendered. It was February, and winter was upon them; the Navajos were destitute. They traveled on foot, in several groups, some led by their headmen, to Bosque Redondo, the reservation created for them and the Mescalero Apaches near Fort Sumner. The march became known as the Long Walk.

The government wanted to turn the Navajos and their cousins the Apaches into sedentary, farming people like the Pueblos. Unfortunately, the land chosen was not fertile, the water brackish, and the area prone to devastating insect infestations. The government's suppliers of food and blankets were corrupt, and many Indians starved to death. The plan was aborted after four years.

The eventual failure of the Bosque was not the result of the Indians' lack of effort, for they worked exceptionally hard—by their own keepers' accounts—to till the soil and grow crops, only to see their harvests decimated by one natural scourge after another. The Navajos, homesick and dispirited by their failures, eventually were allowed to go home, led by Barboncito, whose words are often quoted by the Navajos: "Our grandfathers had no idea of living in any other country except our own."

Though it failed in many areas, the experiment also had some successes. The Navajos learned farming techniques that increased the productivity of the soil. Their skills at silversmithing improved, and would soon become world-renowned. They learned new ways to build hogans and houses. The Navajos changed their dress—abandoning skins in favor of cotton pants for the men and layered long skirts for the women. For the first time, also, they began to think of themselves as a tribe rather than as disparate clans, and for the first time they meted out justice among themselves—outside of the traditional clan responsibilities. The shock and deprivation of being far from home chastened them, and on their eventual return in 1868, this experience helped the leaders restrain the young men who would otherwise have tried to raid again.

Once they were back in their old homes, their population began to grow dramatically, as did their material culture. They were unaware that boundaries for their reservation had been drawn in far-off Washington; nor did they know that those boundaries were subsequently changed, or that in 1882 the U.S. government withdrew an adjacent piece of land for the use of their neighbors the Hopis. The Navajo reservation, which was enlarged several times between 1868 and 1934 to accommodate the rapidly increasing population, eventually came to surround the Hopi reservation. But since no Hopis lived down on the grasslands—their villages were located only on top of the mesas—the Navajos moved into the (seemingly) empty land, following their sheep to better pastures.

Legal maneuvering between the tribes over control of the land heated up in 1958, after nineteen billion tons of coal was found beneath the 1882 Hopi Executive Order reservation. The courts decided in 1962 that the two tribes had "joint, undivided and equal" interest in the land outside of an area surrounding the Hopi mesas. But it was still almost completely inhabited by Navajos.

Legislation passed by Congress in 1974 authorized the removal of those Navajos. The number of Navajos affected, ten thousand, was the total population of the tribe before its defeat by Kit Carson a hundred years earlier.

The Navajo-Hopi problem presents the Navajos with a unique punishment. For the first time in their history, the affected Navajos are being denied a home on the reservation. After Dennis received his degree in sociology in 1985, Ella had begun work on her own degree. By 1988, she too had received her diploma. When she graduated, they could no longer keep their two-bedroom apartment, part of married student housing on the NAU campus. They couldn't move back to Coal Mine

Mesa because the hogans were by then unlivable as a result of age and lack of repair. Ella, adopting her parents' position, was opposed to relocation. For years she resisted and demonstrated and attended meetings in Big Mountain and Coal Mine Mesa where the residents attempted to organize resistance with the help of white lawyers and other allies.

She worked for the Big Mountain Legal Defense/Offense Committee, a group of whites and Indians who lobbied and did legal work in an attempt to change the law. She made beaded jewelry for the office to sell for fund-raising purposes. Year after year, meeting after meeting, she kept up with the twists and turns of the resistance. She opened herself up to me for a book I wrote on the subject, declaring clearly that she believed the Navajo warning that if you sell your Mother, the earth, you and your family will be punished. The Navajos' primary compact with Mother Earth is to care for her and respect her as they would a human mother.

But Ella also felt other pressures. She was college-educated; she wanted her children to have the advantage of the best schools possible. The Tuba City schools, though not as bad as in the days when she attended them, do not offer a challenging education. Ella had also spent much of her life living in the white world and knew the comforts of a house and one's own room, and the security and privacy they offered. She also had defied certain of the old Navajo taboos. For example, in a biological anthropology class required for her graduation, she had handled old human bones—an absolute taboo in the Navajo way. She felt ill during the time the bones were around, and her grandmother told her she shouldn't be touching them, yet she persevered in the class, coming to her own accommodation with her tradition and her future.

Her husband, Dennis, brought up in town, had no objections to returning; in fact he was enthusiastic about getting their own home. He didn't pressure her, however, because he knew that the decision to relocate was hers to make, as the relocation house would be in her name and would come from terminating her rights to her mother's home. But he let her know that he thought it might be good for the family if they had a place of their own.

Ella argued with herself for years. In June 1986 she told me, "I don't want my kids to blame me. I don't just want to move into the white man's world. I'll lose my identity, just become nothing. I could never live with my conscience."

She wanted to believe she wouldn't be forced to make a decision between violating her beliefs and acting in the best interests of her family. "I can't believe they'll really force people to move off the land," she said, "or force them to live on a limited amount of land. I believe something will be done to help the people stay."

Yet although there were many attempts to change the law over the years, including protests, marches on Washington, lawsuits, and presidential emissaries, the relocation commission continued its work, signing up Indians, building them new homes, family after family, removing them from their land, communities, economic arrangements, and moving them into the white world. One after the other, resisters were worn down by the strain of overcrowding, by the livestock inspections of Hopi Rangers, by the cloud of despair that hung over the affected areas.

Ella told me in 1986, "I go to a lot of peyote meetings; I go to a lot of ceremonies for the land. I see these old people there. They sit in there and they cry. And it seems like if I ever went around and just accepted money for [the land], I would be sort of like giving up on them and what they believed in. It would be like I never witnessed their crying for the land. It would just be like turning my back on them."

At another, bitter moment, Ella said, "[What they're asking is] just like giving up your way of life, selling your way of life, selling your religion, selling everything that you believed in, the things your parents taught you. It's like selling all those and turning around and accepting the white man's way, accepting his bribe, which comes in the form of money. I think white people will put even their mother or their sisters on the streets just to get money."

When Ella was feeling hopeful about the future, she said, "I think with an education you can almost make a living anywhere. . . . I know I can make it in the white man's world. And I know I can always keep my traditional teachings even though my children will be brought up in a white man's environment. I know that they can make it."

But then her mind would change again. "All the relocatee families I know, it seems they have given up something that is very special to them. Most of them have lost life in their family. And our traditional teaching says that if you accept payment for the land, you'll suffer for it. I think about that a lot. It scares me. Sometimes I think I should just relocate because it's going to take me years to pay for a house. I should just go, but then I think of that. What good am I if I want to teach Navajo culture and I turn around and accept money for my way of life and the teachings that were handed down to me?"

After Ella received her college degree, she and her family moved into a rented a trailer in Flagstaff for a year while they figured out what to do. They couldn't return home to Coal Mine Mesa. They didn't have enough money for a down payment on a house. But the government was offering them a house—all they had to do was sign the papers. Still, Ella recoiled. She had resisted relocation for twelve years, but something had to be done. In 1989 she decided to go ahead. Her husband and children deserved a home. Something that was their own. "I talked [relocation] over with my father and my mother," Ella recalls, "and they decided, well, you could try it and see what it's like. And I guess it was kind of like a test for me. They wanted to see how it would work out for me."

19

"You Have to Keep Paying a Mortgage for Thirty Years!"

The Bedonies were determined not to fall victim to the relocation commission's shoddy builders, so they interviewed and hired their own contractor, chose a design for the house, and helped out with the construction themselves. The contractor hired Ella's brother Freddie as a worker. So as to maximize the quality and size of house they were building, within the restrictions of the funds provided by the federal relocation commission, the Bedonies bought their own piece of land. It is located in a very nice, wooded, hilly suburban neighborhood in Flagstaff. They hold a $30,000 mortgage on the property, which means a monthly payment of $375, and so the relocation benefit of $66,000 could go completely into the building of the house. Most Navajo relocatees do not take out a mortgage on property—they simply apply the dollar figure of the relocation benefit to a completed house. The allowances are so low, however, that most Navajo families can only afford very small houses in less desirable parts of town. For a family of three or fewer, the benefit is $44,800, for a family of four or more, $66,000. Ella thought it made no sense to go through the trauma of relocation into a substandard house, which most relo houses were. So they decided to take out a mortgage to buy a piece of land, a very strange concept for a people who do not believe in owning land. ("You have to keep paying for it for thirty years!" Ella once said to me in disbelief.)

The Bedonies' house was completed in early 1990. Bessie did not turn her back on Ella or shun the house; in fact, when the family was ready to move in, Bessie blessed it with corn pollen. It is a roomy, two-story home with four bedrooms, a sunny eat-in kitchen, and a living room with a high gabled ceiling. The house also has a two-car garage. Ella planted flowers in the front yard and put down stones and shells around the porch and at the base of some of the trees.

They bought furniture, hung pictures, and moved in. The children were very excited to have their own rooms and several bathrooms in the house. Dennis was now settled in the same town in which he grew up, and in which his own parents have owned a home for decades. Although living in Flagstaff meant a ninety-minute daily commute, he was proud of their house and happy the family had its own home.

But almost immediately, despite her mother's blessing, Ella felt a terrible foreboding. She was afraid she'd made a grave mistake. The first sign was given by her son Kimo. On the reservation, Kimo was a happy, friendly child. He greeted all his relatives with a handshake, was known for his wide, dimpled smile, and was especially close to his grandfather Jack. But as soon as they moved into their new home, Kimo began to hang out with a rough group of teenagers.

During earlier years in Flagstaff, while Dennis and Ella attended college, Kimo had a circle of friends who were mostly black. These children didn't come from the kinds of homes that Ella would have liked. Many were poor and were being raised by parents with alcohol and drug problems. But Kimo seemed happy, and he made and sold tee-shirts decorated with graffiti designs, an activity he much enjoyed and that also earned good money. Kimo is a facile and gifted draftsman. He kept up with his schoolwork, so Ella didn't bother him about his friends.

But when Dennis and Ella moved into their relocation house, when Kimo was eighteen and Buzz fifteen, Kimo's behavior seemed to change overnight. His friends changed. He joined a gang, and began staying out at night and acting up in school, starting fights and disobeying teachers. Ella says, "When we moved to our new house, Kimo really started hanging out with gangs."

Despite the fact that the boys had already spent a good part of their childhood in Flagstaff, relocating appeared to represent a profound change. They began to make fun of Navajo ways —like burning cedar and praying, sprinkling corn pollen in the morning, rituals that help Dennis and Ella feel connected with home and their system of belief—and refused to follow them. "I tried to teach my boys about the kind of things that they should know as young men. They told me, you know, 'We don't need it; we don't live on the rez anymore. And we have no intentions of going back.'

"We tried to get the boys home to my mom's on the weekends for ceremonies and to help out with hauling wood and water, helping with the cattle. You almost have to live on the reservation to feel the culture. You have to walk around the swap meet in Tuba City and meet a relative and shake her hand to remind you of all your ties and responsibilities. You have to tend the livestock and build the fire. And everything we believe revolves around the life we have lived on the land and with our relatives. In the city, it's easy to forget. It's easy to think differently, to think the white man's way, even if you know better.

"I also try to have Indian things in the house, like stirring sticks and traditional hairbrushes and feathers. And I use them to remind the children of our stories and our teachings. It's important to know the Creation stories and the stories about the livestock, how they came to the Navajos. Knowing these things makes up the person that you are. If you know these things, you know your culture, you know where you're coming from and where you're going. These stories strengthen you, help you plan your life, help you resist temptation.

"It's hard to be an Indian in town. Relocation is forcing people away from their culture and into a way of life they can't handle. It's hard to sing the songs about livestock when you have none. It's hard to sing the harvesting songs when you don't have a cornfield. Getting up and sprinkling corn pollen when the sun rises is possible, but only if you have a backyard. Standing in the street sprinkling corn pollen looks strange.

"What we could do was burn cedar and send our prayers on with it. The cedar is like a messenger, carrying good thoughts to the gods. My kids were raised with all these teachings, but in the white world, surrounded by different ways, it was easy to forget. Kimo was getting so much pressure from his friends, he just went along with them."

He started to drink. It was Ella's worst nightmare come true. "None of my brothers or sisters, and there are eleven of us, ever had a problem with alcohol, so I wasn't as aware of the problem as maybe I should have been. I knew there were Navajo families full of alkies—my father's family had that problem. But I thought it had something to do with their upbringing. I was under the impression that our family, which was very traditional, wouldn't be affected by alcoholism. I guess I was naïve.

"But I always kept praying. I took my son's clothes to different traditional Navajo diagnosticians, and they would pray over them and then they would tell me, using what they could sense from the clothes as clues, what was the matter with him and what ceremonies I needed to have done for him.

"My boys felt like they didn't need to learn or go by their Navajo values anymore. They were living in town, and they didn't have any use for it. They didn't want to come back for ceremonies or they didn't want to come back to the rez, they just wanted to stay in town, just live there."

This reaction shocked her. Ella had not anticipated that the boys would respond this way. Perhaps in her own mind, it was an experiment, a temporary move, since all the others in her life had been temporary—a taste of new worlds.

But the move carried a tough symbolic message for her children: We are leaving our land seemed also to mean to them, We are giving up our Indianness.

Kimo's rebellion was ceaseless. "He would start fights with the kids [in school], and he would start arguing with the teachers," says Ella, "and the teachers would call [the] juvenile [authorities] on him. Dennis was getting calls from juvenile. Every day, I dreaded it. Every time the phone rang, I would think it's the school—Flagstaff High School. He was in and out of juvenile all the time. Once he threatened a teacher, and they threw him in the juvenile detention center overnight. As soon as he was out, it would be the same thing again. They didn't do anything to deal with him or try to work with him or try to counsel him. He did have a probation officer. But all he did was report to her and tell her how many hours of community service he'd worked."

"He was on probation for causing problems at school. Threatening the teacher, fighting with somebody. It was always that.

"Kimo had a lot of peer pressure from his friends that he was running around with. My son was going into a lot of things that were really against our teachings."

Kimo's behavior disturbed Buzz, because Buzz saw how much it was hurting his mother and the rest of the family. Buzz "just hated his brother for what he was doing," says Ella. "Sometimes I would catch him crying upstairs, 'Why is my brother doing this? Why is he doing this?' "

To Ella, this trouble was a terrible blow. What had she done? But she felt she couldn't ask her parents for help. She was ashamed. She had brought this on herself because she had relocated. Her parents didn't blame her, but she sensed that her siblings did. "Sometimes I felt like I was unwelcome in my own family by my sisters and my brothers. Somehow I felt I didn't have the right to go home and have ceremonies for my kids or for myself because I had *left*. I felt like I'd sold out, I gave out on the land, I resorted to something that was supposedly an easier way of life.

"A couple of my sisters were really bitter about it. They didn't show it vocally, but I could sense it. And for a long time, I wouldn't come home; I would meet my [mom and dad] in Tuba. I didn't really go out to Coal Mine to have ceremonies or visit. I used to come into Tuba City on Fridays and my parents would meet me here. And I would just visit with them for the day and then I would go home back to Flagstaff.

"Even though that was happening, Dennis and I kept the cedar going all the time and we kept our prayers going at home. We did a lot of things that we did on the reservation. We had our prayers at home. A lot of times I had bad dreams and I would ask a medicine man to say a prayer for me, but I never brought them out where I lived in Flagstaff. They always said the prayer for me at their homes.

"Dennis would tell me, 'It's natural, you know, kids go through that. Boys go through that.' I felt really real bad about what Kimo was doing because my brothers never went through anything like that. They never rebelled. Never got into drinking and moving out, saying they were going to leave home and stuff like that. My brothers never went through those kinds of things. It really started working on me mentally and emotionally. Sometimes I questioned my spiritual side. But I always kept that prayer going. I took my son's clothes to different medicine men, and they would pray for him and then they would tell me, You need to have this other thing done, and I would go and have something else done. I spent a lot of money on these things. It came to the point where we really didn't have the money to spend on these things in the summertime when Dennis didn't work.

"So I started [selling] some of my [silver and turquoise] jewelry as payments for the ceremonies. And it was really expensive." Ella wound up selling most all of the family squash blossom necklaces, turquoise pins, and rings she had been given over the course of her life. Now, when Ella dresses up and wants to adorn herself with silver—to identify herself as an Indian—she wears a Hopi necklace and earrings that she recently bought from a Hopi friend. The irony is not lost on her. As a result of a boundary dispute that was created by the federal government and yet shaped to pit Hopi against Navajo, Ella was forced to leave her ancestral land. Her son then suffered, she believes, as a result of her move, and she sold her Navajo jewelry to help pay for ceremonies for him. And now, because she bought some pieces from a friend, she adorns herself with Hopi jewelry.

Further, as the Navajos are moved off the land, Hopis are planning to move onto it—but some are Hopis who are married to Navajos and have Navajo children. In fact, her own son Kimo is dating a Hopi girl, who could, theoretically, get a homesite lease on the land the Navajos vacated. She could even get a homesite lease for the land on which the Hatathlies live, if they leave. And, if she and Kimo married, what would prevent her Navajo in-laws from staying on their land—which would then be hers? And would their children be Hopis or Navajos? The tragedy and the absurdity of the relocation program is clear when one imagines that in fifty years the land may again be populated by Navajos—Navajos who are married to, or born of, Hopis.

"At one time it got to the point where I really couldn't handle my oldest boy at all. And Dennis would tell me, Just let him go, you know, tell him to move out, let him be on his own." This was advice Ella could not hear. For months, she rejected it. Then, finally, after she'd tried everything else, she asked Kimo to move out.

"I told him that what he was doing was wrong, that we

wanted him to finish school. Why was he so turned off to what we were saying and hoping for him? We wanted him to be a good person. Why was he hanging around these people who don't care about anything or anybody? People who will kill or hurt anybody in their way.

"He would talk back, saying, 'Other parents don't say what you say, other parents let their kids do this or that, other parents buy alcohol for their kids.'

"Kimo said he didn't want anybody telling him what to do. He was his own boss. To me, that wasn't my son talking. It was someone else. Everything was, 'I don't care. If somebody kills me, so what? Who cares?' In the gangs, the way you win honor is by being bad. You gained respect from others when you were bad.

"When I heard my son talking like that, it really hurt me. I don't talk like that and neither does Dennis. Dennis doesn't have a temper. I could understand Kimo joining the gang and hanging out with these people if he'd been abused or neglected, but he never was treated that way. I could never figure out what was wrong with him.

"I told him his friends had brainwashed him. I told him he wasn't talking from his heart but from his mouth. He got really mad at me and he said his friends' parents didn't talk to them like that. I said it's because they didn't care. Nobody cared about them, but he has a lot of people behind him, a lot of people who have high hopes for him, a lot of relatives wanting the best for him.

"He said he didn't care.

"He told me, 'I don't need you anymore. I don't need your help. My friends will take care of me.' They gave him a new home.

Not only did Kimo move out; he also quit school two months before his scheduled graduation. Ella says, "Dennis just kept trying to tell me that he would come back when he was ready, that there was nothing else to do.

"But it really started working on me mentally and emotionally. I thought maybe, well, this is part of what I'm having to go through because I moved off the land. This is sort of a payback for doing that." Ella never told anyone of her horrible conviction. It was almost too much to admit to herself. It was her bitterest, profoundest shame.

Kimo moved in with some friends in a run-down apartment on the south side of Flagstaff. Ella heard through relatives that he was working at the local Safeway.

"I would worry about him, wondering, Where is he, where is he at, what kind of problems is he getting himself into? Does he need any money? You know, those kinds of things that I guess every mother worries about.

"And Dennis would tell me not to do that, to take care of myself, not to get really worn out getting myself stressed out. And I know he was worried about Kimo too, but he didn't want to come out and say it. Sometimes on Fridays I would just leave and come out to Tuba City and go sit with my aunt, and my aunt would tell me, 'Well, you need to have this and that done again,' and I would go and have those kind of [ceremonial] things done for myself. I was really getting stressed out on what my son was doing. About that time I got sick too. I was told I had a tumor and I had to have surgery."

Ella was diagnosed with breast cancer.

20

Cancer:
She Knew She Shouldn't Have Relocated.
She Knew the Price

Ella's first thought, on hearing the word "cancer," was that she wouldn't tell anyone but Dennis. She didn't want the kids to know; she didn't want her parents to know.

Ella didn't need a diagnostician to tell her what she'd done, for in her panic and confusion all she could think was that she'd brought this on herself. She knew she shouldn't have relocated. She knew the price.

As soon as she began treatment, however, her children began to suspect something was wrong. Ella underwent two lumpectomies and then began chemotherapy. After this treatment, she came home sick and exhausted.

"I was going to the hospital a lot and my son Buzz started wondering why. I started my treatment and I would stay there all day. And I guess he told Kimo, and Kimo wanted to know what was happening with me. Sometimes he would call Buzz and I would just be in bed because I'd just got my treatment.

"I finally told my son Kimo about it [over the telephone]. And he told me, 'I hope you don't start running to the medicine people because all they do is they want money, a lot of money. They don't help you. You're not going to get well from it. Just go to the doctors and they can treat you. Besides, you'll be able to understand what's happening with you, whereas a medicine man, he does his sing and then he leaves. He doesn't tell you what's happening or how he's going to treat you or what kind of treatment they're giving you.'

"I felt comfortable going to a doctor too because they take X rays and then they take tests. And like the boys were telling me, I always knew what stage I was in. I felt more comfortable going through that.

"I finally told my parents about it. And then they wanted me to come home. And they were coming up, like, all the time, several times a week. And my sisters started coming around too. And helping me do housework or laundry or taking me where I had to go. But the people who really helped me during that time were my friends, a lot of them were non-Indians. They came out and they sat with me during my treatments at Flagstaff Medical Center.

"Dennis had medical insurance. But once they found out [I had cancer], they didn't want to cover my expenses at Flagstaff. And so we kind of were on our own, and my medical expenses were in the thousands."

The Indian Health Service hospital in Tuba City offers free services to Indians, but they are not equipped to handle serious illnesses. If a patient requires sophisticated treatment or surgery, he or she is referred to another hospital—usually in Flagstaff or Tucson—and the Indian Health Service pays most of the charges not covered by health insurance, if the patient has any. However, Ella, disoriented by the rapid succession of distressing events, didn't get a formal referral before she began chemotherapy in Flagstaff. In time, she began to receive astronomical bills, and between treatments she brought them to the Tuba City Hospital, thinking they had been sent to her in error. But hospital officials told her she had to get a formal referral before the IHS would cover her treatments.

"Here, being a rez lady," she says self-deprecatingly, "I

didn't know it would [cost] so much." Eventually she got the referral she needed, but not before generating bills beyond any measure of what she could pay. Pretty soon she was too ill to worry.

"That treatment was really making me sick. I had diarrhea, I was nauseated a lot; I had no energy at all. Seems like I was tired all the time, even though I would get up and try to do things, try to do my beadwork, or try to sew. Even that took a lot of effort for me to do.

"We went to powwows; we have a lot of friends that go to powwows, and I felt that was a healing place. I would go to powwows and I would just sit there, you know, and watch. I really enjoyed that. And then my friends would come and talk to me.

"During that time, the hospital asked for counseling for my children. And I wanted them to get some kind of counseling from a traditional point of view. So I sought that out myself, for my children from medicine people. They would talk to them. But Buzz denied everything. To this day he still doesn't accept that I had [cancer]. He still doesn't accept that I had it. He would say to me, 'Mom, do this for me. Mom, iron this for me, sew this for me.'

"He knew I couldn't do it. I didn't have the energy. And I'd come back from the hospital when I got my treatments, and I just had to lie down. And I would lie there like all day, and finally I'd get enough energy to get up. And he'd say, 'Mom, why don't you cook, why don't you get up, why don't you clean? Why don't you do something, you just lie in bed?'

"Then he started saying, 'Oh, you're having another ceremony. Mom, you're just spending too much money on ceremonies. There's nothing wrong with you.' He knew I was going to the doctor, and he refused to go to the doctor with me. I told him, you know, 'Sit with me when I get my treatment,' because when they started the chemo, I used to sit up and take it and then after a while I would have to lay down. And I would tell him to sit with me, and he wouldn't go to the doctor with me."

The doctors wanted Ella to continue chemotherapy for at least six months. But after three months of treatment, with all the accompanying weakness and misery, her parents said, "No, don't take it, just stop the whole thing, the medication."

Bessie decided it was time for her to take over Ella's care and to replace her medical treatments with traditional Navajo healing. By this time, Ella believed her mother was probably right: The Anglo ways were surely failing her. She had relocated, generated the ire of her brothers and sisters, lost her son, and now this catastrophe. She no longer had the energy or the conviction to continue on the path she had chosen. Bessie organized a year's worth of traditional Navajo ceremonies, complete with herbs and sings, and even a Chinese acupuncturist from San Francisco.

"I really, really felt better with that," says Ella. "It took a long time for the [chemotherapy] medicine to wear off."

Week after week, Ella went home, taking herbs, having ceremonies, seeing Jerry, the acupuncturist, who gave her more herbs and tried to manipulate the energy fields around her body through other holistic techniques. He also performed acupuncture. Every few weeks, however, Ella went to the Flagstaff Medical Center for monitoring, to check on her condition. The cancer was not returning.

"The [doctors] were really amazed, and they just encouraged me to keep it going. I had to keep going to the doctor for my lab work because I [wanted to have the assurance] that I was getting better. And if the herbal way wasn't working, I wanted to go back to the modern medicine. And so I kept up with my doctor visits. The herbal treatment cost a lot of money, but I think it worked.

"The Navajos have what you call cancer medicine. So I was on different types of herbs having to do with cancer. They work with your blood. And I had medicine people that helped me on my spiritual side, where they talked to me about how these herbs originate and how they thought I got it. They diagnosed me. I went to hand tremblers. And they would ask me, 'Is this what you did when you were growing up?' or 'Did this happen to you?' and I'd say, 'Yeah.' "

Navajo healers fall into three categories. The diviners— either star gazers or hand tremblers, often women—diagnose the nature and cause of an illness and recommend curing ceremonies. The singers, the medicine men who run the many-night ceremonies, are the actual healers and are the most highly esteemed. A third group, herbalists, treat people with medicinal herbs. Some medicine people fall into more than one category.

"They thought the cause of it was way back in my childhood," says Ella. "Navajo people think when you have an illness, it goes back to what you did, maybe you did something in your life that you were not supposed to that was against the natural laws. For example, with myself, my sister and I when we were kids we were herding sheep and we came upon these eggs that were in the ground. We used to find these eggs in the ground, and we used to play with them. But we never told my parents. And one time we were playing and the sheep started to take off. So we wanted to take them with us, but they're really fragile and we didn't want them to break. So she was carrying hers with all kinds of grass in her hands. And I was trying to catch up with the sheep and I had those things in my hand and I didn't want to break them, so I put them in my mouth. I put the egg in my mouth and I was running with it and I swallowed it.

"I just never told my parents that during the summer. So way past the summertime my sister and I got mad about something, and she told my parents about it. She told on me. Lula. So it went back to, like, they say you can get cancer from eagle feathers if you don't treat [them] right, when you clean [them], when you work with [them]. You can get it from any kind of [birds or] poultry. That's why a lot of medicine people don't eat eggs or don't eat chicken. It goes way back, and it has something to do with the lightning too. Lightning will give you sores and is associated with cancer too. A lot of things that we did way back started kind of coming up. Sometimes I think about it when psychiatrists put their patients into hypnotism, and then they talk about what they did; I guess the diagnosticians do something similar. They go into your past."

But the hand tremblers use something like hypnosis on *themselves*—they go into a trance, and the movement of their hands in response to queries reveals the origin of the disease. Star gazers ask questions of the patient, of his past, his symptoms, and use crystals to examine him and help uncover the source of the illness. Diviners work by inspiration; they must deduce which events of the past were injurious and have led to the present imbalance. As Ella says, they are not completely dissimilar from psychiatrists, who also attempt to discover the elements in the patient's past—in part by inspiration—that have led to illness or maladjustment. Ella's diviner identified the swallowing of the bird egg as the probable cause of Ella's cancer. Then a ceremony had to be performed to persuade the Holy Beings not to continue punishing her for breaking the taboo.

The Navajo ceremonies are curing rites, intended to heal physical or mental problems—Navajos don't make a distinction between the two. For much the same reason someone's Navajo name is not mentioned casually, for fear its power will be diminished, and details of Navajo ceremonies are not to be repeated, for fear the ritual will cease to be effective. Ella and her family were adamant on this point, that no details of any ceremony performed over them should be described—for fear their power would be rendered ineffective, or worse. But general descriptions of ceremonies have been published and analyzed by anthropologists and medical doctors, and are also discussed by Navajos.

Most major ceremonies last two to nine nights and require

the medicine man to draw, using colored, finely ground sand, a highly detailed and elaborate painting on the floor of the hogan depicting the Holy People during a scene of the Navajo Creation legend. In addition to making the sand painting, the medicine man will also recite the Navajo origin myth for which the sand painting is an illustration, and sing the ritual chants that accompany the particular ceremony. The instructions for these ceremonies were given to the Navajos by the Holy People at the time of Creation. The performance of the rites seeks to appease the gods for the broken taboo, and then to reestablish in the patient the harmony that existed in primordial time, when the gods spoke directly to humans.

For example, if the patient is suffering from itchy, scaly skin, a diagnostician might say that the affliction reflects a transgression against the red ant people. The patient, at some point in his or her life, may have burned some anthills to get rid of them. But the red ant people played a role in the Navajo's Creation story, and they are holy. The medicine man will recite the story of the role of the red ant people, bring the story alive visually with a sand painting, and sing the appropriate chants to appeal to the ant people's renewed goodwill. A Blessingway usually concludes the ceremony, to bring everything back into harmony.

Sometimes Navajos, especially older people, will resort to traditional healing first, and enter the hospital only when they have become very ill. In the first years of modern medicine on the reservation, in the early twentieth century, hospitals were known as death houses; Navajos went there to die. From the Navajo standpoint, this had a practical advantage, for if a relative died in the hospital rather than at home, the hogan would not have to be abandoned. Precisely because people died in the hospital, though, no one healthy enough to stay away wanted to go there, for fear of contamination from the dead. Also, in those early days, medical personnel were not respectful of the Navajos' own theories of curing, and refused to allow patients to be seen by medicine men. As soon as they could, consequently, Navajo patients would leave.

Robert Bergman, a medical doctor and psychiatrist who treats Navajos and has studied their ceremonies, describes a major sing:

> No one seems to know precisely how many ceremonies there are, but there are many. Important ones last five or nine nights and are difficult and elaborate to a degree approached among us physicians, I think, only by open heart surgery. The proper performance of a major sing requires the presence of the entire extended family and many other connections of the patient. The immediate family must feed all of these people for days. Many of the people present have important roles in the performance, such as chanting, public speaking, dancing in costume, leading group discussions, and many other prescribed activities of a more or less ritualized nature. For the singer himself, the performance requires the letter-perfect performance of 50 to 100 hours of ritual chant (something approaching the recitation of the New Testament from memory), the production of several beautiful and ornate sand paintings, the recitation of the myth connected with the ceremony, and the management of a very large and difficult group process.

Outsiders may think of these arcane ceremonies as simply useless exhortations to inauthentic gods. But even medical doctors acknowledge that "the ceremonies work"—that is, patients usually do better after the ceremonies. This is the result, the doctors surmise, of a powerful, suggestive, and supportive psychotherapy that offers reassurance to the patient, and thus makes him or her stronger and better able to battle whatever troubles him, whether a psychological or physical problem. Many complaints that are helped by ceremonies are of a psychological nature.

Although there is a calm and purpose to Navajo life, it also has its particular anxieties. So many aspects of life are affected by forces the people cannot control, like nature and the whims of the white man. A hundred years ago, a drought could lead to massive starvation. Now, it seldom means death, but it can mean hunger. Constant changes in laws over schooling, taxes, mining, and gambling are made in far-off Washington, yet have profound effects on the Navajo people, who often feel their opinions are not heard. Powerlessness can cause great anxiety.

The requirement to be ever observant of taboos is also stressful. Although the prohibitions on the one hand help protect Navajos from harm, this constant need to avoid violating taboos can itself cause anxiety.

Furthermore, Navajos often live in crowded homes, with multiple familial ties and responsibilities. Resentments can bubble over, perhaps even turn to fantasies of violence. The Hatathlies, like most families, face these problems regularly. There are intrafamily conflicts and jealousies, and differing opinions on whether to trust white people, but they guard their family privacy and do not want details aired. They feel that letting others know about such things can make matters worse. Ella is different. Perhaps her years in the white world—or the hours watching TV talk shows—have made her more comfortable with self-revelation.

The ceremonies help relieve these stresses and anxieties by providing a reason for the patient's distress and then eliminating it. "The patient's evil feelings were not at fault, the myths say; the trouble was just that he was on hand when lightning struck. The proper rite can straighten this out. Thus ritual resolves social maladjustments that might otherwise upset the stability of the group."

Medicine men are usually not very interested in modern speculation about why their ceremonies work. As far as they are concerned, the reasons concern the supernatural. Robert Bergman has observed that

Traditional Navajos talk frequently in symbols: "We are glad you came from Washington to talk with us. There are many mountains between here and Washington," which translates as "Communication with the federal government is difficult. We are glad you are making an effort to improve it." They also reject the notion that they are using figures of speech. They do not attach as much significance to the distinctions among different levels of reality as we do, and like some poets, they reject as stupid and destructive any attempt to translate their words into ordinary language. Though it seems to me that their myths and chants are symbols of human and social-psychological forces and events, they would regard such a statement as silly and missing the point.

Without the benefit of modern psychoanalytic training, medicine men often know many things psychoanalysts do. One hundred-year-old medicine man caught Bergman's attention when the man conducted a sing over a psychotic patient, who then recovered—a recovery the medical doctor called "remarkable and well-documented."

"I don't know," this traditional healer told the psychiatrist, "what you learned from books, but the most important thing I learned from my grandfathers was that there is a part of the mind that we don't really know about, and that it is that part that is most important in whether we become sick or remain well." Bergman was further impressed by the healer's respect for the dynamic unconscious when the latter told him his life story, and how and why he had decided to become a medicine man: As a young man, *he* had been treated by a medicine man for injuries he suffered in an accident, and the man treating him informed him that the accident had been "unconsciously determined."

The psychodynamic underpinnings of the Navajo religion have been appreciated by two of the most celebrated students of the Navajo: Clyde Kluckhohn, a Harvard anthropologist, and his partner, Dorothea Leighton, a psychiatrist, whose seminal work, entitled *The Navaho*, appeared in 1946. Subsequent studies of the Navajos have reflected the great light shed by the work of these two scholars, as well as by the work of Dr. Leighton's husband, also a psychiatrist. The early analytic approach to understanding the culture has benefited the Navajos in the area of medical care, since medical staffs, albeit slowly, have learned the wisdom of making use of traditional healing. The Navajos are extremely concerned about maintaining good health, and they are prepared to spend the time and money necessary to ensure it.

In 1953 the quality of Navajo medical care improved dramatically when Annie Wauneka, a Navajo woman and chairman of the tribe's health department, was asked to explain to Navajos in tuberculosis sanatoriums why it was incumbent upon them to stay until their treatment was complete. She studied the causes of the disease and offered careful and complete medical information to the patients, many of whom then agreed to stay. In the same year, Navajo patients precipitately left a sanatorium in Tucson, Arizona, and Wauneka was again called in. She found out that a tree on the hospital grounds had been struck by lightning, and the patients had fled because of the traditional belief that places where lightning strikes must be avoided. She arranged for a medicine man to perform a Blessingway at the site, and the patients returned. This event led to a growing awareness between practitioners of the two medical systems that they needed each other to best serve the Navajos' health needs. Annie Wauneka won a Presidential Medal of Freedom for her work.

In the late sixties, Dr. Bergman became involved with a school at Rough Rock established to train young men to become medicine men. Research had shown that although most young Navajos believed in the efficacy of Navajo curing, and in the Navajo theory of disease, few could afford the long years of apprenticeship necessary to become singers. The collapse of the livestock economy in the thirties meant that since then almost every young man had had to find wage work—it was no longer possible to be apprenticed to a medicine man for ten years while being supported by the revenue from the flocks. After playing an important role in setting up the school by helping secure funds from the training and special-projects branch of the National Institute of Mental Health, Bergman became a teacher there. He met with the medicine men and the trainees to discuss their different theories and practices of healing and to offer case presentations. The psychiatrist noted that the medicine men knew quite a bit about anatomy as well as some physiology, and that they were very interested in all that was shown to them, particularly microscope slides and pathology specimens. A visit to a local medical center was a great hit: "It was characteristic, I thought, that the two things the medicine men most enjoyed seeing at the hospital were an operation and a particularly good view of a sacred mountain peak from the windows of the psychiatric ward."

While very interested in the hospital, the medicine men also had some suggestions to offer. "They were horrified by the pediatric ward," Bergman wrote, "because the children were so lonely. They kept asking, 'Where are the parents?' They urged that better provision be made for parents to stay with their children. They also suggested that we build two hogans at the hospital for ceremonial purposes. They remarked that they had all performed brief ceremonies in the hospital but that they could do more in a real hogan. They said that the medical staff could see the patients during the sing and could go back and forth if necessary. Their suggestion still has not been followed, but I hope that it will be soon."

The first year of the program focused on medicine, the second on psychology and psychiatry.

During the second year I began discussing psychiatry, and in this area there has been more of a two-sided exchange. We have spent much time on European and Navajo notions of the unconscious, a subject in which difficulties in translation have been great. Navajo metapsychology still largely eludes me, but it is clear that the medicine men know about the dynamic interpretation of errors and dreams. We spent a great deal of time discussing dreams and were pleased to discover that all of us followed the same custom with regard to them. We all, it turned out, spend our first waking moments in the morning contemplating and interpreting our dreams. One of the medicine men gave an example. He had dreamt about an automobile accident and said that that kind of a dream meant something serious was going on within him and that in order to prevent some disaster from happening to him, it was important to perform a chant about it. . . .

My feeling of trust and closeness to this group ultimately became such that I presented my own case, describing some things that had led me to enter my analysis and something of the analysis itself. When I finished this rather long account, one of the singers asked me the name of my analyst and where he is now. When I told him, he said, "You were very lucky to find a man who could do so much for you. He must be a very intelligent person."

Dr. Bergman discovered another area that moved the medicine men when he demonstrated hypnosis to them:

The group ordinarily looks half asleep—as seems to be the custom with medicine men in meetings. This was unnerving at first, until I found out from their questions and comments that they had been paying very close attention. When hypnosis was demonstrated, however, they were obviously wide awake, although at times I wondered if they were breathing. Working with a carefully prepared subject (I was unwilling to face failure before this audience), I demonstrated a number of depth tests, somnambulism, age regression, positive and negative hallucinations, and some posthypnotic suggestions. When I was done, one of the faculty members said, "I'm 82 years old, and I've seen white people all my life, but this is the first time that any one of them has ever surprised me. I'm not surprised to see something like this happen because we do things like this, but I am surprised that a white man should know anything so worthwhile." They also pointed out the resemblance of hypnosis to hand trembling, a diagnostic procedure in which the shaman goes into a trance and his hand moves automatically and indicates the answers to important questions.

When studying the actual multinight sings themselves, the curing ceremonies, Dr. Bergman observed that the ritual "is almost always symbolically appropriate to the case. Pathologically prolonged grief reactions, for example, are almost always treated with a ceremony that removes the influence of the dead from the living and turns the patient's attention back toward life."

Ella's grandmother, who dreamed that the spirit of her dead husband was trying to pull her into the other world, was told she needs a ceremony to help her refocus back on life. The chant and the myth it will retell, when she receives it—in the hogan, in the light of the flickering fire, according to the incantations of the medicine man—will provide a new story, a new mystical experience that will rival the power of her dream and attempt to refocus her back on the living. It is "treatment of a dream by a dream," replacement of one story with another, not unlike the way psychoanalysis has variously been described.

A healing ceremony takes place in a hogan, where the medicine man performs his chants and rituals over the patient. Sometimes relatives will come in and out, bringing water or supplies, or sometimes to participate. Outside, in their trucks, eating, talking, sleeping, are hundreds of relatives. The patient's family is expected to feed these guests throughout the duration of the rite, and their presence is believed to increase the power of the cure. The guests, for their part, believe that they will benefit from being there, from the summoning of the Holy Ones. The huge effort made by the family on the patient's behalf is itself a tremendous psychological boost for the patient, as he sees all his relatives striving to make him well.

Although the activity outside is social and humdrum, inside the hogan spirits are being aroused, primordial time is being rekindled, the Creation of the world is happening anew. Now that the Holy People live elsewhere, it falls to the Navajos to keep order and harmony, and they do so by re-creating the acts of the Holy Ones. The stories about the first days of the world are retold, drawings of significant events are made, and for a few moments, medicine man and patient become holy themselves, embraced in the magic of the world's first moments. Sometimes, at this point, when the patient is sitting on the sand painting, touching his hand to the rendering of the Holy Person's hand, foot to foot, guests will come in and do the same. If they are suffering as well, with a pain in the arm, the leg, the back, they will touch the piece of the Holy Person in the drawing and hope some of its animating spirit will heal them too. At this moment, they have all been returned to mythical time, cosmological well-being. They are redoing the work of the gods, and in so doing they have become godlike; they have returned to the beginning, to the time of Creation, when the gods' strength was manifest.

The ceremonies reflect the Navajos' profound belief in re-animation—that wrongs can be righted, and the individual then freed to continue with life's challenges, better, wiser, and restored to health. Redemption creates the opportunity for one of the most powerful of human dramas—to learn from mistakes and go on. The animating presence of the spirits also provides the Navajos with a tremendous psychological boost in times of stress, a boost that makes the hard steps of continued progress a little easier.

The ceremony provides a climax and a denouement—at the end of the rite, the patient is required to remain quiet and isolated, giving him or her plenty of opportunity to think about the rite, the stories, and the process of healing that has been set in motion. This quiet time allows for visualization of the kind that is known to improve performance in activities as diverse as sports and healing.

The Navajo patient also benefits psychologically from the intense and protracted attentions of the medicine man, a wise and revered person whose personal aura is often quite powerful. There is also an informal interaction that takes place between the medicine man and the patient's family before and during the rite, when the medicine man may hear about or perceive a family conflict, which he may then help resolve.

The ceremonies offer benefits to the community as a whole. The work of feeding participants and guests, and the socializing that accompanies the work, knits families together. The rites also have agricultural undertones that reinforce traditional beliefs about planting and are believed to have an effect on the overall good fortune of the group.

The Navajos keep using the ceremonies because they work. If they didn't serve the people, they would long since have been abandoned or changed. The curing rites helped Ella Bedonie. They made her again feel part of her culture, surrounded by relatives who cared for her, who shared a belief system that offered her some peace and guidance at a time of great turmoil. The ceremonies reassured her of her place in the universe.

21

Witching

The diviners examined Ella and diagnosed a problem involving the breaking of a taboo in her childhood, for which she was treated with a sing. But another diagnosis was also made, concerning Kimo's troubles: witching. Ella explains what she was told: "The [witches] were really working against my parents all these years. See, my parents have a really, really strong belief in the traditional ways and the traditional way of doing things. They really believe in ceremonies. There's no two ways about it. And with us [kids], we went to school. So with us it's different; we have a lot of doubts. And when things don't work right away, we doubt things. If a ceremony doesn't work, doesn't take effect right away, we start doubting things. And then with our kids it's even much harder for them, because they're raised in town and they're not raised around ceremonies as much. And they have a lot of doubts. So they told my dad that all these people, people that know witchcraft, worked against him for many years.

"All his life he's devoted himself, and everything, to his family. We were never involved in drinking and doing a lot of crazy stuff that you see kids and family do. We were always just very close, even though there were a lot of us. He just had a good life compared to other people.

"His own relatives were jealous of what he had. He was so strong in his belief that they started working on us kids, so that one of us would go crazy, and maybe be a womanizer, or somebody that went from one man to another, just started having crazy thoughts, just stuff like that to get you off the road. So they started working on us. Started breaking up our close ties among the children. And when we started having ceremonies, then they started working on the kids. They choose the weak ones to work on."

Witching is a phenomenon strongly believed in by Navajos. It serves an important purpose in the community, in part by providing explanations for ills that do not fall readily into other diagnostic categories. It also provides explanations, as well as an outlet, for antisocial feelings and inclinations—jealousy, aggression, frustration—that are prevalent but forbidden in a society that places such high value on cooperation.

＊

While Ella was undergoing cancer treatment, before she left Flagstaff and moved back to the reservation, she got more bad news about her son. A girl named Wendy knocked on her door one day, and told her that Kimo had been badly beaten by members of a Mexican gang. While he was walking home from the Safeway, a white van pulled up next to him, a bunch of guys tumbled out, and beat him. His face and arms were cut, and some ribs broken. That was all Wendy knew, save the address of a local gang leader whom Kimo knew.

Ella panicked and called Dennis. That evening, they drove to the local housing project where the gang leader lived. Wendy had warned them not to go there at night, but Ella and Dennis went anyway. Ella immediately recognized the man who opened the door, a black man Kimo had long associated with. She had once found a picture of him among Kimo's things. She had warned Kimo about him and had even told the man, one night when he called for Kimo, to stop calling her son. The gang leader, Ella recalls, offered her a stinging retort: "He said to me, 'I can call any time I want to, whether you like it or not. I can do you in. I don't like anyone telling me what to do.' "

"I told him I was not afraid of him because I had a stronger power protecting me."

The black man told Dennis and Ella to go away.

"Don't worry about Kimo," he told them. "Kimo's getting the medical attention he needs in Phoenix." He would tell them no more, and shut the door. Dennis and Ella, greatly disturbed by this last remark, went to the police. The cops told them to stay away from the man, who was known to traffic in drugs and arms. They also said they'd be interested in the photo of the gang leader if Ella could find it. She never did.

The police alerted hospitals in Phoenix, but none reported a boy matching Kimo's description. All Ella could do was wait and worry. She continued to have ceremonies performed for herself and Kimo. As her health improved, so did her hopes for her son.

"All during that time I was having all these ceremonies, and the last one I had I went with my dad to this clan uncle. He did a ceremony, we paid $1,000 to have it. After he did that ceremony, we went to this other man in Tuba. By that time I really didn't have a lot of money, and I had one more bracelet left. And I paid him with that bracelet, and my dad put up $600. This was for Kimo and also for me too, but 90 percent of it was for Kimo, for what he was doing.

"And [the medicine man] told me, he said, 'Don't worry about your son. He's going to be back. In four days. He might come back tomorrow or the next day or maybe three days or maybe on the fourth day. He's going to come home. Don't worry about him; he's okay,' he said. He says all these things that are happening—a lot of it is witchcraft because of what your parents went through [in resisting relocation] and what you're going through and what you and Dennis represent [an attempt to maintain a traditional life in the modern world]. He says a lot of people are jealous of what you do, how you do things, how people look at you. And right now they're attacking the weaker ones, the children. But he says, 'He's going to be back, don't worry about him.'

"So I went back home, and after two days Kimo called me. He said he was in Phoenix and he was okay, not to worry about him. And four days later, he came home. And it was really something, because he'd left with a stereo, a TV, and like he did all his shopping over at the mall. And when he came back, all he brought was a trash bag. And the clothes that he had weren't even his clothes. They were just dingy and dirty, like three tee-shirts, and they were just, like, brown. He just came in and said, 'Mom, I'm home.'

"He came over and gave us a hug, and he said, 'Mom, I want to go home to Grandma,' he said. 'I want to go see my grandma.' "

*

There was just one thing to do before they drove back home, up to Coal Mine. Buzz wanted to buy his brother some clothes. So he took some money out of his bank account; they went to the mall, to Sears, and Buzz bought Kimo some clothes and some shoes.

They brought him out to Coal Mine, and he stayed. Jack and Bessie brought him with them to see a medicine man in Jeddito, who said a prayer for him. The medicine man spoke English and talked to Kimo about his experiences of the past two years.

"From then on," says Ella, "he kind of changed. He wanted to go back to school, he got back into school. He graduated when he was twenty-one. He could have graduated when he was eighteen. Right now he tries to talk to his brother and his nephews. Not too long ago, in fact, three months ago, we had a peyote meeting for him. He said, 'Mom, I want to have a peyote meeting; I want to take my gourd and my fan and my rattle [ceremonial tools for the Native American Church]. I want to take them back to [college in] Tucson with me.' So he asked his grandpa to pray for him. And he invited some people and he invited some of our relatives; they had a meeting. So I don't worry about him anymore."

22

"A Myth Is Just Like a Big Stone Foundation—It Lasts a Long Time"

Kimo's rebellion, his beating by gang members, and Ella's own bout with cancer shook her deeply. Even today, when she speaks of it, she jumps back and forth in time disjointedly, in a monotonous voice. She describes the facts without emotion, and without her usual thoughtfulness and exuberant storytelling. She communicates a massive confusion, an unhinging, a time so upsetting that her world view needed readjustment to account for what had happened.

When Ella decided to let her mother manage her recuperation, she did what many people do when they have encountered bewildering setbacks—she went home, physically and figuratively. And she turned to traditional ways, seeking in them healing and also comfort and some explanation for her suffering. Religion tries to offer explanations for the unpredictable and incomprehensible; the Navajo religion is no different:

> Their system of beliefs . . . gives Navajos something to hold
> to. The old stories bring both the tellers and hearers a sense
> of exaltation by renewing their touch with the world of the
> past and a feeling of security that comes from seeing human
> life as an unbroken chain of events. Myths guarantee the va-

lidity of rites not only by detailing their supernatural origins but also by citing chapter and verse as to who was cured and how and when. They relieve the mind from perplexities by supplying final answers.

As one Navajo said, "Knowing a good story will protect your home and children and property. A myth is just like a big stone foundation—it lasts a long time."

The Navajos' stories make an individual's connection with his forebears clear. They also bring the individual into the reanimating presence of the Holy People: "On the existential plane this experience finds expression in the certainty that life can be periodically begun over again with a maximum of good fortune. Indeed, it is not only an optimistic vision of existence, but a total cleaving to being. By all his behavior, religious man proclaims that he believes only in being, and that his participation in being is assured him by the primordial revelation of which he is the guardian. The sum total of primordial revelations is constituted by his myths."

In the middle of Ella's treatments, she and Dennis moved out of their relocation home and rented it out. They moved back to the reservation. Dennis found a trailer in Tuba City with two bedrooms, a kitchen, and living room. He was eligible for the trailer because of his employment by the Tuba City school district. Nell and Buzz transferred to the Tuba Cityschools. Dennis and Ella hauled up their furniture, art, household items, and clothes; Ella also brought along her washing machine.

Over and over in her mind, Ella thought about what had happened. At first, Ella believed that she was being punished for relocating. She knew the price for selling Mother Earth. But before making her decision to relocate, she had carefully weighed this teaching against the other factors in her life: she had three children and no place to live, the government was offering her a house that she otherwise could never afford, and living in Flagstaff would offer her children a better education, something she and Dennis both valued.

Were these modern concerns really that important? Had she and Dennis been arrogant for imagining that they could violate, without punishment, that deeply held Navajo precept—if you sell Mother Earth the Holy People will punish you? She had gambled that she could have the benefits of both—a better education for her children, a house for the family—and maintain her tie to the reservation and her religious life. She had gambled and lost.

So she moved back home and placed her fate in the hands of her parents. But to her surprise, the medicine men who diagnosed her did not focus on her relocation. Rather, they followed two traditional paths of diagnosis. In the first, they tried to discover what taboos she had broken as a child that might have brought on her cancer. They discovered the violation committed when she accidentally swallowed a bird's egg. She acknowledged the error and was treated for it. She was welcomed back into her community with the full force of its cooperative spirit and effort. Further, the fact that the medicine men did not blame her for relocating, but rather for an act she had committed as a child, lifted an immense weight from her and allowed her to return to Navajo life and start again. The Navajo explanation gave her a chance to start over with a clean slate, a psychological state of grace.

Next the medicine people focused on what had happened to Kimo, but rather than ascribe it to the evils of the Anglo world, they proposed that Ella and her family had become objects of envy as a result of their accomplishments and cohesion. Neighbors or relatives, jealous of the Hatathlies' strengths, their stance against relocation, or Jack's grace and prosperity, could have resorted to witchcraft, taking as their prey especially the weaker, more vulnerable ones, the children. The medicine men did not identify who might have performed the witchcraft.

Witches are humans who do their work in a number of ways. They make powders from corpses, which they then sprinkle on their targets. They can shoot objects into a person—like pieces of bones or little arrows. They can say prayers against someone over poisonous plants. They do their work at night. Sometimes they travel under cover of darkness beneath animal skins, from which they get the name "skin-walkers."

Although the power of witches can be great, it is generally believed that good can overcome their evil work. Medicine men can remove objects that have been blown into people by witches. After Ella's brother Felix, who is now twenty-nine, suffered a bad period of grand mal seizures several years ago, Jack brought him to a Hopi medicine man, who removed a small arrow from Felix's neck. The medicine man's efforts were strenuous, and after the removal, Felix bore a large bruise in the place where the object had purportedly been lodged. Anglo unbelievers call this sleight-of-hand. But Felix slept deeply after the treatment and enjoyed several weeks of relief.

One of the most painful situations in which humans suffer is experiencing pain or confusion whose cause is unknown. Pain without a face is the most fearful of tortures. It cannot be identified or battled. The belief in witchcraft offers Navajos a face to ills that may otherwise remain unclear. If something awful happens that cannot be explained by traditional medicine people or diagnosticians, rather than acknowledge an unanswerable hole in the system or a weakness of the gods, they invoke witchcraft as the answer.

The lore associated with witches provides psychological benefits much like those Anglos receive from fiction, movies, and television. Stories of monsters and cruelty and victims and rescuers allow the listener to identify with the characters and, in the vicarious experience, to feel the aggressive or passive impulses they are constrained from expressing in real life. Just as people like to get scared in horror movies to relieve anxieties of life, or enjoy watching people humiliated and exposed on shows like *Geraldo* or *Sally Jessy Raphaël*, witching also offers stories of aggression and victimization that serve in the Navajo system to dissipate these impulses through storytelling. Perhaps a Navajo man will tell a story of a witch committing incest and in so doing relieve the inclination to act out his own impulses, which would be socially unacceptable and severely punished.

One may express hostile impulses, as well, by becoming a witch: "It is quite possible that the kind of temperament which in the old days found an outlet through organizing and leading war parties finds witchcraft the most congenial substitute. . . . Direct aggression is also expressed, of course, through attacks upon 'witches.' "

Attributing unexplainable events to witches provides a social outlet for hatred and aggression: "The People blame their troubles upon 'witches' instead of upon 'Jews' or 'niggers.' In place of selecting its scapegoats by skin color or by religious tradition, Navaho culture selects certain individuals who are supposed to work evil by secret supernatural techniques."

Ella was prepared to take on the blame for her own illness—she had violated a taboo as a girl, disturbing the natural order, taking inside her body the egg of another creature and thereby preventing that life from existing in this world. And so she had been punished by disease in a part of her body related to reproduction. However, if Kimo's troubles were the result of witching, she doesn't have to blame herself. Navajos believe the victim of witchcraft is blameless. Stories of witching increased in Coal Mine Mesa as more and more families succumbed to pressure and relocated in the mid-eighties. The Navajos sought answers to the family distress and heartache. Witching offered a desperately needed explanation.

But then, what of the blame she felt about relocating? Since this was a subject the medicine men did not address, Ella had to work out her own feelings about whether or not she had transgressed. Ella had simply been following the law and relocating as she had been ordered by the U.S. government. Could the gods be so cruel as to punish her for that? Over time, Ella's view of her illness and Kimo's troubles began to change. She blamed herself less and attributed more blame to the factors identified by the medicine men. The diagnosis of witching relieved Ella of the responsibility for the bad which had ensued from a decision she felt she had had little choice in making. One might say witching is the Navajo explanation of how bad things happen to good people.

In addition to knitting together loopholes in the traditional ceremonial complexes, and offering a structure in which aggression and jealousy can be explained and relieved, witching, and the fear of witching, also serve to maintain order in the society. People who become too wealthy or medicine men who become too powerful are encouraged to be generous with relatives and sponsor large ceremonies—or risk being labeled a witch. This is no small fear, as attacks on witches, if and when they take place, are usually violent and bloody.

The identification of witchcraft as the cause of Kimo's troubles also allowed the Bedonies to retain ownership of their house and postpone for a time the question of what to do with it. They rented it out in the fall of 1990, and later put it on the market. After Ella got better and the family situation settled, they took it off the market. If in fact the medicine men had determined that relocation was to blame, they would have had to put themselves in direct opposition to the U.S. government, which could have caused terrible confusion and panic on the reservation. By identifying Ella's problem as witching, the medicine men avoided this head-on collision with "Washindone," as the Navajos call it.

Ella has not stopped trying to understand her experiences, however. It has occurred to her that at the time the family moved, the boys needed the emotional support of family on the reservation more than they needed their own rooms in their own house or better schools. The boys needed to solidify their Indian identity at home before subjecting themselves to the temptations of the outside world. In retrospect, Ella says, she should not have relocated until they graduated from high school.

23

"Somehow, the Creator Gave Me Another Chance. I Don't Know Why; Maybe One of These Days I'll Find Out"

Ella's bout with cancer was very costly. At the end of the medical intervention, she owed $36,000 that Dennis's medical insurance would not cover.

Ella and her family embarked on a car trip in late 1991, as Ella was recovering. When in Los Angeles visiting friends, Ella called her foster sister Nancy. It was Christmastime and Nancy was delighted to hear from Ella. She arranged a family reunion, with Ella as the surprise present. Ella's foster mother had died years earlier, and her foster father had remarried. Although Ella had not seen him—he is now in his eighties—in twenty years, they had written to each other and spoken on the telephone over the years. Ella was surprised by how much he had aged.

"He was really old," she said. "His hair was pure white."

The family wondered why Ella was resting so much and leaving parties to lie out in the van. Finally she told them about her bout with cancer. Her foster father quickly asked if she needed financial help: his first wife had died of leukemia, and he knew how expensive chemotherapy was.

"He bought insurance to cover all my medical expenses," says Ella. He also didn't want her to be treated at the Indian

Health Service. "He says, 'I don't trust IHS; they're just there to use Indians as guinea pigs.' " He asked his own doctor, a physician from Switzerland who was treating his Parkinson's disease, to examine Ella. The doctor did so during Ella's stay in California and recommended a doctor in Tucson. Ella saw this doctor, and he told her she was healthy, but to watch her diet. "He just really tells me to take care of my diet, take care of myself. But he says it's something that will come up again: 'Maybe in your life, it will show up again. You just have to learn to take care of yourself.' "

I ask Ella if she was surprised that her foster father had been so generous with her.

"No," she said. "He was just that kind of a person. He was real kindhearted. And he used to call me his daughter; whenever I called, I was his daughter. When my foster mother died, I didn't go over there, I just talked to him on the phone. I guess everybody was there when I called. And he said that just because she's gone, that doesn't mean that you shouldn't come around, that you'll always be part of our family because you lived with us, and you'll always be a part of the family. He always said, 'Don't hesitate to ask for anything because if we can, we'll take care of it.' "

Although Ella feels many of her experiences with Anglos have been regrettable, she also thinks some of her relations with white people have benefited her. She received a better education while on Mormon placement and was exposed to cultural and social influences she never would have experienced on the reservation. And although one could argue that her Mormon training confused her and, in the end, wasn't stronger than her own traditional belief, her foster parents did not attempt to stop her when she decided it was time to return home, nor did they deny her their love when she made decisions they thought were wrong. They have remained interested in Ella and devoted to her throughout her life, to the extent of covering $36,000 in medical bills that would otherwise have crushed her and her family.

Ella says her foster father has written to her once a month for the last ten years. When she had first returned home, pregnant with Kimo, her foster parents wrote frequently, but she didn't respond. Yet they continued, in spite of her snub, to drop her cards and letters. In the last ten years, Ella has corresponded more faithfully.

"It was something that I just wanted to forget about, I guess. I felt uncomfortable talking about the church because that's usually what they wanted to talk about. My younger foster sister, she's, like, maybe about two or three years younger than me. We're very close, and she's the one that keeps in contact with me all the time. She calls me and I call her."

She says she was never bitter about the church or her experiences. "I don't think I ever felt bitter about the church," she says. "I just, um, I just kind of felt like I was in the wrong place." When she was still there, however, she did not feel that way. "I never thought about it," she says. Sometimes Navajo friends who were on placement with her ask her if she is still involved with the church, and they invite her to attend services with them. She demurs. She notes that she has a relative who is still active in the Mormon church, but he also attends Navajo ceremonies. "He's able to balance that," she says. He even came to her own ceremonies.

I ask Ella if her parents ever told her their thoughts about placement. Did they regret sending her? Were they glad they did? She says they never mentioned it to her. But they sent Lula, Lenora, and Genny after her.

"I think it was just a good experience," Ella says, laughing. "I mean, I don't have any regrets about ever being on placement, and I think I got to know a family that's just like my family. Maybe because of the faith they had in the church, they accepted me for who I was and they encouraged me always to hold on to my Indian identity. They were always telling me I should have pride in being an Indian person. In their Book of Mormon, I guess we're supposed to be like the Chosen People. The latter days, which are today, I guess, the Indian people are going to be the ones to save the world." Ella laughs again. "They're going to be the leaders. And they have a great lineage, going back. Because of that, the Mormon people have a lot of respect for the Indian people, but then there's lot of Mormons too who really pushed religion on kids who went on placement, I don't know, maybe brainwashed them. But I was never in that position."

Ella's reverence for her family and Navajo ways have become stronger as a result of her journeys in the outside world. It's as if living in exile from her people renewed the urgency of her ties; her faith is stronger now that she's tested it in an alien world.

"I had another chance, you know. I was given another chance. Maybe there was a reason why. My tumor could have really spread to my body, and I wouldn't be here today. But somehow, the Creator gave me another chance. And there is a reason why I was given that chance. And I don't know today why; maybe one of these days I'll find out."

Ella says that as a result of her trials she has become more tolerant. "I look at things differently now," she says. "I live differently know. I think differently. I try to be happy with my family, my sisters, and I try to look at my boys; I tell them that no matter what they do, I'm always going to be their mom, I'm always going to be here for them. Because a lot of mothers, [if] their children do bad things, they'll say, 'You're not my son no more. You take care of your own problem.' But with me, it's different. I would help my kids out of that situation, whatever it is that they're in.

"There was a time in my life where maybe I wouldn't have experienced this chance. Even though it was a bad experience, I was given another chance, and here I am today and I need to be grateful for it. So I look at things that way."

Rather than criticize or dislike people whose interests seem opposed to her own, she tries to understand them. "At one time I really had bad feelings toward white people. In 1978, when the land dispute started, I had really bad feelings toward white people. All these politicians. But today I don't feel like that. They're just doing their job. It's not really their fault, these laws came way, way from back there. Their forefathers are the ones that made these laws. It started a long time ago, and these politicians are just doing their job the best way they can. That's the way I look at it now.

"The Hopi people—I understand why they think this land is theirs. That's their land. And they have that right, they have that right to say that. [And I compare it with the Navajos' stories.] I try to put the [Navajos'] migration stories on one side, and the theories of how they moved around a lot and borrowed from all these different tribes, all these things, and they put it together in a way that fitted their life-style. And it's really beautiful how they did it. It makes a lot of sense. And they must have been really smart, the Navajo people, to put all these things together into a puzzle, all of these puzzles they borrowed from different people. And they put them together to where they fit, and it makes sense."

I ask Ella if she has become more religious since her illness.

"In a way, yes. I think life is very sacred. And when you're given the chance to live here on Mother Earth, you should take care of yourself, your family, live in a more faithful way. Everything has meaning to you; you notice things that you never noticed before. You take time to talk to people, to your relatives, [people who formerly] you might just run by and shake hands with them real quick. You start spending time, stopping by, talking to them, helping them. That's what has changed for me."

Ella's illness and return to the reservation also got her thinking about her legacy to her children, and her own parents' legacy to her. One of her neighbors in Big Mountain once proclaimed angrily at a meeting protesting relocation that she didn't want her grandchildren to learn about Navajo life from an exhibit in a museum. Because of the relocation program,

Ella's children will not be able to raise their children on the reservation, with the sheep, with the corn, with the summer squaw dances, the winter recitations of the animal stories. How much of the Navajo ways will her grandchildren retain? she wonders. How much will they pass on? Will they have any idea how their great-grandfather Jack lived? This is when she conceived of the idea of preserving some of the stories of the old days for them in a book. Perhaps a book is only a step away from the museum, but at least it will contain her own words.

Part Four

24

"Jack, You Are a Fine, Humble Person. This Bundle Is Sacred. You Are the Only One I Think Is Worthy of It"

During the quiet fall days when Ella sat with her father and grandmother, encouraging them to recall the old days, asking them to put words for the first time to events long past and emotions long put away, something extraordinary happened. Rena Williams decided to give away her earth soil bundle. This object, a skin bag filled with soil from the four sacred mountains, contains in symbolic form all the powers and collected knowledge of the Navajos. Rena decided to give the bundle to the child she gave to her sister-in-law to raise, her youngest son, Jack.

Giving Jack the bundle might be equivalent to a white parent leaving all his property and assets to a child who had been given up for adoption and had never lived under his own parents' roof. Rena's choice of Jack was also unconventional because he was raised by a woman not of Rena's clan. Children take the clan of the mother, and the child then learns the myths and family obligations determined by the clan. (Myths and stories differ slightly between clans and families.) Jack was educated by Lilac, whose clan is Tacheenie, or Red Water, and he learned from her the teachings of that clan. Nevertheless, Rena, a member of the Salt

Clan, decided Jack was the worthiest of her nine children and was therefore the one who should inherit the bundle.

Ella wondered if it was Rena's recollection of the old days in their talks together that got her thinking about the bundle and what to do with it. The gathering of the family history had altered its course. Ella visited her grandma soon after she decided to give away her earth soil bundle, and once again Ella turned on her tape recorder.

✳

Rena Williams:

After much thought, I've decided to give my mountain bundle to my son, Jack. I have considered all my children, and I have decided that the youngest of my five sons would carry on this mountain bundle for me. This bundle holds the teachings, stories, songs of our people, our clan, the Salt Clan.

This bundle is very sacred among all medicine bundles. It has sand from all four mountains which mark the boundaries of our land, Dinetah, Land of the Dine. It is our law, the reason for life here. It holds the thoughts of our clan. The white people have a black book which contains stories and songs and instructions about how you should lead your life. This bundle is also our Bible, our directions for life. You cannot drop it; you have to protect it always. In the springtime I want to have a ceremony to transfer this bundle to my son. At this ceremony, it is reopened and renewed. A Blessingway ceremony is held, and then it officially belongs to my son. He carries it on again for our clan, Salt Clan.

If this is not taken care of in a proper manner, it can cause harm to the family. I know I have made the right decision. I can sleep peacefully knowing my son will carry on for me.

✳

Jack Hatathlie:

I feel very honored to have my mother pass the bundle to me. I thought she was going to give it to one of her other children, but she chose me. I know I was not raised with the Salt Clan teachings. I feel good that I am going to have a chance to carry the sacred bundle. This bundle is like the white man's black book. It contains life—the teachings, songs, ceremonies, the foundation of what life is here on Mother Earth. In a humble way I approached my mother and asked her, "Why me?"

She said to me, "My son, my baby"; with tears in her eyes, she grabbed for me and rested herself on my shoulder. "You are a fine, humble person. This bundle is sacred. You are the only one I think is worthy of it. You have led a good life. You had a good childhood. A good mother raised you. Through hardship, you are the man you are today."

While she was holding me, I felt for some reason that maybe she was trying to make up for the times that she never had a chance to hold me as a child. At that moment, I felt a closeness that I had never felt. I feel fortunate that I had two mothers—one who gave me life, and one who gave me my direction in life. Not everyone has two mothers. Now my thoughts are on how I am going to properly accept this soil bundle in a ceremonial way.

✻

Saginey Nez, a clan relative:

I know that Jack was raised by a clan aunt for a reason, a good reason, from the Creator. He was given a firm foundation in life and instructions on how he should lead his life. I look at him as a good, caring man always willing to help. His brothers and sisters are different from him. He takes care of the [Native American Church] fireplace and

*involves his children in the meetings, which is good. Nowadays, it's
hard to talk to your children. But his children listen to him and his
wife. That's the way a family should be.*

*He's a very gentle person. Always talking in a positive and respectful
manner. He respects and acknowledges me, and I think of him as my
own son.*

※

Susie Williams:

*I hear that his natural mother gave him the soil bundle. He really
deserves it, and our family is honored that we had a part in raising
such a person to hold and carry on such a sacred bundle.*

※

It is early morning. The sun has just made its way up over the
horizon, and the red earth is sparkling gold. Dogs bark in the
distance, and the still-cool air begins to tingle with the coming
heat. Ella steps off her bed and walks into the kitchen. She is
dressed and carries a bracelet she is beading. It appears she
has been up for some time. Ella pours coffee from her Mr.
Coffee machine.

She is still thinking about Rena's gift to Jack, and what it
means for her family to receive such an honor. And she is
thinking about the grandmother she is coming to know for the
first time. "I never really felt attached to [Rena] like I did with
my other grandma, Lilac," says Ella. "Lilac was the one who
was around for us, and we spent nights with her. She was
always coming to visit us and stuff like that. She was a real
simple lady. She dressed real simple. She didn't wear a lot of
jewelry. She had a bracelet with a black stone that was given
to her by a grandson, Hoskie, Sally's son. And then she had,
she always had, a coral necklace too, real old coral necklace.

That was what she wore, and maybe a turquoise ring. But comparing her with my real grandma—now *she* was a decked-out lady."

Ella still wonders why her father's blood brothers, who grew up in such relative wealth, should have suffered so many alcohol problems, while her father, whose childhood was poor and filled with hard work, became a responsible, hardworking man. In her mind, the hardship and deprivation he suffered would not augur an auspicious future—revealing a rather middle-class mentality, which is yet utterly Navajo. In her mind, children from a wealthy family would be expected to have better futures, because they were surrounded by more sheep, more food, more *hozho*—at least on the surface. Thinking about her father's upbringing has made her think about the way she has raised her own children, trying to provide them with everything they needed and wanted. She wonders if perhaps that was not the best way.

Her second son, Buzz, has lost interest in school and has been getting into the same kind of trouble Kimo did several years ago. He is drinking, getting into fights, making trouble. He has grown in short order from an impish, animated adolescent into a strapping, muscular young man. Although as a boy he laughed a lot and liked to tell jokes, now his humor has become dry as Tuba's summer dust, and he still makes every effort to maintain an impassive and inexpressive mask on his face. He is a friendly, funny young man among those he knows, yet there is an aspect of him that seems frozen, lacking animation. He seems to have lost momentum and direction. As a boy, he talked about becoming a lawyer. Now there is no talk of college, though he continues to sell his drawings, tattoos, and paintings. Ella says, "He's not doing anything," meaning, he's not applying to art school or getting his work together for shows. He spends a good deal of time with his girlfriend, Sonya, who suffers from a bad case of asthma, and whose mother has a house in Tuba City. Dennis talks to Buzz about the dangers of alcohol, yet Buzz still periodically gets drunk and then fights.

Most of Jack's blood brothers suffered lasting and tortured battles with alcohol. One of them, Ned Hatathlie, made outstanding contributions to Navajo life, serving on the advisory committee to the Navajo Tribal Council, helping to build Navajo Community College—the first college on an Indian reservation in the country—and serving as its president. The Ned Hatathlie Cultural Center, part of Navajo Community College in Tsaile, was named in his honor. But he died at a young age in the bedroom of his home of a shotgun blast. He had been drinking, friends say, and was despondent. He had just been passed over for a job as head of the BIA area office, a high-ranking job in the BIA bureaucracy. It is not clear whether his death was suicide or an accident.

*

"It was about a month ago that my grandma gave the bundle to my dad. I was there with my dad. I went to see my grandma for something. I think I took her some squash and some corn that I fixed. That was when she gave it to him. Her daughters were there too, and two of her sons. She just told him in front of them that none of them know how to take care of something like that. My dad's eyes filled with tears and then my grandma's did too. They just sat there, real emotional, for a very long time.

"She said, 'I raised them and I know them all my life and none of them, you know, have any knowledge of how to take care of these things, these paraphernalias that medicine people have. If I give it to any one of them, it's not going to be cared for. And the way that I cared for it all this time, all my life, it's like putting my life in their hands if I did that. They're just going to let me down. They don't know how to talk about things or take care of anything like that.'

"That same day, I had the recorder in my pocket. I just kinda like turned it on and she talked. Then my dad just talked for it too. She told my dad that now that he has this thing, she knows that her grandkids will take care of her all the time, and she wanted the grandkids to know about it, know how to take care of something like that."

It is unclear who will inherit the earth bundle from Jack, the bundle that contains soil from the Navajos' sacred mountains. None of his children any longer has a piece of land within Dinetah.

25

"I Believe the Native American Church Is the Religion for Our Young People. If You Are Honest with the Medicine, It Will Guide and Help You"

Participation in religious ceremonies occupies a great deal of the Hatathlies' time, energy, and money. In the late thirties, it was estimated that one-third to one-fourth of the productive time of a Navajo man was spent on matters of religion, as was 20 percent of the family's income. One-fifth to one-sixth of a woman's time was spent on ceremonies. Ella's family probably spends a similar proportion of time and funds on religious rites, if not more. Today the Hatathlies not only engage in traditional curing, but they augment it with meetings of the Native American Church, formerly known as the peyote religion.

The origin of the peyote ritual is not definitively known, but it is believed that it began about 1885 among the Comanche or Kiowa Indians in Oklahoma. By 1899 it had spread to sixteen tribes, and by 1955 to seventy-seven in the United States and Canada. It reached the Navajos in the thirties, and has since then proved itself to be enduring and popular. Although it was initially met with great resistance by the Bureau of Indian Affairs, traditional medicine men, and the tribal council, the NAC grew rapidly and now flourishes on the Navajo reservation. It has been estimated that half of the Navajo people are adherents of the NAC.

The NAC makes use of traditional symbols and elements of different Native American ceremonies—eagle feathers, drumming, singing, and tobacco. The NAC also shares the Navajo approach to disease, that the mind plays a large role in the health or illness of an individual. The pantheon of Navajo gods is not addressed specifically; rather the NAC presumes a single transcendent God. And this God is reached directly by each participant through inspiration, rather than by formulaic ritual.

From an outsider's point of view, the peyote meeting, which goes on through the night and combines ritual and songs with prayer and confessional self-revelation, resembles a cross between a religious ceremony and a group therapy session. The patient—sometimes an individual, other times a family—speaks about what is troubling him, and neighbors and relatives offer observations and advice. This is interspersed with singing, ritual manipulation of the fire, offering of prayers with tobacco, and ingestion of peyote, all led by the roadman, so-named because over the course of the night, he will try to bring the patient back onto the road of his life, his true path, and away from the disharmonious, conflict-riddled detours on which he has found himself.

The religion is symbolized by and makes use of the peyote cactus (*Lophophora williamsii*), called "medicine" by the Navajos and usually ingested as a tea. Peyote contains approximately ten alkaloids, including mescaline. Studies of peyote users indicate it is not addictive and usually not pleasurable. Peyote frequently produces nausea, a tightening of the chest and jaw, and sometimes auditory and visual hallucinations. Such effects reinforce the idea that "something is being done to and for the human organism, and [peyote] is felt to be a 'power.' "

The NAC rose in popularity on the reservation during the traumatic livestock reductions of the thirties, which dramatically diminished the Navajos' primary food source and economic activity. To make matters worse, the reductions were carried out without sensitivity to the Navajos' feelings about their sheep herds, without awareness that the herds reflected the family, were in fact considered part of the family. Although most of the livestock was purchased from the Navajos and transported off the reservation, hundreds of animals were simply shot and piled up to rot in the summer sun. To the Navajos, this waste was an unspeakable abomination, and they were shocked and humiliated by it. Observers noted that they had never seen such abject misery in a people as in the Navajos after reductions began.

In prior decades, the U.S. government had encouraged the Navajos to increase their herds, but had not encouraged them to become educated. When the stock was taken away, the Navajos had no training or skills for wage work and were forced to take low-paying, unskilled work. They tried to fight the white man over the livestock reductions, but they lost utterly.

The peyote religion caught on at a time when the Navajos felt they needed additional supernatural power to help them overcome their troubles. Peyotists say they do not pray to God; they commune with Him, speak with Him in the meetings. "Peyotism . . . provides special gifts which compensate for the Indians' lack of status and privilege. If the white man has the Bible and his church, the Indian has direct access to God. If the white man has learning, the Indian has revelation. Peyotism, then, provides mystical paths to knowledge equal or superior to those enjoyed by the majority."

The NAC preserves the essence of the Navajos' central ceremony, the Blessingway, while incorporating ceremonial adaptations that support the changing lives of Navajos. The NAC narrows the size of the important social group from the extended clan to the nuclear family. Hundreds of relatives attend the traditional Navajo curing ceremonies; the peyote meeting, in contrast, involves ten to thirty people. It also reduces the expense, because fewer people must be fed. Ceremonially, it seeks a compromise between Indians' responsibility to their communities and their individual strivings. The leaders of the ceremonies, the roadmen, are usually younger than traditional medicine men and therefore speak English. This means that people who don't speak Navajo can still participate fully. In a traditional ceremony, long passages must be repeated verbatim in Navajo by the patient. Also, it takes fewer years of apprenticeship to become a roadman than to become a traditional healer, thus opening up the profession to more men who must also support their families and can no longer depend on livestock for income.

The NAC provides men with new and significant roles in Navajo culture, roles they have not had (except for medicine men) since raiding days ended in the 1860s. Women control traditional Navajo life, because the livestock is theirs, the family resides on her family's land, and inheritance passes through them. The NAC also offers reinforcement for the men's new role as wage earners. "Superficially then," writes anthropologist John R. Farella, "there are two general types of behavioral transforms which make peyote adaptive to the larger American context. They are, first, the restriction of the active social unit in the direction of the nuclear family and, second, the labeling of the male as the key family member."

The NAC provides a ceremonial framework for these two major changes in Navajo life. After stock reductions, the only way to live off sheep was to compete for the limited grazing land available. This was for the most part impossible, since the government began to regulate livestock family by family. Navajos needed an additional source of income. Women continued to weave rugs and sell them. The men began getting jobs off the reservation, as Jack did, at the Navajo Army Depot in Bellemont, or with the Santa Fe Railroad and at the Page Power Plant. Working off the reservation allows for the creation of wealth, which is good, without striving against a relative, which is bad. But the man must either be separated from his family or bring the family along with him, as Jack did at times, into the Anglo world. But Jack didn't move with his mother-in-law, only his wife and children. Out of necessity, the central family group has decreased in size.

Further, the sheep are less important to the Navajo economy

because of reductions and because the children, who formerly helped tend the flocks, are at school all day. Wages are thus becoming the most important part of family income.

The NAC offers a corresponding ceremonial importance to the younger male wage earners, giving them a ceremonial or "traditional" place in which they are connected with a powerful "female" object—the peyote. The NAC has also helped shift the measure of wealth from sheep to money.

The NAC, like traditional Navajo healing, also uses a sophisticated intuitive psychology. In the NAC meeting, the patient is encouraged to speak about what is on his mind and in his heart. The night-long ceremony is marked by various stages, some of which are determined by the effects of the peyote— nausea, depression, and then fatigue. There is a beginning, a middle, and an end during which the stories are told, much as certain rhythms may develop during a psychoanalytic hour, with revelations, dramatic declarations, and emotional outbursts taking place at key moments in the process.

The physical effect of the peyote on those who ingest it has been described as follows: "In all but its mildest and most prodromal forms, the peyote experience is characterized by a feeling of the *personal significance* of external and internal stimuli. The user is prompted to ask of everything, "What does this mean for me?" Similarly, the psychoanalyst encourages the patient to put aside the sounds of the other voices telling him who he is and what he should be, and encourages him to listen to his own heart in the roar of interference produced by those who came before.

The result is paradoxical and counterintuitive: listening to the self produces a deeper understanding and appreciation of the outside world. Navajo peyotists say, "I used just to live from day to day, but now I *think*." Anthropologist David Aberle explains, "When this comment can be elaborated—and often it cannot—it usually turns out to mean that one's self, one's aims, one's relationships, and one's ethics have become matters for reflection, and have somehow taken on a new dimension of meaning." Is this not the effect of the journey to find the self by any method? And like any other profound influence, peyote has no end to its revelatory power. Say users, "You can use Peyote all your life, but you'll never learn all there is to know about Peyote."

Peyote is a symbol of the Church, a means of communication with God, a power in its own right, and a cure of unique potency for spiritual and physical disease. Peyotists use the generic Navajo term for medicine, "*azee*," to refer to Peyote. To a Navajo, "medicine" refers not only to herbal or Western medicine but also to the entire complex of ritual that . . . [invokes] supernatural power for the benefit of the sick. When Navajos call Peyote "medicine," they refer to its inseparable physical and spiritual potency. Peyote—its ritual and itself— is a gift of God for Indians.

Jack Hatathlie, whose last name means "singer," is a road-man for the NAC. He told his daughter Ella that he believes the NAC is the future for young people. It allows young men an opportunity to become healers and religious leaders, and it provides an opportunity for change that is typically Navajo. Rather than rejecting the Anglo influences that have permeated Navajo life, in a ceremonial shift it brings these changes into the tradition. NAC also provides a framework for the incorporation of modern morality into Navajo philosophy, and it strictly forbids the use of alcohol.

Although they are different, traditional Navajo religion and the NAC do not conflict with each other. Many families use them together, as do the Hatathlies. Some families will hold a peyote meeting in hopes it will increase the effectiveness of a traditional ceremony. Whenever a family member is sick, Jack will ordinarily arrange both traditional curing ceremonies and a peyote meeting for that person.

In a traditional curing ceremony, the patient is healed by contact with the Holy People during the retelling of the origin myth, in a reconjuring of the first sacred moments of the world. This contact with the primordial reanimates the patient, and the gods are expected to act according to rules of compulsion. In a peyote meeting, the people also believe they are communing with the divine, though here it is conceived of as a single transcendent, all-powerful God. God is appealed to with inspiration rather than compulsion. The patient is healed through self-revelation and self-examination.

The positive effects of the talking cure in the peyote meeting—the relief that comes from airing buried thoughts and feelings, the support of those who come to understand the confusions that are causing the patient pain—are enhanced by the belief that another One is hearing, that He is all-powerful and in a position to heal. The physical effects of the peyote on the body reinforce the idea that a power is working inside the patient. Says Ella, "It's medicinal, it directs our prayers, it's kind of a mediator between the Creator and us."

The NAC has been called a nativistic movement, an attempt to reassert or perpetuate an indigenous culture in the face of outside pressures to assimilate. There is some suggestion that Blessingway, the central element in traditional Navajo ceremonies, is also nativistic. It is important to remember that Navajo culture and religion are highly composite, and that pieces of other Indian cultures were integrated wholesale. The Navajos displayed their genius in the strategy of incorporating the new by making it traditional. Different becomes the same once it is incorporated into the ceremonial framework.

Navajo scholar David Brugge suggests that the development of Blessingway may have served some of the same purposes several hundred years ago that the NAC serves now:

> It is very probable that Blessingway . . . was the core of a nativistic reassertion of the Athabaskan way of life with mech-

anisms for the integration of foreign elements that were compatible with it. The "ceremonial break," a concept that pervades many aspects of Navajo life, was probably one of the mechanisms to Navajo-ize non-Navajo traits. . . . It was through the development of simple mechanisms of this sort to allow for the symbolic Navajo-ization of foreign traits that gives Navajo culture its incorporativeness, so that entire technologies can be integrated into the culture without causing basic changes, and the culture can be adapted relatively easily to changing conditions.

(The "ceremonial break" is a mark in a design that makes a "break" in the completion of the design. Almost every Navajo rug, for example, will have a thread that extends from the center of the design out to the edge of the rug, allowing the "spirit" of the design to escape.)

The peyote ceremony also takes one further step. Whereas traditional healing tries to alter supernatural forces that are causing illness in a patient, the peyote meeting does not attempt to change the outside world, but only the mind of the sufferer—and perhaps of his family. The NAC ". . . is redemptive, rather than transformative, in seeking a major change in the soul of the believer, rather than in the social order." This is also a useful mechanism in a people who are very concerned about feeling well, yet who have very little political or economic influence and power.

The NAC provides a framework within which Navajo culture can absorb elements of the twentieth-century Anglo world while maintaining the essence of what is Navajo, which is the Blessingway and all that it suggests. But even Blessingway, it seems, emerged from an attempt to assert what had previously been essential to the culture in the face of overwhelming changes from without. The central message of Blessingway is "the only permanence is change." To be traditional is to believe in Blessingway; to be traditional is to believe in change.

✴

Jack Hatathlie:

I was given the Native American Church fireplace on Labor Day, twenty-two years ago, when I was forty-two years old. It was given to me by a request made by my relatives that were NAC members. Sometimes people request to be roadmen, or sometimes some men just start running these meetings.

I felt it was an honor for me to be asked to be a roadman. To help my people in times of need in prayer was a special calling for me. The title, to be a roadman, was not just for me, but my family and relatives. I went through a lot of hardship with my life and also my health, so this was something special I was blessed with from the Creator, I thought.

I had problems with my gallbladder before I was a roadman. I underwent an operation to remove my gallstones, but somehow I had infections that kept recurring. I had many medicine men that had sings for me because the medical doctors told me they couldn't help me, so they referred me back to traditional healing. I used many medicine men for sings, stargazing, herbs, and hand trembling. Finally, I resorted to just eating this herb peyote for healing. I had meetings, and in those meetings I would consume a lot of medicine. At times, I didn't know what was happening because it was working on me. I would vomit it up, but I still would drink or eat more. Finally, I was able to keep it down. I wanted to be healed, because I had a life ahead of me; I was still young with small children. I had nine children then; Theresa was a baby. My family needed a healthy father to provide for them. I had plans and dreams of a good life for my little ones.

I was told that if I wanted to be healed I could not hold back: I needed to give myself up to the medicine, eating as much as I could, even if it meant throwing it up.

I thought and prayed in this way when I had a peyote meeting for me to get well. My relatives came and also prayed for me, crying so that I could get well. My faith in the medicine was strengthened even more at this time, because early in the morning when they brought the water in, my pain was gone and I sat up where before I had been lying down. Today without a doubt I know the Creator works through the medicine, and I have seen it work miracles.

I had two more baby girls after this, so I now have eleven children, and I credit all the good things that have happened since then to the fireplace.

I have run meetings for people young and old for almost any occasions. Sickness, births, thank-you meetings, education meetings, and so on. You can set up a meeting for just about anything.

Today, I am grateful to have had an opportunity to have this fireplace. I raised my children in the way of the fireplace. They all have meetings occasionally for different things. They know how to conduct themselves in the meetings. My boys are now grown and help me when I run meetings. Freddie and Fred both work taking care of the fire, Glenn [Jack and Bessie's second son] *is always the drummer, and Felix sometimes drums and takes care of the fire. The girls sometimes bring in the water, or usually they cook and take care of things outside. So all in all my children are active in NAC. It makes my wife and me very happy that the fireplace is going to be carried on for us.*

There's a lot of good teachings in it. I feel it's for everyone who has a humble heart. I've seen many non-Indians come and use this sacred herb. They learn to respect it, learn to pray and sing in the fireplace. It makes me feel good. I don't speak English, but in the meetings I don't need to explain to the non-Indians. There's always the silent communication that we are praying together and for a purpose.

When I was given the fireplace, an Oto Indian from Red Rock, Oklahoma, came and conducted a ceremony for me. The fireplace came from his wife, Levon. His name is Truman Daily, and today he is ninety-four years old.

He told me during that special meeting that it's up to me what I do with the fireplace. I can take care of it the right way or I can misuse it. There were two directions I could take. [By] misuse, I mean I could go and hold a beer can or wine bottle in one hand and then try to pray on the other hand.

He told me, "Take care of this fireplace. It will give you directions to where you will lead your children. Use it for your family. You have a big family. One of these days, you will see your children helping you, praying and singing with you, then you will realize what I'm talking about."

So I believe that when you believe in something and pray together, your family will be strong. I try to be a good role model for my children. Always encouraging and giving them the support that they need.

We're very proud of our children. They all have good lives, good families, good education, and they all respect the fireplace.

✳

There are different stories about how peyote came about. As it was told to me, a woman was lost from her band and wandering around. She was so tired from looking for her band, she lay down, and as she lay helplessly watching the buzzards above, she heard a voice. The voice spoke to her and said, "Eat the plant that is growing beside you." She pulled out the cactus and ate the top part of it. Strength returned to the woman immediately.

The woman was given a direction back to her people. When she got back, she gave the plant to her people and showed them how to use it.

The fireplace that was given to me goes back to Quanah Parker, a half-blood Comanche Indian leader. He brought the religion into Oklahoma. Quanah Parker's mother was an Anglo woman who was captured by Comanches as a young girl. She grew up among the Comanches and married a Comanche. Later, after her husband was killed in a raid, she decided to go back to her people. She left Quanah Parker behind to learn the Indian ways. She took her daughter with her. She was accustomed to living in the open and later died of homesickness for the land and people she left behind.

Quanah had a vision of how the fireplace should be set up. Peyote *was used fresh and green. Dried peyote was either ground and mixed with water or simmered and made into tea to drink. Cedar or sweet grass is used for incense to purify. Native-grown tobacco rolled in corn husks is used because smoking was and is part of every Native American prayer ceremony.*

Different types of feathers are used. We believe that birds have different kinds of powers. Birds like hawks, water turkeys, cormorants, scissor-tailed flycatchers, flickers, and sometimes parakeet feathers. Eagle feathers are the most popular because we believe them to be the most powerful. They are cleaned and held together by buckskin and beaded. They are used to bring special blessings to oneself. Smoke and birds or feathers carry prayers with them as they ascend.

Peyote as the sacrament is always present. We never smoke it. I've never heard of it used that way.

When there's a meeting, an altar as a moonshape is made [with dirt on the floor of] the tipi or hogan. A deep groove is made in the middle, which represents the road of life. On the crest of the moon, Father Peyote is placed, representing the power of belief. The Father Peyote was always very sacred, sometimes passed from father to son. Prayer is not directed at Father Peyote, but through him, as the representative of the sun as intermediary to the powers above. He speaks for us. In peyote way, there are no priests or ministers. Any man who wishes to pray, prays. A roadman conducts the ceremony, prays and sings before other participants. He invites people to help him pray.

Anyone can set up a meeting for any occasion. Peyote, cedarwood, and a feast after the meeting is provided by anyone setting up the meeting. You ask someone to drum; that person becomes the drummer throughout the night for anyone wishing to sing. A fire chief takes care of the fire throughout the night, making sure it keeps burning, keeping the smoke down. He goes out and takes care of who comes in and goes out. A roadman's wife is the one who brings in the water in the morning, offering a prayer to conclude the ceremony.

Outside in the cook shack, food is being prepared for the next day. Usually, something light is served after you get out of the meeting—cookies, coffee, tea, orange pieces, doughnuts—a light breakfast. Noon-

time is when they have the big feast. Water again is brought in and drunk before food is eaten because it represents a new day and new life which women bring.

I believe the Native American Church is the religion for our young people. It's not complicated; it's very simple. Nowadays young people are not learning the songs and chants and prayers of our medicine men. It's a process that takes years of training to be a medicine man. Everybody is stressing education so all can be able to make it in today's society. I even had to work to support my family. This way of praying, the NAC, is good for young people. If you are honest with the medicine, it will guide and help you. You have to be sincere with it, take care of the songs and respect one another in the meeting, I tell my children.

As Navajos, we have incorporated many of our stories and teachings into NAC. Here again, I always stress positiveness to the young people—to take care of themselves, because you never know what's ahead.

This fireplace has been good to me. It has taken care of my family. It has brought me happiness in my grandchildren. Now I look forward to being a great-grandfather. I've had rich blessings in my life with no regrets.

*

Peyote grows in Texas and Mexico, and the Navajos travel to purchase it a couple of times a year. Before a family departs, a meeting is held to bless the trip, during which time people who need peyote pray, explain how much they want, and pitch in money for the trip.

"All the time they're [on the way] down there, it's constant praying, no time to sightsee," says Ella. "It's just singing and praying all the way down there."

The Hatathlies usually buy their peyote from a woman in Texas named Amanda Cardenaz. "She's an old lady now, and she knows my dad really well, because we've been down so many times," says Ella. Sometimes the peyote has already been harvested and sacked, other times the Hatathlies must dig up the plants themselves. Peyote is a short, hairy cactus composed of flesh and roots, both of which are consumed. The flesh is in the shape of a small sphere resembling a pincushion. The cost, including trip expenses, is about $100 for four pounds, and rising steadily. One needs about a quarter-pound per meeting.

"Down there, you do a lot of praying, but praying for a certain reason," Ella says. "If one of us [kids] went, we represented the young people. If you were a student, you represented the school, and you were kind of like a representative. Sometimes you had meetings down there. Amanda Cardenaz has her own tipi. They set it up, and they run meetings down there."

The driver heads straight back to Arizona, again no sightseeing or visiting, and the trip ends with another meeting, this time to distribute the peyote.

"When they're fresh, you take the roots off and you can dry them separately, but the top part, the green one, you can cut it up in slices, like peaches, then hang it on a thread to dry. When it's dried, then you can grind it coarsely.

"And when I was growing up, you took it dry. But nowadays, people mix it with water so it's not so dry. Sometimes they make about two gallons of the tea, sometimes one gallon. It takes about a dozen, dozen and a half [buttons] to make the tea.

"Or you can eat it just fresh, slice it up and eat it fresh like that. Or you can make it into tea with the fresh ones, boil it and separate it from the tea and drink the tea."

Ella doesn't remember the first time she had peyote, as she was so young.

"I grew up with it since I was a baby," says Ella. "I guess we used it for different reasons. Whenever one of us got sick, my parents would give it to us and say a prayer for us. When we were going somewhere, when we needed a blessing right away, maybe my dad would take out his [ceremonial sticks and fans] and give us medicine and he would pray and we would go on our way instead of having a big meeting. Like when we were at NAU, we would go to my dad and he would pray for us and he would give us medicine. It's for any purpose, it's for anything."

Like Blessingway, peyote meetings are sometimes held to celebrate happy events, like birthdays or Mother's Day.

"For the kids' birthdays, we take them to a medicine man we know to have a birthday prayer for them, and they take the medicine. Like for Danielle about a month ago—she was at school and all of a sudden, she blacked out. And the nurse didn't know what happened to her. So we just brought her back and we took her to one of our friends who's a roadman, and he prayed for her and gave her some of that medicine and just encouraged her. A lot of times, there's a lot of jealousy, especially among young people who try to do something for the community, or sometimes, maybe, there's some kind of jealousy toward parents and they try to get at the kids. Having prayers like this all the time gets rid of those things."

Ella says the medicine has no hallucinogenic effect on her. Nell says it makes her very sleepy.

"Kimo, he takes a lot of it, I guess, when he goes to a meeting, and he says it doesn't really bother him. But I guess in a way, when you're doing something wrong, somehow that medicine works on you and you start hallucinating. I don't know what the correct word would be, if it's hallucinating. I think hallucination is a white man's word for getting high on something that you take. It's a different word than we would use—we say it's working on you. Maybe you drink all the time, or don't take care of your family, and you start getting sick— I guess the medicine is warning you."

Ella has been going to a lot of meetings lately. A lot is going on in her life, and she goes to the meetings to seek help and guidance. In January she was hired to teach preschool at a small, privately funded school for young children in the Gap, a town twenty miles northwest of Tuba City and separated from it by a huge, serpentine rock escarpment. Ella's father used to herd sheep in the Gap, a dusty, hilly area whose populace suffers a lack of tribal services because of its isolation. Most of its residents are not educated, and the drinking problems among the men are very bad. Most of the Gap's residents earn a living selling crafts along U.S. Highway 89, which connects Flagstaff with Lake Powell to the north and is heavily traveled by tourists. Ella teaches half a day, four days a week, and must rise very early to catch a ride to school with the other preschool teacher.

Ella is also taking classes in Navajo language and linguistics at Navajo Community College to improve her understanding of the structure of the language. And she is also concerned about Buzz, who doesn't seem to be making any plans for his future. He has been dating his girlfriend, Sonya, for three years now, but isn't talking about marriage. He works two jobs—as an auto mechanic's apprentice and in a library in Tuba City— but he has not taken any training for a vocation.

"When I go to meetings, I try to go as much as I can, and I've been going more than I usually do. I go because I feel I need help; I go in there and pray for my boys, especially Buzz. And when I go over there, it makes me feel better. If I go to the meeting and I pray maybe something good will happen. And when I first got my job at the Gap, it really made me tired all the time, so I would go to meetings every weekend, maybe in a row, for a month, and I thought about my job and I prayed for my job, hoping that a good thing is going to come out of it, and that I would be able to help somebody. Also, about the school and the classes I'm taking. I want to be able to understand more about culture, more about the old way, the dialect. I go there and I pray about how I want to learn to write better and better myself in that area in the cultural context. I go for that reason, and then my daughter, she's got this [powwow princess] crown, and she's kind of young and she really didn't know the responsibility that was behind it, how she really has to watch herself because she's a role model—everybody's looking at you, everybody's ready to say something negative. So I tell her about these things, and I go to the meetings and I pray about it. And I would like to get my family more involved in going to the meetings.

"Even though I'm tired, I don't want to let that excuse be the reason I don't go to meetings. I don't let that be an excuse. I go in there, I go in there maybe as kind of endurance for myself. I like to go in there to listen to other people talk, especially traditional people. Maybe there's a meeting for young people, maybe they're having some kind of problem, and they're having that meeting for that purpose, and [the old people] talk about how they should fix it and how they should get help or help themselves. I just kind of listen. There's a lot of kinship in there, talking about each other. I like it when they offer a traditional teaching. I like to listen to the songs, now they're using Navajo words. And I like to go there to hear the young people. Some of them really sing, and some really know how to pray, using the natural things, the elements that make us alive. I like to listen to them instead of 'Jesus, God.' I like to hear them pray. It makes me feel good to know they're trying to carry on the best way they can—it may be next week I'll see them, they're drunk, but at least they're trying."

*

"If I was going to have a meeting for my family, usually my dad would help me, and [my brothers and sisters] will say, 'We'll get you some wood.' And they get oak in Flagstaff, and they prepare it in the traditional way—they'll make an offering to the oak with corn pollen before they start cutting it down. They'll bring it home and they'll trim it to a certain size.

"And maybe one of my brothers will say, 'I'll help you set up.' If it's in a hogan, then they'll help clean it up and maybe put the stove in there and all the floor covering inside, sheep-skins and blankets to sit on. And then someone might say, 'I'll help you fix the corn husks,' cut it up like that for the smoke. And someone else might say, 'I'll help you with the tobacco,' and another, 'I'll bring some medicine.' So everybody kind of helps us put it together, and maybe my sisters will say, 'I'll help you with some soda; I'll bring the salad or potato salad for the morning meal.' And I'll go to my Hopi friends for the morning breakfast, corn, traditional foods; I'll go down there and get blue corn meal—they use blue corn meal; they make it into a mush. Or I can get sweet cake from them, puberty cake. They make it a different way [than do Navajos]. I can get that from them. I can get dried kneel-down bread from them if I don't have any. And sometimes I get bread—she'll make me yeast bread; she'll make me traditional Hopi foods to eat the next day. Different ways she makes traditional foods for me.

"Then we usually take a roll of tobacco and give it to whom you want to ask for a prayer, to pray for us. You give them the tobacco and tell them the purpose of the meeting: 'This is why we want you to pray for us.'

"You can buy tobacco in the stores, or traditional people sell it. It's from the mountains—traditional smoke. And the wrapping is corn husk.

"We give it to the person and he smokes it, and sometimes we'll give him money, maybe $100 for coming to our place. Then we go back, start getting ready the wood, the place, making sure we have enough food, enough meat, butcher a sheep maybe. Then we let our relatives know, our friends.

"The evening of the meeting, you feed people before the meeting, it's a courtesy to feed people. If it's in a tipi, we put up the tipi poles and put canvas around it. And then about nine, ten o'clock [at night], we just go in to the meeting and everybody sits.

"After everybody sits, then everybody gets one of the corn

husks, and then the tobacco is passed around and everybody rolls a smoke. After some time, you tell the relatives about the purpose of the meeting: maybe it's for your children to go to school and learn, maybe for your job or family. You thank them for all the things that you got during the year, and pray for the future. You talk about that. And you acknowledge all your relatives by kinship, by clan. And then after that, everybody starts praying at the same time for you. Everybody prays out loud, 'My grandfather [Peyote], [I pray] to have a good life, a good home, take care of the fireplace, [I pray for] her dishes that she uses to feed her people, her home, to take care of the children so they can have a good life, know kinship, so they can know their culture, show respect to their relatives.' That kind of stuff.

"They all pray at one time, until the last person finishes praying, which is about one hour. It's about an hour, really loud, everybody. Then after that they pass the medicine in the bowl, either as powder or as tea. Everybody drinks some. It doesn't matter how much you drink, as much as you want.

"And after everybody gets the medicine, they pass the sage around. The sage represents life, plant life. And everybody sniffs it and blesses themselves. After that goes around, then the instruments are passed—the cane, the rattle, and the fan. The cane [which is beaded and decorated with horsehair] is the cane to your life, your cane to old age. And then you have your fan, [again beautifully beaded and bound to look like a wing,] which is sometimes an eagle fan—it carries your prayers up [to the Creator]. Then you have your rattle, which you use to accompany yourself when you sing.

"And they start passing [the rattle] around, and anyone who wants to sing can sing with that. And then there's a drummer; he takes care of the drum. And he sits next to whoever wants to sing, and they sing a song. And it goes all the way around like that. Anyone can sing whatever song they want. The drummer goes to each person as they're singing. He goes around maybe twice, and then they pass the medicine every so often. And everybody drinks the medicine. And then during that time, whoever wants to pray can pray with that medicine and the tobacco. So whoever wants to pray will have a chance to pray with the tobacco.

"Everything is acknowledged in there, like sometimes you'll say 'Mother Peyote' or 'Father Peyote,' 'the Fire,' 'Grandfather Fire,' 'Grandmother Poker,' 'the Fire Poker,' 'Our Mother the Water.' Indian people think everything is interrelated, that's why everything is as a whole in there.

"At any time in there, if anybody wants to give you advice, they'll give you advice, they'll pray for you. Or maybe somebody comes in who has a problem of their own, and they'll pray about it. During that time, the roadman will remember him in his prayer, while he's praying for us at the same time. Everybody prays for themselves too, besides us.

"At about midnight, they stop everything—all the singing, all the praying stops—and then they have a special prayer, a special song for the midnight water. And usually whoever takes care of the fire brings the water in. He also prays for the purpose of the meeting. Maybe he'll give some advice, and then after that, after he finishes, then somebody else will be given a chance to pray, and then finally it comes to us. We get what they call the main smoke. And we pray with that, and we pray for the purpose of why we wanted to set the meeting up, not for anybody else in there, but just for the purpose of the meeting. We say that prayer together; then if I want to pray in my own way, I pray in my own way. If my boys want to pray in their own way, they pray in their own way. Out loud—it doesn't matter how you pray. It's really up to you how you pray."

Anglo observers speak of the aesthetic beauty of the peyote meeting. On the floor, the roadman builds a crescent-moon-shaped altar of moist sand. He makes a ridge along its crest, from tip to tip, which symbolizes the road of life, along which the participants will pass over the course of the evening. The roadman will move the Chief Peyote, a large and well-formed peyote button, across the arc of the altar during the course of the night.

After prayers are said and the tobacco smoked, the fireman will burn the butts. The burning of the tobacco remnants serves to extinguish the sins confessed; it is a purification. The fireman tends the fire, which is built in the middle of the circle, and he organizes the red coals, sometimes rearranging them into the shape of a heart and sweeping up the ashes, sometimes forming them into shapes, such as crescents, eagles, full moons.

The rhythm of the ceremony moves from the excitement and hopefulness of the opening and the discussion of the evening's purpose, to a period of struggle and pain and anxiety from midnight to the early morning, and then a resurgent hope with the arrival of the morning water and the food. The fire, constantly stoked and fed, creates a visual focus for the participants, as do the beautiful ceremonial instruments. The magnificent eagle wings are fanned rhythmically before the fire, guiding the smoke with the prayers up to God. (The eagle flies higher than all other birds, and thus is the most sacred.) The singing and the drumming can be extremely intense, with the song and the hope beating through one's entire body.

There are certain fixed ritual elements in the ceremony, like the arrival of the water at midnight and in the morning, the ritual purification of the instruments, the distribution of water for drinking, certain prayers and songs. There is also room for unplanned events—a confession, advice, a prayer. At certain times, incense is burned and whistles blown to invoke the attention of the supernaturals. After the morning water and before the traditional light breakfast, the mood gets more upbeat and positive, the struggles of the night give way to the hope of the dawn and a return to harmony. After the initial light breakfast, at 7:30 or 8:00 a.m., a bigger meal is served at about noon. More prayers are said, and thanks offered to the participants.

Some roadmen and participants will mention Jesus; others won't. Some roadmen keep a small crucifix or other Christian medallion in their peyote kits—wooden boxes, often made of cedar, in which they store and carry their paraphernalia. As Ella says, "They say that He has many names, but He's the same person."

26

"Buzz Always Asks Me,
Why Do I Have to Work So Hard,
Why Am I Always Working in the Field,
Why Don't We Just Buy the Corn?"

It is harvest time in Navajoland, the start of weeks when farmers will gather the bounty of the summer, the round, sugary red watermelons; the firm, bright zucchinis; the bushels upon bushels of corn that have sprouted like miracles out of the dry red dust. Although the appearance of the fruit and vegetables seems inexplicable in this arid climate, they have been coaxed and cared for and prayed over since springtime.

The work began soon after the last snow, when the fields were plowed under, old plants loosened and uprooted. Later in the spring, tumbleweeds and other dead brush were gathered up and burned. Then, hoeing, backbreaking labor in which every last green weed or grass peeping out from the tilled furrows must be removed so that every drop of moisture held by these fields will nourish the crops and nothing else. Then the fields are plowed again, and furrows made. Planting: Bessie and Jack walk through the furrows, carefully pressing seeds that they have saved from last year into the soft soil mounds. Behind them, someone smooths the soft loam over the seeds into small mounds of dirt.

Months more of hoeing and weeding will follow, and in the

one plot in Tuba City, near the highway, where irrigation is available, the Hatathlies will pay for water and make sure the channels are clear and strong so as to make best use of the water as it comes tumbling through the pipes.

Since the Navajos use no insecticides, there are various battles with bugs and worms throughout the growing season, some winnable, some not. One fight that is winnable is digging out worms from the base of the corn plants. This requires work from everybody. The family members stand side by side, pushing away the dirt and peeling back pieces of the stalks to root out the worms. Ella has taken the opportunity of long stretches digging worms to talk to her father about some of the stories she remembers him telling her when she was small.

"He was telling me about how things are different today. How people are really changing. He told Danielle that she needs to start digging worms. Every year she used to dig worms in the field, and this year she says to me, 'Mom, I'm not digging no worms this year. I'm not a little girl no more.' "

"And I said, 'Well, it's not a little girl's job. I said anybody does it.' She said, 'No, I'm not going to do it.' And I said, 'Well, Grandma said they already have plans when we're going to dig worms.' And she said, 'No, I'm not going to do it.' "

Bessie was not thrown by Nell's declaration. She told Ella that when Nell returns from Canada, where she is visiting with friends, she'll have other chores. "The crops will be ready when she comes back, and then she'll have to fix the corn," she told Ella.

Nell had a puberty ceremony last year, known as the *kinaalda*, which is celebrated when a girl reaches menarche. As part of the ceremony, Nell learned to grind corn and prepare traditional corn dishes. This is a rite of passage into adulthood whose symbols relate to growth and fertility. She is "molded" by another woman—Nell actually lies down on blankets, dressed in traditional clothes, and an older woman, while talking to her about the responsibilities of being a Navajo woman, runs her hands over her as if she were sculpting her out of clay, as Changing Woman made the Navajo clans out of lumps of her own epidermis. Ella chose Annie Begay, from Coal Mine Canyon, to mold Nell.

All that Nell remembers about what Annie told her was that she should help around the house and keep herself clean—a subject Nell knows quite a bit about, as most of her day is spent in the bathroom, washing her hair, or before the mirror, scrubbing her face and putting on makeup. But Nell doesn't want to be a woman yet.

"I didn't want that ceremony," Nell says, "because I didn't want anybody to know I was growing up."

She went ahead with it, however, because her grandmother and mother wanted her to. "I think when I reach twenty, I'll be a lady. I like to run around and laugh real loud, and that's not ladylike. Sometimes after school, I wear jeans and a big shirt. And sometimes my mom gets mad; she says I need to dress appropriately. But I don't like to dress the way other people tell me to dress. I just want to be myself."

In spite of her embarrassment at the acknowledgment of her maturing, Nell performed the tasks required of her with attention and diligence—although, to preserve her attendance record at school, she cut the week-long ceremony short a few days, with her grandmother's approval.

The ceremony, a variant of the Blessingway, required Nell to develop real skills. Last year she ground corn with a traditional stone, or *metate*, and then made a sweet corn cake.

It is said that every Navajo house should have grinding stones. According to old legends, "The stones are said to keep the women of the household happy and healthy and to increase the length of their lives. The stones also cause members of the household to have good thoughts. And the stones protect those members."

One thinks of the various appliances that have been developed to make modern life easier for the homemaker. And in modern times, with both parents working and children to care for, there is hardly time for grinding corn. But it is not hard to see that grinding, strenuous as it is, must have made Navajo women very strong, and the exercise undoubtedly made them healthier, if not always happier. As the women ground and cooked, they sang the traditional corn songs, which reinforce the Navajo teachings.

In this way culture has been passed for the most part of human history—through oral tales and songs, transmitted during cooperative work or during storytelling. This is how children absorb the values of their parents, by watching them work and hearing the stories they tell. Traditional Navajos believe some stories should never be written down, but passed only by word of mouth. They believe that writing them down changes them, changes their meaning and the feelings with which they should be heard.

Nell's Navajo education has only begun. Says Ella, "Since she's had her [first] puberty ceremony, this year she has to learn how to take care of the corn and harvest the corn and dry the corn and learn how to make several types of meals from the corn herself. Before she had help, but this year [for her second ceremony], she's got to do it herself. She has to learn to make kneel-down bread. She's got to make it just right."

Kneel-down bread is an extremely practical food that, once prepared, can be kept for most of the year without refrigeration—and through the winter, when fresh food supplies are not available. The corn must be picked when it is young, when the kernels are still small and tender. The corn is cut off the cob and then ground, not with a *metate*, but in a steel grinder, the sort that screws onto a table and is commonly used to grind meat or fruit.

The soft ground corn is placed in the tender pieces of the corn husks, which are then folded up like a tamale. The little packets of ground corn in the corn husks are laid side by side in a square pit that's been dug into the ground. Tin foil is then put over the husks, and hot ashes laid on top of the foil. The bread cooks in a half-hour or so beneath the hot coals.

Nell must learn how to tell when the corn is ready, because if she waits too long, the corn will be too dry and too tough for kneel-down bread. She must learn to choose what pieces of the husks are best for wrapping the corn, and she must also save some of the tenderest inside husks for rolling tobacco for ceremonies.

"My dad always says that when you have children, your teaching should start from the cornfield," says Ella. "That's where life starts—you know, corn is life. And a lot of teachings are centered around the corn, and it's everywhere in all the legends. Everything we had, all the ceremonies, corn is there. So it's like a great, big, major, important element to the Navajo way of life, especially on the women's side. So they say that when you work your corn, you polish up your mind, you learn to develop your mind to make it strong and not make it weak. Same as the sheep.

"You teach yourself to resist temptation. Like you teach yourself, if you're working the corn and say there's something going on in town, you really want to go to. Should I go and leave my corn until tomorrow? If you leave your corn until the next day, something might happen to your corn; that's what they say.

"My dad always makes sure that we take every corn kernel off the ground when we work with corn. Corn is a person, because it's food to us, so you can't waste it, and when you waste corn like that—like I see it in the schools, where they paint corn and use it for art—that's a form of waste. You shouldn't do that. So that's why my dad said, when people talk about tradition, working a field, having a field—that's being traditional. That's where your teachings come from, your mind and your whole being. That's what you call a traditional person. That's why he really emphasizes planting and utilizing the corn in the right way and taking care of it.

"Buzz always asks me, Why do I have to work so hard, why am I always home, working in the field. Why don't we just buy the corn? Buzz doesn't like to work down here, hoeing, being out in the heat, because it's not 'cool' down there to be seen in the corn, down in the field, and his friends might see him. I was telling him it's part of learning. Because a lot of our legends, a lot of our stories, all come back to the corn. And we were brought up to believe that corn is life. As long as you have corn, you're never going to go hungry.

"There are things you should always have, like a cup of corn in your hand or a corncob in your hand, because then the Holy People will know they're going to always bless you with corn even if you have nothing else to eat; as long as you have corn, even a cup of corn from the cob, then you can roast it and feed your children or make mush with it and feed your kids with it. Corn is very, very important for our lives. And my dad says that if you have children or are a teacher, you should know these things. He says that a lot of your thought, and the way you look at life, it's all from the cornfields and from being out there working. You think about all the things that you were taught, all the things that you were brought up with. And that's the reality for you when you are out there working.

"And I tell my son that my dad taught me a lot of these things. And I had a lot of questions. I asked a lot of questions of my dad. And he tells me a lot. When I was small I grew up with them. And I regret the times growing up when I didn't really pay attention. A lot of things I don't remember, and I ask my dad and he expands on it. When I'm out in the fields, all the things my dad taught me, I think about them. If I don't go out there, I don't really have the full concept of what he's really trying to tell me. When you're out there you think about a lot of these things."

After the kneel-down bread is cooked, the packets are taken from the fire. If they're opened to eat right away, one will find a pillow of steaming cooked corn—like tamales. It can be eaten plain, with a little butter, or with meat or salsa. Red peppers can be sprinkled into it. It can also be dried and later broken into bite-sized pieces and steamed, or placed in soups or stews. In a world without electricity and freezers, this is a good way of preserving food.

Butter is not a traditional foodstuff, and the Navajos have never made it themselves. The older ones know about it, though, and call it *mantegia,* from the Spanish word *mantequilla.* The traditional Navajos don't use it, as they can't keep it for any length of time without refrigeration. Of course, Ella and Dennis keep butter in their trailer, in the refrigerator.

And since Ella has electricity and refrigerator and freezer, she has developed a modern version of kneel-down bread. "I started putting chili [salsa] in it last year," she says, "and then I started cooking my hamburger and draining the fat from it, and mixing the hamburger and the corn and the chili and cooking it like that and just making kneel-down bread [with the mixture]. I wouldn't dry that. You'd have to eat it just that day or put it in the freezer. It's wrapped in the husks, like a tamale."

The corn that is not used for kneel-down bread is left to grow a little older, and then harvested, husked, and put on the roof to dry. After it has dried, the corn is separated by color— red, blue, yellow, and white—and the kernels are scraped off the cobs into barrels, where they will be stored. Later the kernels will be ground and mixed with wheat flour to make corn cakes. The blue corn is ground into flour for piki bread—a rolled, flaky bread akin to phyllo that is made by the Hopis.

One can also make many other things with the dried corn: "You can put it in soup; it's got a different taste from hominy. Or you can grind it and make it [into] a cream for your coffee. You can grind it really fine. And then you can make pudding with it too. Like pudding with sweet corn that you make for puberty ceremonies. You don't mix it with anything; it has a sweet taste to it, that fresh dried corn.

"You can make blue marbles with it." Blue marbles are made

from dried blue cornmeal mixed with ash from burned juniper wood. Hot water is added to the mixture, and it is mixed with Navajo stirring sticks. Once the mixture is malleable, small pieces are removed and rolled in the hand to make marble-sized balls. These are then boiled and eaten. The juniper ash acts as leavening, like baking powder.

Fresh corn—corn that is harvested when it is mature, but not dried—can also be baked. Says Ella, "In the old days, they used to make a big hole in the ground, and they use to build a fire and that fire would go all day. And it would get real hot and then they would clean it out and then they would put the corn in there, and then they would cover it up and seal it and then the fire would cook it all night. Unhusked corn. You can do like a truckload at a time." And the fresh corn can also be roasted over the charcoals and eaten from the hand. Indian corn is denser and more fibrous that the sweet corn Anglos are used to eating. One picks the kernels off one by one to eat, rather than running one's teeth across the cob—and each kernel is a small mouthful. Half a cob is more filling than a whole cob of sweet corn.

Almost every piece of the plant is used for one thing or another. The stalks are cut down after all the corn has been harvested, and everything green is fed to the sheep and the horses. The hair tassels on the top of the corn are saved and ground into a powder that is believed to help children avoid colds in the winter. Some hair tassels themselves are also saved—tossed into a boiling broth, they add a fresh-corn taste.

There are some pieces of corn that don't develop properly —they are very small and don't develop "teeth," as Ella puts it. They just have small, partly developed bumps, which are made into medicine by Ella's mother and administered to children who have trouble with stuttering. According to the Navajo idea that like cures like, the small, undeveloped "nubs" have a similarity with the words that stumble out of a young child's mouth, words that are improperly formed.

There are some parts of the corn that are not eaten—worms that bury themselves into the kernels are cut out and thrown away. Also, says Ella, "There's a mold or something, I don't know what it is; it's like a mushroom and it's black. It's a kind of growth on your corn, and we don't eat that. When you get that, they say it means your children have been going to the bathroom in the field."

As Ella tells these stories, she is reminded of some Navajo sayings:

"If you sneeze, it means that somebody is talking about you."

"If your cat is licking its paws, it means that somebody is coming to see you."

"If your dog sits with his back toward you, it means he's thinking about you; maybe you've treated him bad."

"You're not supposed to eat in front of your animals, your dog or cat, because it's supposed to affect your digestion. Every time you swallow, that cat or that dog will swallow [while looking at you] and you're not going to get full of whatever you're eating."

"If your shoestrings are untied, that means that your husband or your wife is flirting with someone."

"If you kick yarn, it means that during the day somebody is coming to see you."

"If you have hiccups, it means that you are hungry for mutton."

"If your eye itches, it means somebody's going to hit you in the eye."

"If you fart and laugh about it, your face will get real saggy when you're just a young person."

"If you're on your moon [period] and you're an adolescent like Nell and you scratch yourself, you get scratch marks on your body." (Nell is listening and she groans.)

"And when you're on your moon [Nell sighs with embarrassment] and you're a young person too and you laugh, you will develop age lines."

"And then they say that when you're a young girl like Nell, you're not supposed to laugh and carry on, get out of hand. They say that's a sign that you're not stable in your mind."

"Then they say you shouldn't joke a lot when you're just a young person. And you shouldn't joke about other people too, like your clan brothers. You can joke about them but not to overdo it."

"Then you're not supposed to joke with your sisters. I guess up to a certain extent you can make jokes, but you can't overdo [it] because sometimes a fight will break out among your sisters."

"If you're a girl, you can joke with your paternal grandfathers like they were your boyfriends. And they can joke with you too—they can talk about being jealous of somebody calling you—or if you have a boyfriend, they can display signs of jealousy towards that boy or they'll pretend that they get mad at that boy or they'll pretend like they'll get mad at you. And they can make jokes like that. And they'll joke about maybe going off together."

※

During the heat of the harvest, when Ella was making fifty kneel-down breads a day for two weeks, she brought her grandma down with her. "I ask her things and she talks. She sleeps a lot. She said she'd rather stay down there."

As Ella talked with her grandmother, people drove in from the road to trade mutton for melons and corn. Some dropped by and hung around long enough that Ella offered them a bite to eat—a few pieces of kneel-down bread and a slice of watermelon on a hot summer day.

Ella was excited by a visit from Lew Gurwitz, a lawyer from Boston who years ago helped the Navajos organize and begin their long battle against the relocation act. He stopped by on his way to British Columbia, where he was representing another tribe in a battle over fishing and land rights. These visits always excite Ella; she loves to keep up with her friends. Gurwitz, tall and barrel-chested, with long flowing white hair, resembled a younger Marlon Brando. He brought along with him a German woman and her children. The woman stayed with Bessie for a week, helping with the corn and chores at the house. Ella offered high praise for the woman: "She was nice. She took part in everything. She helped with everything that we were doing down there." Guests who work hard and do not shy away from Navajo ways are much welcomed.

Her children loved playing in the irrigation ditches by the field in Tuba City. "They just went wild," says Ella. "That water was running, and they went in there and they were muddy all over. They played and played in there, in the water." Jack and Bessie have another couple of cornfields nearer to their house, as well as this large one along the highway in Tuba City, so they were working constantly all summer at one field or the other. Gurwitz's visit recalled Lee Phillips to Ella's mind, another lawyer who has invested a great deal of time and effort to help out the Navajos. Though Gurwitz went on to work on other Indian issues, and died suddenly in September 1994, Phillips remains in Flagstaff, helping the Navajos continue to battle relocation. Ella is fiercely devoted to Lee, who is in his late thirties, wears his hair in a ponytail down his back, but fancies Italian neckties and stylish suits—which he wears with cowboy boots. Ella worries about Lee's being so far from his home, Ohio. She worries that he hasn't yet found a wife, and worries that he works too hard for people who can't pay him. She calls him every time she is in town, but he typically doesn't return phone calls for several days, so she hasn't seen him in months. She thinks she'll cook him up a batch of zucchini and bring it to his office.

Ella tells me that she has a perfect woman picked out for him—Annie Begay from Coal Mine Canyon.

"I told Lee he had to come down and get Annie. He won't have to worry about her cheating or stuff like that. Whenever he comes back, he knows she'll be home. And he can even have one of those dugouts at the bottom of the canyon as his own bachelor pad." Ella shrieks with laughter.

Ella looks down at her arms and exclaims about the damage the sun has wrought on the complexions of her family. "Dennis is just black," says Ella. "He gets really black. I got little bumps all over my arm because my arms are really sunburned. I got real red. It's like heat rash."

Ella tried sunblock and sunscreen, but none of it worked. She says, "It doesn't work on Indians, I don't think."

27

"Why Go Someplace When You're Still Crying Inside"

Fall and winter are miserable. There is rain and wind and illness, including a flu that hits like a sledgehammer, sending many elderly Navajos to the hospital. The water from the rains is causing the dirt roads on the reservation to turn to soup, making transportation difficult if not impossible in some areas. Water runs in rivulets, forming new washes, altering the shapes of roads. The driveway leading to the Hatathlies' home from the highway now looks like a five-lane freeway—of mud—as vehicles try to avoid the ruts and puddles by plowing through the sodden grass to make new routes. Mud sticks like cake batter to everything in sight and hardens like plaster. Shoes and boots are ruined, livestock hobbled and dismayed.

Sand has washed out from the roads onto the grasslands; animals have wandered to high ground to escape the water. School has been canceled, and the Hopis are dropping emergency supplies of water and hay and warm clothes down to the Navajos from planes.

"It was really something," says Ella. "The field in front of my parents' house was just one big lake, and Van's trading post nearly floated away. The sewers overflowed, and Moencopi Wash is full of water.

"There are dirt roads that are completely washed out; there'll be big old streams cutting through a road. We had livestock drowning. Some people were evacuated too, from the Leupp area, Tolani Lake area. They wanted to take Annie out of the canyon, but she refused. She said, 'No, you're not taking me anywhere.' "

Annie rode up to the top of the canyon on horseback and then hitchhiked into Tuba for supplies. "Her horse just hobbles on," says Ella. "She goes back down. It's just a big mess out here on the reservation. It's good the rains came; they just came too much. It's been going on for four, maybe five days. It's a lot of water. There are little dams all over the place. The only time you can go anywhere is at night or early morning, when it's still frozen."

The Hopis also suffered. The roofs of several houses in Moencopi caved in. "You know how the roofs are just kind of flat?" Ella asks me of the traditional Pueblo dwellings. "The sand kept washing away. I guess they kept putting more and more mud on top, but pretty soon they were covering them with plastic. And then the plastic was holding the water, and pretty soon they just gave way and they had emergency teams working down there. The Red Cross was out there, too.

"People covered their hogans with plastic too, and my dad was out with the tractor making trenches away from the house. They tried to make [the water] go to the field behind the house. But it was a lot of rain. Then they covered the corral with plastic too, to protect the animals. It was really pouring."

The Navajos are accustomed to periodic disasters like this. Almost every winter a state of emergency is declared on the reservation as the result of heavy snow or rain that prevents people from getting out for supplies. Most Navajos have enough food stored to last them for days. But the animals need fodder. In spite of the enmity that has developed between the Navajos and the Hopis as a result of the land dispute, almost every winter the Hopis provide for the Navajos who are living on Hopi land. Ella's mother doesn't realize she's getting help from the Hopis because they now have legal jurisdiction over her land. She said, "The Navajos never bring me food, but the Hopis really took care of us."

Ella stops by her grandma's house one day, and Rena lets her know she's been very anxious to see her. "You said you'd be back the next day," Rena scolds her. "You said you'd be back the next day with the tape recorder, so I thought about what I wanted to tell you," she says. Day after day Rena waited, after Ella's last visit, but no Ella. Finally, she started asking her grandkids if they'd seen Ella around Tuba City. But here she was, after all that time. Rena told her again, "When you came to see me, you told me you were going to come the next day, and I kept thinking about it, and you never came around, so I said, maybe it hasn't been a day for you yet."

"Maybe it hasn't been a day yet for me!" Ella tells me, laughing at her grandma's witticism.

The rain goes on and on. In summer, the Hopis and Navajos pray for rain to nourish their crops, and when their prayers are answered, it often rains and rains until there is no place for the water to go. There are two rainy seasons in Arizona, in July and January. Although the volume of water makes problems in the short term, the winter rain is good for the crops. The moisture is stored in the sandy washes and helps the crops survive the long, parched summers.

It is a time of much illness and distress in the Hatathlie family, and Jack is busy arranging rite after rite. One of his sisters, Agnes, the eldest of the five girls, the baby that had just been born when Jack was given to Lilac, has been diagnosed with pancreatic cancer. She knows the cancer is incurable, so she didn't tell her family she was ill, realizing that Jack and Rena would spend a lot of money on ceremonies. And, sure enough, as soon as they found out she was sick, Jack began to organize ceremonies.

Because of her daughter's illness, Rena has again put off the ceremony she was planning to rid herself of the influence of her husband's lingering spirit. Rena is very sad about Agnes, and she spends much of her time sitting at home and crying. She is sad that her daughter didn't tell her sooner, so the ceremonies would have had more time to work on her.

As the shortest days of winter become longer and the hope of spring begins to scent the air, another flu hits. First Bessie and Ella, then Kimo in Tucson, and eventually Dennis and Jack. The weather turns foul again, and the wind rips a piece of metal off the Bedonies' trailer.

In April, Agnes dies.

"Too many things have been happening," says Ella over the telephone. She sounds terrible; she is hoarse, weak. She sounds as if she hardly has the energy to talk.

"How's your grandma?" I ask.

"Upset. The people over there are talking to her, taking care of her. I guess it was just kind of real shocking to her. To the end, I guess, she thought [Agnes] would be better."

Rena had been especially close to Agnes, her being the eldest girl. Agnes had lived close to her mother her whole life, and Rena depended on her.

Ella has hardly any time to tend to her own family, because immediately following Agnes's death, one of Dennis's aunts—his mother's sister—died unexpectedly. Ella and Dennis had been visiting her in a Phoenix hospital, where she had been taken for what the family thought would be a routine gallbladder removal. But on opening her up, the doctors saw she was riddled with cancer. They closed her up and transferred her to the Phoenix Indian Hospital, but something happened on her way over.

"They don't know what it was," says Ella. "Maybe she had a clot or a hemorrhage, or a heart attack or something. By the time she got to the Indian Hospital, her blood pressure and heart rate were way up. She was in critical condition, and so when she passed away they said they wouldn't release the body until they did an autopsy. The state wanted to do an autopsy and the family objected. But they wanted to know in case somebody was at fault. And they did and it was all over inside her, the cancer, everywhere. She was seventy-eight."

Dennis's aunt had lived in Abilene, Texas, for most of her life and had recently moved to Phoenix. After all her years away, she was about to return home to the reservation. She knew this was where she wanted to live out her life.

"She never complained," says Ella about their visit with her after the cancer had been found, but before her fateful ambulance trip. "She joked and stuff like that, and told everybody to go home. She just wanted to go to sleep; she was tired. We were with her. She talked to everybody. We were with her Friday, Saturday, Sunday. She knew she was dying. She talked about it, said for everybody to take care of their families—that she just wanted to go. She was tired."

In the background, Dennis is beating rhythmically on a drum. Ella says they are about to go to a meeting to discuss Dennis's aunt's funeral. She sounds out of sorts.

"Too many things are happening," she keeps saying. "My dad's aunt, his real aunt, she has pneumonia; I guess they found her by herself. They flew her to the hospital in Crownpoint [New Mexico], and my dad is trying to go out there and see how she is. My dad's aunt. He's got one living aunt. My grandma's sister."

Ella feels bad that she hasn't been around to help her father, because complicated negotiations concerning the autopsy of Dennis's aunt, the transport of her body up to the reservation, and the burial have absorbed and continue to make demands on her and Dennis's time.

"The meeting tonight is for Dennis's aunt, over at my sister-in-law's, over by [the town of] Rare Metals. We're going to talk about what we've done so far and the arrangements with the mortician. And the services, what time it's going to take place, what type it's going to be. And Dennis is going to tell them, because they've been drinking and fighting and arguing over their mom's belongings. So he's going to tell them how we think about the family, the Indian way. And then they're going to talk about where they're going to have dinner, the services, and what's going to happen there, who're going to be the pallbearers."

It seems that Dennis and Ella have already paid most of the costs. And Ella has sewn a skirt and blouse for the woman to be buried in. Ella isn't very coherent about this. When I ask if any of the other relatives will contribute money to pay for the burial, she says "I don't know."

"Were they all drinking?"

"I don't know. They just say, 'We don't have that much money, but we can get flowers, you know, a Pendleton, what she's going to wear.' [But] I made her outfit for her, a whole outfit."

The woman is eventually given a Christian burial at Red Lake, twenty miles north of Coal Mine. Buzz and Nell ask Ella all kinds of questions about the unfamiliar religious rites. "Why are they wearing crosses around their necks?" asks Buzz. "To keep away witches?" And Nell wants to know if the plus marks (the crosses) are placed on the graves because the people underneath them were particularly good. Ella realizes with surprise that her children know very little about Christianity. "You kids need to read the Bible," Ella tells them. "Don't you know anything about Jesus?" Buzz gives her a blank look.

I can tell Ella is very worried; I have never heard her sound so tired. Later I find out that Dennis has paid all the costs, and that it has become clear that he will not be reimbursed by the family. Although this is all the money the family had saved for their summer expenses, Jack explains to Ella that she can't talk about it, because that would suggest they regretted spending the money, and the person who had passed away would therefore never be able to rest.

Ella understands who will bear the burden of providing for the family for the next months—she is the one with the skills to pick up cash with beading and other handicrafts. But her mind is on her own family. She didn't even get to see Agnes before she died. She was in Phoenix with Dennis's aunt. Her own seemingly endless battle with the flu is also very worrisome, and she has an infection in her earlobe that hasn't gone away for months, despite her treatment of it with a topical antibiotic.

"You sound very tired," I tell her.

"Oh, I am. I've just been running around, sewing, just really tired. Also my sickness and then trying to be everywhere for everybody." As usual, Ella has been carrying on an inhuman schedule. Thursday night last week, she attended a peyote meeting her father organized for Agnes's benefit. Jack let her out at 6:00 a.m. after the all-night ceremony, whereupon she headed straight up to the Gap for work. That evening, Dennis and Ella headed down to Phoenix—a six-hour drive—to visit Dennis's aunt, who had just been admitted to the hospital. They visited her for three days, and then after her surprise death, they got back in the car and drove to the reservation, and arrived at 3:00 a.m. Ella went to school at 7:00 a.m. that day, and on returning to Tuba City at the end of the day, she gathered together some piki bread to bring to Agnes at the hospital. Ella had had only a few hours of sleep over the past four days.

"I went to her room and there was nobody there. I left that room, I thought they kept moving her around. And this lady, one of my relatives, who was in the hospital, was walking. And she said, 'Oh, she went home. She went home Saturday,' she told me. I thought, wow, she went home! And she said, 'Yeah, she went home.'

"I didn't think about it in any way, and I went over to the desk and I asked the doctor when my aunt was released. And he just looked at me. He said, 'She died Saturday.'

"I didn't know. I had just got back from work. So I went over to my grandma's and everybody was there.

"It seems I just haven't had time to be with my side of the

family. We were supposed to go to the Gathering of Nations in Albuquerque. We had reservations for three days. And we just put that off. And my dad came by and I talked to him. He's been feeling really bad for almost a month now—just about what's happening with his family, with my aunt. He had hoped until the end, because he had all these [ceremonies] going. . . . Even during the week he had peyote meetings, and I went over there. But they just like—I guess, I guess, he, maybe he had hoped. . . . He said there are such things as miracles."

Ella's voice is a thin croak, and she is coughing almost nonstop. I ask her if she's been to the doctor. She says yes.

"Yeah. They took my blood, did all kinds of tests on me. I got another mammogram done. I'm supposed to get a letter any day, or they're supposed to call me or something. I went over there yesterday to check on it, and they said that the results haven't come back yet."

"Are you worried about that?"

"No. Not really."

"When was the last time you had one?"

"It was during the summer. I think it was August or September, when we were doing harvesting."

Ella doesn't hear about the mammogram for months. She knows she should go back to the Flagstaff Medical Center and have another one done, because the mammogram performed in Tuba City was done in a van by a woman who appeared unskilled. While adjusting the equipment, she pinched Ella's left breast between two heavy plates. Discharge spurted out. This is the breast in which she had earlier had the cancer. The woman looked alarmed and scolded Ella for not letting her know she had a problem.

Shocked, Ella replied, "I assumed these were professional services." Ella tells me she has noticed some discharge for a couple of months. The doctors at Tuba City told her it probably wasn't anything serious, but that she should bypass the tribal mammograms and get one at the Flagstaff hospital.

But now that the family is so strapped for money, Ella is

loath to go for medical tests. Her friends urge her to do so and even help her financially to relieve the pressure. Ella seems frightened.

Tonight, yet, she must meet with Dennis's relatives. She and Dennis have already written a eulogy. But there are still arrangements that must be made.

"Us Indian people, we have a lot of respect for the people who pass away. Seems like with Anglo people it's not like that. They just have the funeral and that's it. They don't really bother with it. With us, it's different. We get together, we talk to one another. This is the time that we talk about death, how it was a long time ago, and what happens when somebody dies. At no other time do you talk about it. And my dad came and talked to Dennis about it."

Ella and Dennis have canceled their own plans to go to Albuquerque to the Gathering of Nations, and Nell has canceled a giveaway—a giving of presents to fellow powwow dancers that is an offering of gratitude for good fortune. Nell will not dance either.

"Why go someplace when you're still crying inside," asks Ella, "and try to enjoy yourself? It's better to do all your crying at one time, let go little by little. Like when a person passes away, it's four days—that's when you stay home and be with your family.

"And then after the funeral too, maybe up to a month, you don't really travel a lot, just kind of stay around the house, stay home. And then after a month, you can go places. It's just showing respect.

"Too many things happening," she says again, coughing. "I tried to talk to my dad. I just thought, well, it's not really the time to talk to him. I'll try to talk about happy things with him, try to be with him—you know, buy him something to eat every so often. I think he is the strongest force for the family. And his mother really depends on him. She really kind of like found him to do this and that, and said, 'I want you to do this,' even though everybody had given up. It was his mom and him, they just really [kept trying to do ceremonies and prayers for Agnes]."

Bowing to an urge to decorate the grave site in some fashion for Dennis's aunt, Ella looked for flowers. Although the mortician's wife owns a flower shop, by the time they got over there, it was closed. Ella bought some plastic flowers.

"My dad looked at them and asked, 'What did we get that for?' We said we were going to take it out to the grave site."

In the old ways, a man's saddle would be placed on his grave, and sometimes his horse shot over it. The dead person would be wrapped in blankets and buried without a coffin. Ashes to ashes, dust to dust. Nothing was to interfere with the disintegration of the body and its reunion with the earth. His horse and saddle were left for him, some say, so he wouldn't come back to look for them. Others say, "We give to the dead to show respect, to indicate that they were loved by those who survive."

The plastic flowers—that was almost incomprehensible to Jack.

28

Back to Flagstaff

In April, worn out from the deaths and the rain and the flu, Ella checked into the Indian Health Service Hospital in Tuba City. The doctors determined she was dehydrated, and they put her on an I.V. "I've got a cough and tickles in my throat," she says, "and whenever I lean over it feels like my brains are going to fall out. Then my waist was just hurting, my stomach. I didn't know what was wrong with me, and then I was going to the bathroom a lot. I thought I had a urinary infection, but then I thought, no, it's not like that—and just body aches, so I went to the hospital."

She thinks she may have become dehydrated as a result of a bout of diarrhea, and she also suffered from a yeast infection. Her mother is still sick with the flu. Ella bought her a bag of throat lozenges and told her to keep one in her mouth all the time. Ella still hasn't gone to Flagstaff for another mammogram.

Meantime, on the eastern part of the reservation, the "Navajo flu" is identified as a killer of a few dozen people in the Four Corners area. The television news networks rush en masse to the scene. Every night for several days, each of the networks manages to portray the Navajo people as reactionary, ill-mannered, ignorant, superstitious, and opposed to science and medical knowledge. They interview elderly Navajos who say that the medicine men will know what is causing the illness, that the medicine men must be consulted. The reports, which the Navajos watch on television, make them look stupid, and they don't like it. Thereupon, the Navajos refuse to speak any more to reporters.

As it turns out, the medicine men, gathered together by Navajo President Peterson Zah, provide the crucial bit of information to help medical investigators track down the cause of the illness. They tell investigators that they knew that something was happening because the piñon nut crop this year was excessively large. Instead of one blooming, there were two, even three. Navajos gather the piñons that fall from pinecones, roast them, and sell them, so they are highly attuned to the state of the piñon crop.

The scientists soon realize that rodents, which also gather the piñon nuts, were also more abundant this year. And eventually, the ailment that caused acute respiratory failure and sudden death in handfuls of people—even young, healthy people in the middle of dancing or shopping at the market—was identified as the hanta virus, which is carried by rodents and dropped in their feces. In the arid climate, the organism becomes airborne, presumably on dust, and is inhaled.

This is only one of the latest signs to the traditional Navajo and Hopi people that the earth is severely out of balance. They see the natural disasters—floods, hurricanes, volcanic eruptions, illness—as marks that Mother Earth is reacting to the abuse of her body and bounty. Navajos no longer talk about this in an excited manner, because it is old hat to them. They have been predicting terrible scourges as a result of the white man's abuse of nature for years and years.

The Navajos have never had trouble in trying to "justify the ways of God to men," to use Milton's phrase. They are like many other religious people in believing that natural scourges are warnings from God for misbehavior.

Ella suddenly announces that she and Dennis plan to move back into their relocation home this summer.

"What?"

She speaks in circles. I don't know if she's unsure of how she feels about this decision, or whether she knows in her heart but won't say. The illness and rains of the past winter have contributed to a feeling of foreboding hanging over the family. Ella's lingering illnesses, the discharge from her breast, the deaths of two relatives, the family's loss of their summer funds, and Ella's hesitation to get a mammogram are bad signs. The decision to return to the house whose building was the starting point of so much family distress seems an almost reckless gesture.

I ask Ella why they have made the decision to move back. She answers in a very soft voice.

"Dennis thinks we need to do other things as a family. Do other things for the city of Flagstaff, like for Native American families. He thinks we got what we came for, and now we need to go back to Flagstaff."

"And what did you come back for?"

"To get treatments for my health, the traditional way, because of my mom."

I think of her current medical troubles, and I wonder if they are a sign. The reasons she offers for returning are Dennis's. They are vague and a tad grandiose. Before I can ask again what Flagstaff offers them, she says, "I guess we miss being in Flagstaff. And then [Dennis's] mom and dad—he thinks a lot about them because they're sick all the time. And he can't do very much being here, especially [for] his dad; it seems he always wants Dennis up there. He calls him, wants to know why we don't visit. Why we haven't come. He just needs a lot of help, help around the house, cleaning up around the back, stuff like that. Just little things—and just for companionship. I think he really misses his kids, and he feels Dennis understands him a lot. And I think that's why I want, Dan wants, to go back to Flagstaff."

Dennis's father's Alzheimer's is worsening. Although Dennis had a troubled relationship with his dad, he has taken responsibility for his father's care. Dennis says that his father never played with him when he was a child. "He never really showed me affection." Dennis says this was due in part to his father's own difficult childhood. "He was raised really bad. On the rez. His father was a very violent and mean man. And if [my dad] did anything wrong, and he tried to run, his father would saddle up the horse or just go bareback and chase him down and drag him, slap him, knock him around. Talk about child abuse!"

One of the reasons Dennis stopped drinking was that he saw violent tendencies of his own emerging after he and Ella had begun their family. "Once in a while it would come out and—I'm still working through recovery to work on it."

Ella thinks that Dennis wants to make peace with his father. He feels further that his and Ella's attentions have been focused on Ella's side of the family for years, and now his family needs some help.

"Maybe he feels that there's so much he missed out on growing up, because he grew up with real strong Christian teachings. And now it's different with his family. I guess they still believe that stuff, but it's not intense like before." In fact, as his father has aged, he has spontaneously remembered Navajo stories and songs, and is drawn to share them with his son Dennis, the only one of his children who has learned traditional ways. It is Dennis whom he wants around him now, as he gets sicker, and as his mind searches for an anchor.

But Ella, I get the feeling, would rather stay near her mother.

Finally, she says just that. "I would like to stay around the reservation because I would be closer to my family. I have more opportunities to participate in whatever's happening around

there in terms of ceremonies. I know everybody around here
—I feel at home here in Tuba City. And I feel that if I stay
here, my kids have more contact with reservation life than in
Flagstaff, where they wouldn't have that.

"But then in another way I think Flagstaff offers better ed-
ucational opportunities. We're close to the university, where
we can take advantage of classes there. And maybe the school
has more to offer to kids that live in town. But then again
there's a lot of things that I'm afraid of too, like there's a lot of
gang activities, and in the school district I know that Danielle's
going to be under a lot of peer pressure, even though I tell her
every day, you know, 'Show respect for yourself, and whatever
you do and whatever you say, you represent your people.' And I
know it's kind of hard for people that young to think that way
sometimes, because you're under a lot of peer pressure in Flagstaff and the activities you do in Flagstaff are very different from
those in Tuba City. I don't really want her hanging around
video game centers. I really don't want her getting involved
with dances or going to movies with her friends, staying at her
friends' for the night."

"What's the matter with movies?"

"You never know what happens there. Somebody might
say, Let's ride around for a while, and she might jump in with
some friends from school and you never know what's going to
happen. That's why I tell her I don't want her to get into anyone
else's vehicle unless you know that person."

"Do you think Nell would get out of the vehicle if she felt
unsafe?"

"I think she would, but I'm always afraid: What if she gets
off at a place where she has no access to a phone? That's what
I worry about the most. Like this summer, we weren't going
to get a phone and I told Dennis, well, you know it costs money
to have it hooked up, maybe $90 or $100. But then again, I
think about it, she wants to go swimming, she wants to get
involved in gymnastics; I don't mind that. There's ice skating

there in Flagstaff. I really don't know what kind of friends she would have in Flagstaff. I don't know what kind of families they'd be coming from, and I'd feel much more comfortable if we had a phone. That way she could call us.

"So far we've never had a problem with that here at school; usually up here we know the parents of her friends at school. They're usually employees at school, or somewhere along the way, Dennis knows them. I don't think I've ever let her stay overnight at anybody's house. If one of her friends wants to stay overnight, I'll talk to the parents and they'll stay overnight. But I don't think she's ever stayed overnight with somebody in Tuba. I know her friends have asked several times. But I worry about it. Like this other girl, she's really grown up. She wants to have Nell over sometimes. Dennis is kind of hesitant because he knows that family, and they drink quite a bit. She's got brothers who drink and the mother drinks and the father drinks. I say to her, What if the situation develops that the whole family, they all start fighting? What's going to happen? You might get hurt. Or maybe they might chase you in the vehicle, maybe the mother would chase you in the vehicle and try to take you somewhere, and she might be drinking, and you never know what might happen on the road. And like Fridays, [traffic's] really heavy sometimes, especially during the dances.

"I tell her driving around is not a recreation. You never know what's going to happen; there's a lot of drunk Indians on the road, and it may not be your fault. So she's got sense in her. She's always said that 'whenever I do something wrong at school, Daddy always knows. I don't know what it is, but he has this ability in his head to know when something's wrong.' I guess because of that too, she behaves. She's actually a pretty good kid compared to a lot of girls I know.

"And at the same time," Ella continues, "I don't want to be too strict on her too. So I don't know. There's some friends she has in Flagstaff, some friends that we knew; they go to powwows; they live outside of Flagstaff. Some of them are kind of older, like the ones she went to Ontario with. She used to hang around with those girls. They're teenagers."

"Nell's a teenager," I remind Ella.

"She always says, 'Mom, I'm a preteen.' "

"She's thirteen?"

"She'll be fourteen in September."

"She's a teenager."

"I guess so."

As Ella goes on, she sounds sad and wistful. I feel that she doesn't want to move back at all but is doing so because Dennis wants to. She made this choice once already and paid dearly for it.

Ella suddenly starts to talk about her parents in a remorseful tone.

"There's a lot of things I did that I regretted, a lot of things that maybe I said that hurt somebody without realizing it. But the one thing I never did was, I never talked back to my mom and my dad.

"I have a lot of respect for them. Sometimes even to hug my mom or my dad or just say their names: 'my mom' or 'my dad,' I get a lot of feeling. I kind of get really emotional about it, maybe whereas anybody else wouldn't. Because I attained that understanding in my mind that, God, this is my mom and dad, and they're not going to be here forever, and I have to spend time with them and enjoy being with them, try to get as much as I can out of it. And to me, I look at them as having a good marriage. My mom never got mad at my dad. My dad always took care of my mom. I never saw my mom or my dad fight about anything; late at night maybe I heard them talking about things, what they wanted to do, like have a ceremony, or something like that.

"Maybe that's where I picked it up from. Way late at night when I wake up, Dennis and I will talk about things, something that we saw different about the boys, or we're suspicious about something—how are we going to approach them, what can we say to them, that what they're doing is wrong, it's not good for their bodies. And we're doing all these things and we're trying to help them, but they need to help themselves."

"What things do you regret?"

"Um. I guess maybe not listening like I should have, way back, to a lot of teachings. To me it was 'Oh, again, the same thing,' and I would be playing, I tried playing, and I never really asked questions. A lot of the old language, I didn't pick up like I should have, and today I have to write it down to remember it. Because you don't hear it anymore. And I regret not knowing a lot of ways to prepare traditional foods like dyes, plant dyes—my mom knows about all these things. I never really took time. I guess the interruption was school. School, you had to be in school, nine, ten months out of the year.

"Only two months we were home, but all that time was spent herding sheep and then taking care of my siblings."

Ella pauses. I wonder why she is speaking about the things she missed, the lessons she didn't learn as well as she might have. I wonder if her melancholia is related to her thoughts of returning to town.

✳

Ella pulls a load of laundry from the washer and hangs it up outside over her garden. Back inside, sitting at the kitchen table before several plastic boxes of beads and metal earrings she will cover with beaded designs, Ella starts to talk.

"I don't have a perfect family; there's no such thing as a perfect family. I always think that if you really want to do something with your life, I think it all has to do with your mind, how you want to live your life, how you want to make your life work. You have to start thinking about how you're going to take care of your family, because that's always first, how you're going to survive. You start doing those things.

"And then, like Dennis and I, like I'm at school now and I'll be at school during the summer. I don't have to go to school, but I want to take advantage of a lot of these things that are offered through Navajo Community College, like Navajo philosophy, foundation of Navajo culture, these kinds of things. A lot of the teachings that I see presented in these courses, I've heard [about] from my family. From my family, it's always coming out in Navajo, Navajo way, Navajo philosophy. And now I guess I'm getting interested in ways of how to present it in English. Using English words, the terminology.

"I guess, maybe five years down the line, I'm thinking about getting a job at NCC, maybe teaching culture or teaching tradition to people of my kids' generation, because it's lacking, it's not being taught in the schools and the home anymore.

"They're trying to get it in the school. But when they give it in the school, I think it's really different. It has a lot more meaning if it's presented from way deep inside. If you have a feeling for what you're teaching, you present it more, and there's much more understanding in who you're teaching it to.

"Maybe a lot of people my age don't think about it; just talking to people [I get the impression that] some of my relatives don't really have that feeling for their culture. I'm at that age where I have a lot of feeling for it now. I know why it's so important. And maybe one of these days, I might have a class and I might tell these young people, 'This is why.'

"Like [during] the time my kids were growing up, I talked to them about the way I was raised, the culture. I don't know, they just, maybe it was the way I talked about it or the way I presented it. Like today I think, maybe I could have done it differently."

None of Ella's children speaks Navajo fluently. The stories she wants to preserve, the stories her father tells her, are not ones her children know well. She sees the needs in the children she teaches at the Gap, who suffer because their parents, addled with alcohol and under pressure from the Holy Roller churches they attend, have turned away from their Navajo ways.

"The people I work with are so backward," Ella says. "I never thought I'd say anything like that about people. Like we had a job interview for a janitor for a job at the school? And I sat on the interview committee because I had to speak Navajo to them and interview them. And we had a lot of people. Some young people came, some parents, and you know, we asked, 'Why do you want this job?'

" 'Oh, I want coffee money,' some said.

" 'What would you do if you were done with your job cleaning and mopping everything before your four hours is up? Let's say you finished your job in two and a half hours. What would you do for that hour and a half?'

"And then they'd say, 'I'd just sit around. Until my four hours is up.'

"We hired the one who had an answer like 'I'll find something to do, like pick up trash around outside.' He gave us what we thought were the best answers. I mean, like, we asked questions like, 'If you were to have problems with one of the teachers here, how would you solve it?' And then one of them said, 'I'd just go over and tell her off. I'm right all the time.' This guy was about, maybe thirty. You practically have to lead them around and say, 'This is what you should say; this is what you should do.' Today we were talking about maybe having some kind of service training for the parents. And teach them what to say in an interview."

Ella thinks their problems come from having a foot in each culture—Navajo and Anglo—but knowing almost nothing about either. They hear things on television about how Anglos live, but they don't really understand those ways, and they never learned Navajo values because the churches in town have influenced generations into thinking their ways were evil.

The man they hired for the job arrives early in a pickup truck with several of his little daughters. They sit and play in the truck alone during the day as he goes about his chores. He is tall and carries himself with a dignified, elegant carriage. He wears neat jeans, a tee-shirt and cowboy boots. His skin is very dark, and his face deeply pockmarked. His face expresses fear and hardship, the fear that comes when you know you are doing everything you can and your children are still going hungry. One can see how important this job is to him; he comes hours early and stays hours late, looking for additional things to do, clearly determined that no one will catch him unprepared. His wife has started as a teacher's aide, earning about $5 an hour. They are expecting their eighth child.

"I mean, it's kind of like isolated there. In Tuba City we have a lot of traditional people, right? And in Gap they have a lot of Christianity influence. And it's a lot of the Holy Roller stuff. They belong to the Navajo Baptist Church, and then there's the Pentecostal. And then there's another one called the Church of God. They're all interrelated. I think they're just teaching the wrong thing.

"These people don't really know what the concept of Christian is. I mean, these people fight and they—they go to the church and they think that [Navajo] culture is not important. 'We don't want Navajo taught here,' they say about the school. 'We want our kids to have a white teacher. We don't want Navajo teachers.' That's what they say.

"I don't know what [that Holy Roller church] is or what they like about it," she says. "I tell them that a true Christian is like this: they go by the word of God, the Ten Commandments. I say, 'If you're a true Christian, you don't go and pick fights with your neighbors; you don't go and put down people.' I mean, that's what they do. They get themselves involved in all these different arguments. They fight among themselves.

"You know, that culture is phony; that's the way I look at it. They're so confused about what being a Christian is, you know, even the traditional people, some of them have turned to Christianity. Some of them say there are also good teachings in the Navajo way, but these young people, they go to church—and that's all they believe in, and they leave that Navajo behind, and that's why they're not really teaching their

kids the values of being Navajo, and that's where all the confusion starts. But it's so, it's really sad.

"They don't understand Christianity, and they've given up
their own ways. Many of the Navajos in the Gap don't speak
their own language. And they don't want their children to learn
Navajo ways. The parents, they think that Navajo is going to
hold their children back; they don't think it's important that
they know the culture."

The first thing Ella taught her little three-, four-, and five-
year-old students was their clan affiliations. She sent papers
home to their parents and asked them to identify the mother's
clan, the father's clan, and other affiliated clans. Ella then made
a chart on the wall showing each child and his or her important
clans, so the children would become familiar with them, and
would learn how to greet each other, "Hello, my son" or "Hello,
my grandmother." Ella quickly realized that even the other
teachers and administrators did not know their own clans, and
they used the traditional greetings improperly.

The children responded to Ella quickly and powerfully. She
brought in traditional clothes for them to play with; she brought
in a cradleboard and pictures of traditional people. She read
stories to them from books, and has endeavored to get better
toys and learning materials in the classroom. Most have very
short attention spans, and many were unfamiliar with toys and
crayons. She began to teach them Navajo words, but looking
around the classroom, it is clear that the children's needs are
quite basic. Several of the children have large and visible burns
on them—a not uncommon occurrence in homes with no electricity. The children get burned by fire or by hot oil used for
cooking. Some are being abused by their parents; a few have
bruises and cuts on their faces. Every day Ella examines the
children. Unobtrusively during story time or while they are
playing, she approaches them and speaks to them in her soft,
soothing voice, and if she sees bruises, she asks them about
them. Sometimes, if she knows a child has been abused in the

past, she'll ask if they have any sores or bruises, even if she doesn't see any.

Ella believes that Navajo culture can support them, nurture them, give them the teachings they'll need to start their lives. But they're not getting Navajo teaching or much else at home. Since their parents sell on the roadside, no one is home to care for them. Most of the mothers work beading or stringing necklaces when they are not selling. It seems a pattern in the Gap that the women give the money they earn to their men, and the men spend the money on drink and trucks, and then smash the trucks.

Teaching the children of the Gap, Ella thinks of her own children and wonders if she has been successful enough in instilling Navajo values in them. Perhaps she wasn't strict enough. Perhaps the harshness of her father's boyhood is the way to make a respectful, hardworking, well-balanced adult.

And yet, the forces of modernity continue to press on them all. The Bedonies are living in a cramped trailer in Tuba City when they own a four-bedroom home in Flagstaff. Why not place Nell in a better school? Why not live in their own house?

In some ways, her struggle itself is truly Navajo—trying to find a way to bring into her traditional view of the world those aspects of a new culture that are beneficial. But Ella's dilemma is not really knowing if a new house, better schools, and more contact with whites are in fact beneficial, or whether they will lead her and her family down a misleading and dangerous path.

"There was always that between me and Dennis. Dennis came from a border town family. I came from a traditional family. Seems like there's always that fine line between us. I always want to be more involved in my traditional things, ceremonies. I want my kids to be really involved, even if it's not directly related to my family. I want my kids to be there. Because I feel it's important that they at least know what's happening—just watching it and seeing it—what's happening. And then seeing how people help one another by sharing.

I just talk to them about it, and they don't really understand it. They should be giving to one another, helping one another; that's the main reason why you're here [in this life]. If you feel you have more than what you need, then give it to somebody else. If I just talk about it, I don't think they really comprehend it.

"But if I show them, they're *there* and they *see* it, not so much as me saying look at that person helping that person, but them *seeing* it, being *there*, being part of it. I think that would really make them understand more."

Dennis believes that the kids can retain these beliefs without daily reinforcement on the reservation. "Dennis says, Well, you know, I believe those things. We don't have to be there to believe in those things. We support them and whatever is happening, but we don't need to be there."

But Ella knows what it means to live away from the reservation. It is difficult to keep the feelings and Navajo frame of mind in a different setting. She seems to be trying to argue herself into a position that just does not feel right to her heart. She has agreed to move back down to the relocation house, but when she thinks about it, her thoughts go home to Coal Mine Mesa. Speaking about the advantages of city life leads her to speak of regret about time lost with her parents, lessons that weren't learned as well as they might have been. Thinking about moving to town leads her to think about teaching Navajo culture and how important it is to feel the culture, to see the ceremonies and the customs at work while participating in them. Yet she will likely not teach Navajo culture in Flagstaff. In a way, moving down does answer a traditional call: Dennis's desire to care for his ailing father, a most Navajo of desires. But unfortunately, it keeps Ella from tending her own.

"I never actually learned how to weave," says Ella, taking the conversation, it seems, off in a very different direction. But soon I understand she has not changed the subject at all.

"Just through the years I would see my mom do it, and

sometimes she would let me help her, so I already knew how to do it. It's like every day she was weaving. And we saw it all the time; we saw it all the time. It was like making fry bread maybe, slapping it back and forth; we saw her doing that. When it was time for us to do it, I already knew how to do it, just by watching her. Now I think maybe I should put down all my beadwork and really get myself into weaving, 'cause when I'm weaving, my mom is there with me, she's part of that process." Ella's voice becomes soft here. She stops for a few seconds.

"And when I go to Flagstaff, I feel that by weaving, my mom's going to always be there with me, because this is part of her, I got this from her. It's not something that I'll have for a little while and lose. It's not like jewelry: I can take care of it as much as I can, but then I might lose it, or someone could steal it and it would be gone and never be replaced. But this weaving, it's different. I have it and I'm always going to have it; as part of my mother, I got it from her. Even though she's not around, that part is going to be always with me."

29

Summer

It is May 3, and I have a hankering to call Ella on the telephone. After a few minutes of chatting she reminds me that the next day is her birthday. She will be forty-one years old. I'm hit with a pang of remorse because I have forgotten her birthday. However, I remind myself that I will be out in Arizona in ten days, and I'll get her a present when I'm there. I quickly realize that I did the same thing last year. I just happened to call her the evening before her birthday. I think this is strange.

"What are you going to do tomorrow?" I ask.

"Go to work," she answers.

"Is anyone taking you out to dinner?"

"I don't know," she says, but her tone rings with an excitement, with the promise of the unexpected, though she says nothing particular has been planned. I am reminded of Ella's ineffable good humor and the excitement with which she greets life's twists. How ebullient she becomes when embarking on an adventure, and how ready she is to do so at a moment's notice.

"Alvin says he'll buy me a pizza," she says of one of her nephews, Lula's son. "He's really cute. In fact, he said, 'Auntie, your birthday's coming up, huh?' "

He knew because his brother's birthday is the same day as Ella's.

"He says, 'I know 'cause of Mike's birthday, and I'll get you a pizza.' " I ask Ella if she thinks he'll make good on his promise. She says she doesn't know, but the odds aren't bad, since he works at the local pizza parlor.

I ask Ella what she would like for her birthday. Without a moment's pause, she says, "A car just like yours, but a convertible, so I can zoom down Main Street with the top down, so the wind can rustle through my short hair." She laughs and laughs and laughs.

I ask her if she might think of something a bit smaller. Every time I ask, however, I get the same answer, and the same delightfully hysterical laughter.

Ella tells me that she has not gone to Flagstaff Medical Center yet for another mammogram.

"Dan tells me it all depends what they say, but I could go to the VA too. I guess he called the VA today in Phoenix and he's supposed to find out more information tomorrow. More and more I'm thinking, I'll just go back to Flagstaff even though I have to pay."

I try to impress upon her the benefits of quick action. If she has a problem in her breast, she'd best know about it quickly. She has spoken of the discharge for almost four months, and though the doctors in Tuba City have tried to reassure her that it is probably nothing, they have advised her to get another mammogram. She says she knows, but she doesn't want to know. Perhaps she is scared, though when I ask her if she is, she says no.

"I finally got my gold tooth," she says cheerfully. "It's on the side. I had a temporary one so they could get this one. And I got it the other day. Every time I chewed, the other one came out. And pretty soon it was in no shape to be back in my mouth because it would crunch. Buzz came in and he was asking me for some money, and I said, 'I don't have any money to give you now.' And he goes, 'Well, as soon as you go to sleep, Mom, I'm going to take your gold tooth, and I'll go pawn it.'" She laughs. She loves to repeat the wacky things her kids say.

Otherwise, Ella is still tired and sick. "Yeah, I don't know, maybe it's the coughing in my head. Every time I look down I get dizzy-like. And my stomach hurts all the time. I'm coughing too. They took my blood tests, and then I went down there [to the hospital in Tuba City] Wednesday for another one. They want to do another one just to make sure. They said that sometimes if you have an infection, a bad infection inside, it shows up in your blood. If it's in your blood, in order to treat it, I guess they treat your blood."

When people enter the Tuba City Hospital, they aren't always able to see a doctor. "They have a lot of interns there from the military," Ella says. "And then they have physician's assistants. Only if you have a major kind of illness—then you're assigned to a doctor, and you'll see that one doctor all the time. Otherwise, if you're pretty healthy, if you get a bug here and there, they assign you to a physician's assistant and then you go see him whenever you go to the hospital."

Ella says there are only two doctors in the adult ward in the general clinic, so if she needs to see a doctor, she often has to wait; if she wants to see her own doctor, she may have to wait a few days. She can't always keep the appointments they make for her, because of her job or family responsibilities.

"If you go in for an emergency, you might see an eye doctor, or you might see a bone doctor. But if it's really serious, they call somebody who's on standby. And they usually come down. If it's an accident or something really bad, then they call another doctor. Or they fly you out to Phoenix or Flagstaff or Gallup [New Mexico]." Most Anglos would not tolerate the kind of care the Indians get at Public Health Service hospitals. But Indians make good use of the hospitals, which serve as primary-care facilities. One of the reasons they have embraced modern medicine is its effect on infant mortality. In 1945 only one of every two children was likely to live to school age. In 1967 more than 98 percent of children lived to enter school.

Navajos are aware, however, that they often receive less than blue-ribbon care. For example, the hospital will not perform root canals. They will pull a tooth, but they won't do the surgery necessary to save it. This is undoubtedly a cost-cutting measure, yet the Navajos pay exorbitant prices for dental work. Ella went to a private dentist, one who seems to have a monopoly on the Navajo market—and paid hundreds of dollars for her gold tooth.

Ella seems calm about her health, as if she had decided to put her fate in the hands of the gods. However, she tells me that the other day, while she was in Basha's supermarket, she felt a sharp pain behind her knee. She stood still and massaged it. Slowly it seemed to pass, but as it moved, it hurt badly. Ella went to the hospital, and a nurse told her it might be a blood clot.

I fear what all her friends and relatives fear, a return of the cancer. I worry about it now because Ella is thinking of returning to Flagstaff, a move that previously caused her such distress and illness. She still hasn't had a comprehensive exam from her own doctor. She has told me for weeks that she had an appointment at the Flagstaff Medical Center, but she has not yet gone.

She is trying to stay on the low-fat diet that was recommended for her, at least her version of the low-fat diet. "I used to really like to eat meat, like roadside. I haven't eaten that since maybe the last time you came," she says, about mutton and mutton sandwiches.

"I get hamburger, that real lean kind? And I make soup with it. I put all kinds of vegetables in there. I cook the hamburger first, and then put water in there and all the vegetables in there, some tomato sauce, and then I add red chili, the kind you buy frozen. Baca's red chili. You can buy it in the freezer department. They have like mild, medium, and hot. I usually get the hot, and I add so much until it has the hot flavor. Everybody likes it. I usually make a big pot that lasts for like three days."

Since Ella has been ill, Nell has helped out. "I just come home and lie down, and Nell's making her soup and she says, 'Gaa, Mom, soup again?' I buy those thin round steaks, and sometimes she slices them up and puts all kinds of vegetables, like cauliflower, broccoli, zucchini, carrots, potatoes, and sometimes she puts [in] that beef broth. So she likes to do that."

Ella says she does the shopping with Nell. "I usually ask the kids, 'What do you want?' and I get what they want. [Nell] was making Hamburger Helper. And then pretty soon Buzz got tired of it. And now she says, 'You don't like it? Cook yourself.' " In early fall, Buzz returned from Tucson, where he had moved in with Kimo. The plan was for them to live together, but Buzz came home so his mom could cook for him. The sight of the empty refrigerator in the apartment he shared with his brother depressed him, so his adventure, living with Kimo, ended quickly. Kimo has persevered at Pima Community College, trying every term to save up enough money to transfer to the University of Arizona. But every term something else happens to set him back: his apartment is burglarized, then he ruins his car engine by letting it run out of oil.

A week after Ella's birthday, she sounds a little better. I ask her how she celebrated the day, and she says her sister Budge sent her some flowers via the district office of the school system. Someone at the Gap school office called her, and she went over and picked up the flowers. They were sent from the one floral shop in town.

"It was a rose she sent me, and some little carnations. They close up and open up."

On the night of her birthday, at about ten, after she was in bed with the lights out, she heard some singing outside her trailer. She woke up enough to hear that the song was "Happy

Birthday." She figures it was some of her sisters and their kids. "I heard the kids outside. I guess they parked on the side of the trailer, and they sang 'Happy Birthday.' I let them just drive off." She sounds tickled about it.

A few days later, she tells me she has been examined by her doctor in Tuba. She says, "Sometimes I hear bubbles in my nose, and there's nothing there. They just gave me some antibiotics. And they put a tube in my throat down into my chest, and they drained some green stuff out of my lungs, I guess. They said they heard wheezing in my lungs. And they took an X ray of my chest and it was just, kinda like, grayish. And they told me when you have a real bad cold sometimes it's like that. So for that wheezing in my chest, they put a tube in there and drained some of that stuff out. They said on Tuesday I'm going in down in Flag."

She is still having a yellow discharge from her left breast. "He asked me if maybe I, like, injured myself recently, like maybe with the kids, since I work with the little kids, if any of them bumped me. Sometimes he said when you have surgery and something like that happens, you'll get infections. Sometimes that will happen, sometimes the scar tissue tears."

"Do you remember that happening?"

"I don't remember. I try not to have them on my left side —I try not to play games with them that will injure my left side, because I always think about that. I'm always careful about it. And he said sometimes if you're moving stuff around and you put a lot of pressure on your breast to move something, he said sometimes that'll do that too. But for my cold, he said it was what was going around. He said there are people that have been hospitalized that have had it for that long. People come in all the time and say they've had it for a long time. One of my co-workers says she's had it for three months. It's all over the reservation. A lot of people have it."

In another week or so, Ella seems fine. But she still does not get another mammogram in Flagstaff. I can't tell if it's the money that's stopping her or fear. I tell her I will pay for her medical costs. She won't accept my offer.

※

On May 15, I arrive in Coal Mine. Ella and I drive down to Flagstaff to inspect the Bedonies' house, which has been vacated by its tenants. Dennis, who came down before us, has already gone through the house, checking for damage, and has found that the carpeting has been worn badly in several places, by dogs it seems. The tenants were not supposed to have animals in the house. The garage floor has been stained with oil in several places; it looks as if someone was working on cars in there.

The house, now starkly empty, has the feel of many new houses in Arizona—the walls are Sheetrock, the concrete floors covered with thick carpet, no particular design or style evident anywhere. The bathtubs are made of molded plastic, as are the sinks. Vanities are made of wood with bronze hardware that is too elaborate. The high ceiling in the living room is a dramatic element, though, and the kitchen opens into a breakfast nook area that is sunny and roomy.

The renters constructed a redwood pen for dogs around the back door, which they have left behind, and Dennis says he's thinking of dismantling it and using the wood to make a boundary fence for the property. The lot isn't really landscaped, and the yard is not delineated by any markers. The area is very hilly, surrounded by woodlands. Most of the houses are similarly upscale, similarly modern, with natural-wood exteriors. Across the street is a large expanse of conservation land.

After looking through all the rooms and noting the stains on the carpet, the nails in the walls, the damage to paint, Ella whispers to me, "It seems like a rental house to me. It doesn't seem like a real house."

The house has a ghostly, impersonal feel. I wonder how

much this has to do with seeing the evidence of other inhabitants, and wondering what took place in the house while
strangers were there. The house now contains other people's
stories, stories Ella will never know. I think how coming into
your home to see the marks of other inhabitants, while a shock
to anyone, must be particularly uncomfortable for Navajos, for
whom the house has been blessed and made sacred.

A few minutes after Ella and I arrive, Buzz, his girlfriend,
Sonya, and Nell walk in with a Big Foot pizza, a pizza the size
of a doormat. We eat it and drink Cokes standing up around
a counter in the kitchen—there is no furniture yet—while the
family discusses the big event of the night before: Nell's prom.

Buzz razzes Nell about her date, who brought three girls
with him.

"Three girls?" I ask. "If he brought three girls, who was in
the prom picture with him?"

Nell looks up delicately from her pizza, sips her Coke, and
says, "All of us."

"All of you at once?" I know Navajos are different from
Anglos in many ways, but I can't imagine this being acceptable
to any teenage girl.

"No," Nell looks at me as if I'd just started reading aloud
from the telephone book.

"We each had our picture taken with him. And then we
had one of all of us."

"You should have seen them dancing," Ella says, giggling.
"They wouldn't get near each other."

"They all had their shoes off; those girls were limping
around in their heels," says Dennis, shaking his head. He was
there as a chaperone. Buzz drove around outside, to make sure
Nell didn't go out for some air with anyone, as if she would.
She says she hates boys. Toward the end of the evening, Ella
escorted Nell to the carnival—a show of rides (a Ferris wheel
and others)—that was set up in Tuba City that weekend.

Nell wore a beautiful bottle-green gown. (She calls it "environmental green," Ella tells me.) It is satin, fitted at the bust and waist and descending into a full skirt. She wore long white gloves and white high heels (there wasn't time to dye the shoes to match the dress). Nell wanted to buy a rhinestone necklace and earrings, but Ella nixed that. Instead, she bought some rhinestone studs and inserted them into the bust of Nell's dress and onto her gloves.

Later, I see the dress draped over a straight chair in Nell's bedroom in Tuba City. It looks used, deflated, without life. In contrast, I notice Nell's powwow outfits hanging in the closet, six or seven of them, in heavy plastic garment bags. They are alive, full, vibrant. I think back on the relocation house, and it seems to share some of the qualities of the prom dress. And I think that Ella is right; Nell would have simply lost the rhinestone earrings and necklace somewhere. She would never lose one of her beaded moccasins or her bag beaded in a dramatic, big rose, whose outline was drawn by Buzz. Nell's ceremonial items don't become worthless next season, stuff for the swap meet. When she grows out of the moccasins, they will be saved, as will the bag, when Nell sees another design on another dancer that catches her fancy. She will bead a new one for herself, and the old one may wind up in Ella's classroom, where the children will swarm around Ella, eager to see the Indian things she has brought for them—the old velveteen baby dresses, the cradleboards, the moccasins, the bags—the objects that have deep and resonant meaning for them, the things that tell them who they are.

✳

It's time to get a birthday present. As we drive down to Flagstaff, Ella mentions that she does not own a single dress, so I think maybe she'd like one. But she says no. We go to the old center of town, to her favorite trading post, Puchteca, and look at the smaller work of some of the Navajo painters. Most of them are too expensive for me. Then she decides we should head over to Wal-Mart, recently built in a newly developed area of town not far from the Bedonies' house. The store is gargantuan; Ella has long been a bargain hunter, and Wal-Mart offers some of the best prices in town.

Nell goes off from us and returns in a few minutes to the cart with shampoo and some compacts. She has taken to wearing white powder on her face to make it lighter. In the last two months Nell's appearance has changed dramatically. She is suddenly a beautiful young woman. She wears lipstick and lines her eyes delicately with kohl. Her features have become graceful, exotic, Asian, mysterious. She has also lost most of her childish mannerisms. Her transformation has taken place, it seems, overnight. She is immensely self-conscious and spends hours in her bathroom washing and scrubbing. Ella says she has gone through a year's worth of Mary Kay facial scrub in several months.

I think of the white powder and the scrubbing. Is she trying to make her face white? Then I suddenly remember a conversation I had with Nell eight years ago, when she was an adorable five-year-old. We were in Sedona, and her parents were looking around in a store of Indian crafts. Nell and I sat outside on the balcony of the building, in the shade, surrounded by pots of pink and white vinca.

"Will I be white when I grow up?" She asked, looking right at me with her big brown eyes. I was startled.

"No, you'll be a beautiful brown color, like you are now," I said. Nell looked at me as if she didn't believe me, as if she knew better. She said, "Well, when I get out of the bathtub, I look whiter. So I thought that when I get older, I'll be white." I look over at Nell now, who has grown up so much yet is emblazoned in everyone's mind as an utterly winsome five-year-old, and I wonder what is going on in her head about her skin color. She has rather steadily complained to her mother about her features. For a while she hated her eyes because they turned up too much, she thought, at the outer corners. "I look like a cat," she said. Then she thought her nose was too big. I once saw her late for the grand entry of a Tuba City powwow because she had taken so much time braiding her hair until it was perfect.

Nell regularly wins powwow events across the reservation. Boys pursue her in school, but she won't have anything to do with them. In fact, even though she was a junior high cheerleader this year, she asked her mother to make her a special uniform with a longer skirt; she thought it immodest to wear the short pleated skirts the other girls wore.

We continue to tramp through the store. Ella has said that she doesn't have any good pots and pans, so she decides on a set of Revere Ware. Nice shiny pots with copper bottoms— a set of untarnished new pots to welcome her back into her home. I ask her if she's sure there isn't anything more personal she'd like. She says no. Nell gets impatient as we stand at the checkout line, and goes outside to wait. Ella looks at the compacts of light powder Nell has placed on the counter, and tells the cashier not to ring them up.

✺

It quickly becomes clear that the decision to pay the costs of the burial and transport of Dan's aunt had severe consequences for the Bedonies. It left them without a cent for the entire summer, the summer, no less, that they were planning to move to town. Ella and Dennis go looking for jobs, but the school district in Flagstaff won't hire them for temporary positions, and the jobs on the reservation pay better, so they don't want to sign up for permanent ones.

Ella has thought about borrowing some money from her father, but when she finally gets around to asking him, he says, "You're two days too late." He tells her he has just paid off his tractor and lent money to one of his sons to buy a new vehicle. Ella just laughed, because this always happens. She knows when he gets paid, and she always waits and waits before asking her dad for a loan, and by the time she asks, he's usually already spent it.

Jack advised her not to fret about their summer savings. "Don't worry about it. That's the last thing you should worry about," he said. "You'll always get more money. You buried Dan's aunt and now that's done. Money will always be replenished."

Unfortunately, the burden falls on Ella to earn the money. Though she is still weak from her various illnesses, over the summer she will be up all hours of the night beading and making jewelry to sell. Dennis is unsuccessful in finding summer work. An anthropologist talks to Ella about a job at Walnut Canyon and Montezuma Castle, heavily visited historical sites that feature ruins of the ancient Anasazi people around Flagstaff and Sedona. She tells me that he wants her to do research, and is willing to pay her a salary of about $30,000. I ask her for more details, but she doesn't know them. She misses a meeting they have set up for an interview, and calls him a few days later. In spite of the missed appointment, he is still interested. She wants to know more about the job. It seems that Ella would be asked to give talks at the sites about the ancient cultures that inhabited the places. What would the research be? She wasn't sure, but the job would involve some travel and some instruction of tour guides. It sounds like a very substantial job to me. If she took it, it would help their financial situation greatly, and might be a stepping-stone to other things.

A few weeks later, she mentions the job again, but doesn't sound interested in it. Finally, she decides to turn it down. "Why?" I ask.

"It just sounds like it's a lot of work, and not something I want to do, I don't think. I found out it was going to take some traveling. I don't want to do that, I'm scared of driving. Down to museums and different places where they have dwellings—

like Canyon de Chelly, Betatkin, Montezuma Castle. I guess they have people who come from different historical societies all over the world; they come and they make appointments to be at a certain place on certain days, and they want to come out and find out about the kind of people that used to live there."

"So you'd have to give speeches to them?"

"Yeah, and go through the rooms and go through . . . show them artifacts, and that means skeletons. I don't want to do that. I want to stay far away from that sort of stuff."

The prospect of that kind of work disturbs her. Also, she would have to work on weekends, which she doesn't want to do.

So it looks like she'll be back at the Gap next fall, where the children so desperately need good teachers. Ella says she has received some letters from the children. "Just a lot of scribbling and pictures," she says. One little boy, Christopher, sent her a special letter with an enclosure. Says Ella, "He sent me a leaf."

In this decision I sense a struggle within Ella over whether to step full force into the white world and accept a substantial, demanding job or to maintain a more familiar pace and way of life. The struggle was a brief one. The white world offers untold possibilities, but possibilities that require five-day workweeks, full-time, day after day. At the Gap, she can be absent for a day and replaced by a substitute. Fridays, there are no classes. The work at Gap is familiar, it is important to Ella, and it is close to home, offering Ella opportunities to stop off and see her parents. It conforms more to the rhythms of her life.

The anthropologist is not the only Anglo eager to hire Ella to work for him. One day at the Gap preschool, when Ella was leading a parent orientation, the editor of the Lake Powell City *Post* happened by and was so taken with Ella's words about the schoolchildren that he asked her to write a column for him. She did so. He asked her to do one every week, and she wrote several. Between writing the column and interviewing her relatives for the book, she is developing considerable writing skills. She says one day she'd like to write a book. But she'll turn the recorder and camera lens around. "I want to write a book about a white person, a white Jewish woman," she says, giggling her expectant, delighted giggle, then roaring with laughter.

✳

Before arriving at the Gap, which lies thirty-five miles northwest of Tuba City, one is accompanied by a massive rock escarpment that winds like a serpent alongside the road, ever-present, arching and rearing its body and revealing the delicate colors of its underbelly—red, purple, yellow, ochre, green. Ella compared the beauty of this rock to the artwork of the preschool children.

"*Ya'at'eeh* [hello]," she wrote, in one of her articles for the Lake Powell City *Post*.

> Gap school is a unique school situated in what most people call an isolated place. To the school staff and students at Gap school, it's the most beautiful place in the whole Dine reservation. The beautiful cliffs on the east side are like a bulletin board displaying the artwork of nature. The red formations of rocks look like blocks that the children play with at school. The streams on the land are like the paintings of the children as they freely express themselves with a paintbrush. The rolling hills, some in circles, oblongs, squares and triangles, display the creativity of our children as they play with Play-Doh. The whole land formation with its beautiful colors to us are like the artwork of our students at Gap school.

✳

In July, Ella signs another contract to teach part-time next fall at the Gap, a job that brings her a far lower salary than that offered by the anthropologist. The family still must make it through the summer, however. In addition to beading and selling at the roadside swap meet, Ella tells me they are getting into the wholesale jewelry-buying business.

"I got some money together, and we bought a license and then we bought some jewelry, silver jewelry, and we sold over at the powwow downtown, the Flagstaff Days. And then we had some left over, and then Danielle placed first [in the powwow dance competition] and she got over $300, and she said, 'Let's go to Fort Duchesne, and I'll pay for it.' It's way over there in Utah, an all-day drive. We left at six in the morning and got there at five at night.

"We just had a little bit left, so we just sold what we had. But it's expensive just paying to sell, we didn't really make a profit, so that [money] went." But they were excited about the possibility of a new means of earning money. Ella has to increase her inventories of merchandise, and that requires investment of money, but she has seen other people make a living selling jewelry this way at powwows and other gatherings.

Now, they are back in their Flagstaff house. Ella is beading; Dennis is with his parents at their house. The Bedonies have brought a few things down from the trailer in Tuba City, but they haven't moved everything. They have installed a new phone in Flagstaff and turned off the old one in Tuba. Ella has to leave her number unlisted, or relatives and friends will call collect and ask her to pass on messages to people on the reservation who have no telephone.

The Bedonies' plans about living in Flagstaff are slightly incoherent. Nell plans to go to school there, but both Dennis and Ella have jobs on the reservation. Ella, when she lived in Tuba, had to leave at 7:00 a.m. to get to the Gap on time, and this schedule exhausted her. Now she'll have to leave at 5:30 a.m. to get to school on time.

Already, the Bedonies' decision to move back into their Flagstaff home is causing major changes in their lives and in their interaction with family. First, they decided in the spring not to plant their cornfield. It is impossible to tend the field if they live ninety minutes away. So the field will lie fallow unless one of her sisters takes it over. But Ella's move back to town has stirred up some of the jealousies and resentments expressed by her sisters when she first relocated. Ella went ahead and paid for the irrigation fees, even though she won't have a cornfield there, to avoid aggravating her sisters, who are again reacting as they did when she first relocated. When they see her coming, they leave or turn their backs on her.

"A lot of times I didn't want to come home because I didn't want to feel hurt like that," says Ella. "I'd come and then everybody would just leave, you know. And then I'd hear from other people what they were saying about me, and about me selling out and that I don't belong out there any more, and I shouldn't have a part in any family discussions."

Some of her sisters are grumbling about the expense of the new ceremonies, suggesting that she wouldn't be sick if she hadn't moved back to the house.

But Jack and Bessie do not blame her for her troubles. "My mom and dad don't think about me that way; they don't talk about me that way. Every day I wake up thinking about them because I came from them; I came from their flesh. Now I come here all the time because I want to see them, and I want to spend as much time as I can with them. And they tell me I'm from here, I grew up here, and I'm a part of the land here. I'm a part of everything here.

"And I come here, I come here for healing. This is where I feel strong. When I'm in Flag sometimes I don't feel so strong, and sometimes I'm weak, and I come here, and I take in all this fresh air and I feel good. I go to the corral with my mom, and we laugh, and that's healing for me. But I'm not going to ask my brothers and sisters for forgiveness. When I have my ceremonies, I'll be over here at the hogan, and I'll see them over at the house, and they bring things over there to help with the ceremonies, but they don't come in and say anything to me. Maybe they're ashamed, or they don't know how to approach me or something. I don't know what it is this time, but I don't feel any way towards them. If they want to talk to me, fine. I don't hold anything against anybody. I just want to live each day the way my mom and dad want me to."

How they want her to live is unclear. How she will live in a Navajo way in Flagstaff is unclear. But she is trying to sort these problems out. She is helped by her wide circle of friends, many of whom are white. When she was undergoing chemotherapy, it was her Anglo friends who sat with her and helped her. Her sisters and brothers said they didn't want to see her in that condition.

Navajo teachings, while extolling the virtues of good relations between relatives, also take note of the fact that there are often strains among blood relatives. Although Navajo ways aim at an ideal—you should treat everyone as if he were your relative—they also acknowledge that everyone doesn't always live up to that ideal.

One day, Jack came by Ella's house in Flagstaff and told her he had noticed how many friends she had. "A couple of weeks ago, [my mom and dad] came to pick me up," says Ella, "and I had people here, Anglo people, and one of my friends was cooking, and one was washing for me, and one was trying to help me do my beadwork, and after they left, I [told my dad,] 'They're not my family, but they come and check on me all the time.'

"And then he says, 'I notice wherever you go, you always know somebody, or somebody's always hugging you or shaking your hand, or always happy to see you. When I see that, I see myself,' he said. 'That's the kind of person I am.' He says, 'You have a lot of friends, and your sisters and your brothers, they're not like that. You have the gift, and that's making friends; you have a lot of friends from all over the place.' And he says, 'That's good. They're the ones who are always around for you when we're not here.' He was telling me that. I think it's true.

"And so, you know, in our way too, they always say that people that are no blood relation to you, they're the ones who become closest to you. They're the ones that will help you. And I think it's true. My dad used to tell me these things. It's just part of Navajo teachings, and I hear it all the time. The person who helps you will not be your own sister, will not be your own brother. It'll be somebody else."

And so, Navajo ways once again open themselves up to adaptation, to adjustment. The new friends are often better relatives than the real relatives. So in the Navajo way, they become relatives. Ella says, "Now if I met someone who was in no way related to me, even by clan, then I would adopt a way of acknowledging her, maybe, like, we're not related clan-wise, so we'll just be sisters. We'd just become sisters." The system doesn't crack. It isn't destroyed or made invalid. It opens up and absorbs the change, so the fundamental value can be retained: be good to your relatives, be good to your friends. *Hozho* adds to *hozho*. What is good for them is good for you. What is good for you is good for them. Egoism and altruism are not opposed.

30

The End

It is nearing the end of August, and I call Ella in Flagstaff. Nell answers the telephone. She and her mother and Buzz and Sonya are sitting in the living room watching *Geraldo*. "It's about people who have been married more than nine times," Nell says. "That's stupid!" Her father is in Tuba City, staying in the trailer. "We're all alone here," she says. Their life, it appears, in this big house, has become focused on one spot in one room: in front of the television.

Nell has started school, and she loves it—particularly the food. She tells me that there are several small restaurants at West Side Junior High, which offer a variety of menus. "There's, like, a little restaurant in the back where you can eat, where you get your fries or soda or shakes. In the morning, they sell doughnuts or breakfast, or you can get the other kind, the regular breakfast [in the cafeteria]."

She has three lockers (two for P.E.), for which she must remember the combinations, and there are vending machines in school for snacks. "You can eat in class," Nell says, "chew gum, drink pop. But you have to clean your own mess up."

Aside from the interesting things, like the food, the fact that her gym uniform's too short, that the boys lead the girls through exercises in P.E., and that they stretch and lift weights, she says that the schoolwork is demanding and that she likes her teachers. She sounds very excited, and says she likes school much better than in Tuba City.

"Have you made any new friends?" I ask.

"Yeah, I got lots, a lot of Spanish friends, and two white friends, and one Indian friend." Nell says that the school is predominantly Hispanic and black, with only about ninety Indians —Navajo and Hopi—and a few whites.

Nell has big plans. Next year, she wants to attend private school in Prescott, Arizona. Then, she's fantasizing about going to Jamaica to perform Indian dances. "All those foreign places I want to go. I *love* different places. When I'm in twelfth grade, I want to go somewhere to go to school—somewhere far away. But my mom won't let me. She says, 'It's too far.' And then she says she's going to come with me. My dad said the same thing. I want to go to Italy. Maybe I'll go to school—you know where you can get a good education is, um, Japan, because the kids there are more advanced. I want to go there. I know how to speak French, Spanish, and a little bit of Navajo."

For college, Nell is thinking of Princeton, Yale, and Georgetown, because if she goes there, she says, she will get a better job.

Buzz asks, "When are you coming up so we can go shopping?" This is his standard line, delivered deadpan, though he expects a laugh from me. Nell says, "Christmas is coming up. I want something *extravagant*."

I ask Nell if her mother's started up at the Gap. "No," she says, "she resigned."

I am very surprised. "Why?"

"She wants to stay home; she's a professional seller. She sells silver jewelry."

After a few more minutes, Nell turns the telephone over to her mother. I ask Ella how she is and she says, "Good," though it doesn't sound so good.

"I'm not working. I resigned the day I was supposed to report back to work. I was really looking forward to it and made a lot of plans with people out there, and then we just couldn't find anybody to stay with Danielle here. We could commute, but Dennis leaves at 5:00 a.m.—to get out early. And then he gets back at 5:30 p.m., and Nell catches the bus at 7:12 a.m., and then she's home at 2:15 p.m., so there's nobody to stay with her. And Nell's becoming a teenager, and I need to be here for her. So . . ."

I ask her what she thinks they'll do up in the Gap without her, on such late notice.

"I don't know. Dennis took my resignation up, but he was telling me there's no motivation out there. All the new stuff I ordered—we were going to have everything brand-new—it's all still in boxes. And I guess [the other teacher] Louise is going to go out and recruit for her kids; she was going to teach kindergarten, and I had preschool. But somebody did replace me—they've got somebody temporarily there. Dan was telling me they might close the school. So I don't know.

"I just really—it really bothered me for a week. Not going back. I just had a lot of things planned, a lot of things I wanted to do with the kids, with the parents. . . . I just felt really bad about not going back. It really bothered me. And now I guess I've kind of settled my mind, but I just keep thinking, well, my priority is here.

"And besides, Dennis—he'd rather have me stay home, 'cause it was just too much on me too, going back and forth. It was too tiring. And then to commute from here it would be worse. We even had it [worked] out to where Louise was going to wait for me at the junction [near Tuba City] in the morning [to pick Ella up after her commute to Tuba with Dennis and to drive on up to the Gap]. So, I don't know. But I like what I'm doing now. I'm getting my inventory up, and I made a lot of contacts with people who make jewelry. And Dennis says in the garage we're going to set up our own shop. I'm going to start doing my own jewelry. So . . ."

Somehow, I'm not surprised that she isn't going all the way to the Gap now that she's moved to Flagstaff. But I am shocked that she waited so long to let the school know she couldn't honor her commitment. I think of a little boy in her class whose father was a hopeless alcoholic, violent and suicidal. One night he tried to strangle his wife, the boy's mother. After observing that incident, and getting beaten himself, the boy stopped talking for almost a year. But slowly, painfully, with Ella's close attentions, he began to talk again. This little boy had few words, but he had one for Ella, which he pronounced clearly and perfectly, especially when he climbed into her lap for a hug. He called her "Mrs. N'zhonie"—"Mrs. Beautiful." Who will help him this year?

And what of the other children, most of whom come from extremely poor families? Although she will not be there with them this year, hanging on the door of her classroom is a poem her students wrote. It reads:

> *I love my language.*
> *My language, I am learning.*
> *My language is hard, but I'm trying to speak it.*
> *I like my language. My language sounds like a song.*

✱

In the end, Ella felt that her primary responsibilities lay with her own family. I wonder how much her decision not to go back to work was affected by concerns about her health.

I ask Ella how she's feeling. After a long pause she says, cheerfully, "Good."

"That was a big pause," I say.

"Well, I'm on medication again for my blood, for my blood count, my white cells, jumping around—so they gave me medication for that. Infection in my blood. So I've been on that for about a month now. It has to do with my white cell count. It goes up and down. It's for my white blood cells, but they gave me medication too for being anemic, slightly anemic."

I have no idea what this means, although I remember she was on a drug for reasons she described in a similar fashion after her bout with cancer two years ago. I ask her more questions, but she can't tell me the name of the drug or any more information about what the doctors found.

"Did you go for another mammogram?"

"Yeah. I had another one down in Flagstaff Medical Center. It was okay. They kind of like—that leakage that I had? I probably bumped something, and there was some kind of infection, so they gave me medication, so I have to go back for that every two weeks to have them check it again."

Step by step, their life is becoming more Anglicized, but then, how could it be otherwise? She's decided to become an entrepreneur, and has begun buying and selling jewelry. Her son Kimo is also getting into business. He is staying out of school for a semester to study for a real estate license, so he can earn enough money to pay his way through the University of Arizona. For the past year, he hasn't been able to transfer out of Pima Community College because he didn't have enough money, and Dan and Ella didn't have enough to help him.

The editor of the Lake Powell *Post* has called Ella; he still wants her to write a column for him, even though she is no longer working in Page. She was noncommittal. For one thing, he doesn't pay. She says she would like to take a journalism class, and had signed up for some extension courses in Tuba and is upset now that she cannot take them.

"Oh, well, now I'm in the jewelry business," she says, "and I like it."

Ella says: "Maybe Dennis will take a second wife. I told him, Wouldn't it be nice if he took a second wife, and then she could stay home? I'm at the age when I want to go places now—the kids are grown, and I don't have [as much] responsibility. I want to go, go, go."

✳

In January, Ella finds a lump in her breast. She does nothing about it for weeks and decides she will not have a biopsy, though that is what the medical doctors suggest. She will not go to the Flagstaff Medical Center. "That's the last thing I'll do," she says. She drives to Santa Monica with a clan aunt for treatment by Jerry Kwon, the acupuncturist and holistic healer who had worked on her throughout the latter stages of her earlier bout with cancer. And since then he has come to Tuba City several times to work on her and other Navajos who want healing. At those times, Ella's living room is jammed—the Navajo people very much appreciate his healing techniques, and drive from all over to see him. People, mostly old, traditional couples, sit silently while others are treated, awaiting their turn. He gives them herbs, uses a glass of water to diagnose ailments according to energy fields, and performs acupuncture. They pay him what they can.

Ella tells her parents about the lump, and they schedule a ten-day ceremony. I talk to her every few days for several weeks. Though I try to suggest as often as I dare the good reasons to have a biopsy, she is adamantly against it. One day in February she calls and out of the blue announces that she indeed had a biopsy. Two tumors were removed. A week later, she calls to say they were benign.

She is still headed back to Coal Mine Mesa for the ceremony. The medical doctors suggest she might consider having her breast removed to avoid the chance of more tumors and the risk that another one might be cancerous.

"Like the Amazon women," she says. "I'll think about it."

✳

A few months later, Ella, Dennis, and Nell have settled into their new lives in Flagstaff. Dennis still enjoys his job counseling kids at the Tuba City elementary school, and he spends a few nights a week up at the trailer, to spare himself and the car the ninety-minute drive to Flagstaff. Kimo is still seeing his Hopi girlfriend in Tucson, where they are both trying to finish school. Her parents do not approve of her dating a Navajo, though Kimo goes up to the mesas and tries to help them out by gathering wood and performing other chores. She is about to graduate from the University of Arizona, and Kimo's still working, trying to get enough money to transfer to the university, where he plans to get a degree in criminal justice. Rena finally got the ceremony she needed to remove the influence of Joe's ghost, and she feels much better, but she has yet to give Jack the earth bundle in the traditional spring ceremony. Last spring the ceremony was impossible because of all the sickness.

Jack and Bessie continue to fight relocation, each in a different way. Jack attends countless meetings, listening to the Hopis' offers for a negotiated settlement, then the Navajos' objections. Bessie is tired and maddened by the issue, and refuses to listen to any of it. She plans to stay on her land, period. One of her neighbors once carried a sign whose message she supports. "The Creator Is the Only One Who Is Going to Relocate Me."

Buzz is living in the trailer in Tuba City. He still works for Davis Chevrolet as a mechanic's assistant, and his second job is now at Basha's supermarket bagging groceries. He has several cats, a sharpei, and a turtle that lives in an aquarium. Buzz says, "I have to have two jobs because of my vet's bills."

Dennis brings live goldfish for the turtle to eat. "Buzz says [the turtle] gets excited when you put fish in there," says Ella. "But when I look at him, I don't know, he doesn't really look like he shows anything at all. But Buzz says his eyes move real fast and then his tail starts moving. That's when he says you can tell the turtle's excited." The turtle's name is Hurry Up. And Buzz has a nickname for it, as well: War Pony.

I ask Ella, "How should I end the book?"

Ella thinks about my question for a few seconds and says,

"Write this: She's moved back into her house with her white picket fence and the yellow roses. She's now attained the great American dream. And she asks, 'So this is what everybody works for? Then what?' "

Then she starts to laugh.

31

"And So It Is That When One Doesn't Know the Traditions One Has Nothing to Light One's Way"

Children, I want you to know how I think. I'm very old, and what I have to offer you is getting scarce. The old people's knowledge is that by which one looks up and sees the world after the sun has risen. By means of knowledge, one makes one's way through the day from the time the first light is seen in the East until the darkness rises and finally the world becomes dark. At that time, one can no longer see.

And so it is that when one doesn't know the traditions one has nothing to light one's way. It is as though one lived with a covering on one's eyes, as if one lived being deaf and blind. Yet when one knows the traditions, one has vision to see as far as Black Mountain and beyond, to see all the way to where the land meets the ocean. It's as though one's vision becomes as good as that. I long for you to realize what it is that your ancestors had, and how it is that some of us old people still live our lives.

If you would only come to know our words and take the time to think them over, you would come to know that they were true and valuable. These teachings are of a kind that you would someday want to use in teaching your own children. But hardly any of you will listen to us anymore, even though there are now so many of you. And so it is up to those few of you who do want to learn. You will never be alone.

You'll learn one thing after another and the old people will help you. Then the more you learn, the more you'll be able to tie things together and to understand.

And so it is up to those of you who are really interested to listen and to make sense for yourselves of what we say. Then you will come to be respected and sought after for advice . . . people will think of you as a living sparking fire.

How to Make a Cradleboard

Jack Hatathlie:

"Ella asked me how to make a cradleboard. And I will explain it. You go and look for a tree that is fully mature. You make two diagonal cuts on one side of the tree down low to the ground. You make another cut on the back side of the tree. This lets you fell the tree in the right direction. After the tree falls, you cut off the small limbs and branches.

"After cutting those off, you measure the trunk and cut it into thirty-inch and thirty-two-inch sections, so you actually cut three sections from the tree. You then cut down a small cedar tree that would be for the rainbow—the headpiece. You cut one twenty-eight-inch section from this small tree. You find another tree that's already a dead log. You place a section on the log at a spot where there is a curve or dip in it. You put the thirty-two-inch piece against the log and then place a little stick between the log and the section of cedar so it won't rub when you begin cutting the pieces of cedar trunk into boards.

"Sometimes it's better to put two holes in the ground and to put two large sticks in the holes. This makes an X, and you can put the log in this to help hold it.

"You then cut the logs into boards about one inch thick. You cut the logs into boards. You cut down the middle of the logs, but you don't cut it all the way through. You make a shallow straight cut, so that when you cut deep in the log the saw won't cut crooked. You cut two boards out of each log.

"You don't use the outside pieces because they are too small. You take the middle two boards to make the bottom of the cradle and to use for other parts too.

"You dry the boards for a couple of weeks. After two weeks, it's time to cut the pieces for the cradleboard.

"The pattern for a cradleboard comes to you while in the process of making it. You make marks for the holes that need to be drilled. I used to heat a metal tool and keep putting it on the hole until it burned through. These holes were for the leather ties that hold the cradleboard together.

"It's very important that when making a cradle, you don't use two types of boards. You can't use wood from two different cedar trees to make the two back boards of the cradleboard. You can use wood from other cedar trees for the rainbow.

"First you drill the holes in the cradleboard about three-sixteenths of an inch in diameter. You then cut all the pieces of the cradleboard with a handsaw. You cut the bottom board out first. Next the rainbow pieces. After you cut all the pieces, you sand them and smooth out the edges. You sand the rainbow real thin, to about one-quarter inch. If the rainbow is too thick, it won't bend. After you finish sanding the rainbow, you put it in hot water. The water soaks into the board, making it easy to bend. You slowly bend it. Sometimes you can tie the rainbow with a string after it takes the shape of a rainbow, and you let it dry several days.

"You cut thin straps of leather, and you use that to tie the boards together, using a square knot.

"The first boards you tie together are the earth and dark-sky boards. Then you tie the broken rainbow to these on the backside to make the two back boards stiff. You then add the short rainbow, which is for the baby's footrest. You have to tie the rainbow and the bottom boards together in a certain way.

"After all the boards are laced together, you can have the mother sew one-inch-wide strips of cloth. These make the lightning bolts, which are attached to the sides with string. The sunbeam is laced through each of the lightning bolts.

"When the cradleboard is finished you put *chiih*, red ochre, on it before you put the baby in. This *chiih* has been with our people for a long time. My daughter Ella even says they find these among the cavemen's burials, so it dates a long way back.

"*Chiih* is red. It represents our people, our Mother Earth, our power and strength. When you touch this red ochre on different parts of the cradleboard, you ask for protection from all the natural elements because it was made from a living plant.

"You make a small mattress that would fit the length and width of the cradleboard, then you lay blankets on top of the mattress, three baby blankets. You place your baby in the cradle and wrap the blankets around it. You take the sunbeam and lace it through the lightning bolts, wrapping your baby snugly in the cradleboard. A cloth can be tied to the rainbow to cover the baby's face when it's asleep.

"I raised all my children in cradleboards. I encourage my children to use the cradleboard and to know the parts of the cradleboard.

"I was raised in a cradleboard, and I still have that board. My oldest grandson, Kimo, used it for a while. You can rock your baby back and forth—other siblings can care for the baby while it's in a cradleboard while you do other things. You can stand it against a wall or anything. The children can play around and the people can watch. If it accidentally falls over, the rainbow will protect the baby's head.

"I don't see it around a lot these days. I just hear a lot of stories that a baby fell off the bed and injured itself, or the baby fell out of its crib."

How to Butcher a Sheep

Jack Hatathlie:

"You need a sharp knife, bowl, and a rope.

"First, pick out a fat sheep. You can tell if it's a fat sheep or not by feeling and rubbing its tail. Then throw the sheep on its back, tie all four legs together with the rope.

"Hold the sheep's head back and cut the sheep's throat. Put a bowl under the sheep's head so the blood can drain into the bowl. When there's no more blood coming out, put a piece of wood under the head, to keep sand out of it. Then untie the legs and sprinkle ground white cornmeal from head to tail while praying, praying to the sheep that your family needed to eat, and praying that you will have many more sheep.

"Next, cut a slit in the chest area all the way down to the anal area. Starting at the chest, start cutting away the skin from the meat. Make sure that you don't cut through the skin. When you're done skinning the front part of the sheep, you cut crosswise at the knee joint. Cut deep enough so that you can cut the joints apart. Make a slit from the knees to the chest part of the sheep—start cutting and peeling the skin back. Do the same thing for the other side. Go to the back and cut at the joint, and also cut the skin open from the hind leg to the middle. Start cutting and peeling the skin again. Keep turning the sheep on its side and cutting the skin away from the sheep. Go back to the neck section and peel all the skin away down to the tail.

"Cut open the neck section and pull the esophagus out. Pull it out until it's long enough to tie in two places. If you don't, the bowels will start coming out.

"When the skin is completely off, spread the sheepskin nearby. Tie the hind legs of the sheep together with the rope. Hang it up on a strong post or tree. Cut open the stomach area making sure you don't cut the intestines or stomach. Make a long slit up and down, enough so you can get all the intestines and stomach out. Pull it all out and place on sheepskin. Go inside the sheep and cut the lungs and heart out, also the throat. Hang on a nail to air out. Cut the head and feet off the sheepskin. Build a fire and singe them.

"Separate all the intestines, uncoiling them from the stomach. Tear off all the fat from the stomach and hang out to dry. Cut the large stomach out and dump the waste out. After separating the intestines, start cleaning them. Pour warm water into them to thoroughly clean them. Wash all others with warm water. Wrap small intestines around the big intestines. Stuff the pancreas with chili or onion and pin the opening with a nail.

"Cut the liver into slices, cut the lung in half, and also cut the heart and all remaining attachments to the lining of the lung, throat, and so forth.

"All the insides can be eaten roasted. Sometimes, you can cut all the attachments to the throat, liver, and lung in small pieces and fry them in oil or boil them. They say the insides are always to be eaten first if the sheep is going to be replaced by the Holy People. These are usually eaten first anytime a sheep is butchered.

"The sheep's head and feet are cooked underground until tender, and the meat is eaten. Eyes and tongue are usually favorites. Brains can be eaten if they're not going to be used for tanning a buckskin.

"The small joints of the feet of the sheep can be boiled until all the muscles are gone and the bone comes up brilliant white. The bones can be used for toys for children. They usually vary in size, but four feet can usually make shapes that resemble a family. I had them as toys. No one has them now."

HOW TO MAKE BLOOD SAUSAGE

4 diced potatoes
2 cups diced meat
1 can corn
½ cup diced fat
1 large onion
1 tablespoon crushed chili
2 carrots
2 cups crushed white cornmeal
1 teaspoon minced garlic

"Knead the blood clot together. Drain all the blood out into a separate bowl. Throw blood clots to the dogs.

"Put all the ingredients into the bowl of blood. Mix together and pour into the large stomach of the sheep.

"Put the stomach into boiling water. Boil forty-five minutes, turning occasionally so it won't stick to the bottom. Slice and serve with hot coffee and tortillas."

HOW TO PREPARE THE SHEEPSKIN

"Stretch it out on the ground and nail it in. Dry four days or more. Rub with a rock until it's soft. Your bed is ready.

"In winter, when you can't dry sheepskin because of the cold, you can eat the skin.

"Heat a heavy skillet. Cover the skillet with the skin, wool on the outside and the skin next to the skillet. After a few minutes, start pulling the wool from the skin. Because of the heat going though the skin, it will come off easily. Repeat until all the wool is off. The skin will shrink to half its size. Slice into four-inch strips, two inches wide. Roll with strips of fat inside and salt it. Roast over hot charcoals.

"Fat can be used for the blackening ceremony. Fat mixed with ground ash, rubbed over the body during ceremonies, will ward off bad spirits that are giving you nightmares.

"Bone marrow saved in a jar can be rubbed at ends of hair or used as hair grease and will condition and give strength to the hair.

"Baby goatskin, peeled from the head to the toe without knives, can be made into water bags. Goatskins were used as snowshoes.

"Sheep were butchered when special guests came; they are used in exchange for ceremonies, traded for goods, sold for cash, and are used to feed people who attend ceremonies. Nowadays it's hard to butcher a sheep because I have no sheep to bring [because of the land dispute]. Our lives have always revolved around sheep.

"I'm talking about sheep, and now I'm hungry for mutton."

Notes

Page

xiii   "It could be said": Mircea Eliade, *The Sacred and the Profane* (New York: Harcourt Brace Jovanovich, 1959), p. 11.

xv   "there is no other way": Ibid., p. 165.

xix   "I am conscious": Caryl Emerson, *Problems of Dostoevsky's Poetics* (Minneapolis: University of Minnesota Press, 1963), as quoted in David K. Danow, *The Thought of Mikhail Bakhtin* (New York: St. Martin's Press, 1991), p. 59.

4   "The group of roots": Leland C. Wyman, *Blessingway* (Tucson: University of Arizona Press, 1970), pp. 209–10.

9   "The world exists because": Eliade, *The Sacred and the Profane*, p. 165.

23   "among the most primitive": Ruth Underhill, *The Navajos* (Norman: University of Oklahoma Press, 1956), p. 5.
    "Their homes were shelters": Ibid.

25   "From . . . hints of myth": Ibid., p. 23.

52   Good and evil coexist: Leland C. Wyman, "Navajo Ceremonial System," in *Handbook of North American Indians*, vol. 10 (Washington: Smithsonian Institution, 1983), p. 536.
    "Man . . . forms part": Eliade, *The Sacred and the Profane*, p. 165.
    "Openness to the world": Ibid.

Notes

53 "people live . . . on": Leo Tolstoy, *A Confession and Other Religious Writings* (London: Penguin Books, 1987), pp. 19–20.

55 "repeat the paradigmatic": Eliade, *The Sacred and the Profane*, p. 32.

56 "Every construction": Ibid., p. 57.

58 "Changing Woman": Gladys A. Reichard, *Navaho Religion* (Tucson: University of Arizona Press, 1983), p. 21.

59 "growth, adaptation, and re-animation": John R. Farella, *The Main Stalk: A Synthesis of Navajo Philosophy* (Tucson: University of Arizona Press, 1984), p. 185.

  "the song of songs": Gerald Hausman, *The Gift of the Gila Monster* (New York: Simon and Schuster, 1993), p. 31.

76 Many Navajos who could not speak English: Emily Benedek, *The Wind Won't Know Me: A History of the Navajo-Hopi Land Dispute* (New York: Alfred A. Knopf, Inc., 1992), p. 211.

100 "The children were wrapped": Reichard, *Navaho Religion*, p. 543.

104 "One of the worst things to be said": Gary Witherspoon, *Navajo Kinship and Marriage* (Chicago: University of Chicago Press, 1975), p. 88.

  "Once while I was": Ibid.

127 "after they had dwindled": Book of Mormon, 1 Nephi 12:23.

  "their scales of darkness . . . delightsome people": Book of Mormon, 2 Nephi 30:5–6.

  A leader . . . Arizona sun: Jerry Kammer, *The Second Long Walk* (Albuquerque: University of New Mexico Press, 1980), p. 64.

130 Navajo myths and stories: Reichard, *Navaho Religion*, pp. 41–45.

  "Christianity strives": Ibid., pp. 45–46.

153 Indian children who tried: Helen Sekaquaptewa with Louise Udall, *Me and Mine* (Tucson: University of Arizona Press, 1969), p. 137.

172 "In Navaho life": Reichard, *Navaho Religion*, pp. 124–25.

176 "One of the things . . . If their lips are moving, they're praying": Telephone interview with Jon Norstog, July 13, 1993.

180 "The Navajo 'economic theory' ": John Ladd, *The Structure of a Moral Code* (Cambridge: Harvard University Press, 1957), p. 244.

183 For hundreds of years: Peter Nabokov, *Indian Running* (Santa Barbara: Capra Press, 1981), p. 9.

"ancient knowledge": Ibid., p. 16.

"Running was something": Ibid., pp. 100–01.

184 "There's no comparison": Ibid., p. 101.

One Indian coach: Bertram Gabriel, "Running to Nowhere," *Sports Illustrated*, vol. 51, no. 22 (November 26, 1979).

185 "It seemed the Tarahumaras": Nabokov, *Indian Running*, p. 185.

187 "nearly eight hundred thousand": Edward H. Spicer, *Cycles of Conquest* (Tucson: University of Arizona Press, 1962), p. 216.

It is estimated that: Ibid., p. 217.

188 "Our grandfathers had no idea": Gerald Thompson, *The Army and the Navajo* (Tucson: University of Arizona Press, 1982), p. 153.

188–9 The Navajos learned . . . tried to raid again: Ibid., pp. 164–65.

189 Legal maneuvering between . . . and other allies: A full explanation of the dispute can be found in Benedek, *The Wind Won't Know Me*.

209 "No one seems": Robert L. Bergman, "A School for Medicine Men," *American Journal of Psychiatry*, vol. 30 (June 1973), p. 663.

210 "The patient's evil feelings": Clyde Kluckhohn and Dorothea Leighton, *The Navaho* (Cambridge: Harvard University Press, 1946), p. 170.

211 "Traditional Navajos talk": Bergman, "A School for Medicine Men," pp. 663–64.

"remarkable and well-documented" to "unconsciously determined": Ibid., pp. 663–66.

212 In 1953 . . . for her work: Robert L. Bergman, "Navajo Health Services and Projects," in *Handbook for North American Indians*, vol. 10 (Washington: Smithsonian Institution, 1983), p. 674.

213–15 "It was characteristic" . . . "treatment of a dream by a dream": Bergman, "A School for Medicine Men," pp. 663–66.

215–16 A healing ceremony . . . to make him well: Alexander H. Leighton and Dorothea C. Leighton, "Elements of Psychotherapy in Navaho Religion," *Psychiatry*, 4 (1941), p. 522.

217 The Navajo patient . . . then help resolve: Ibid.

223 "Their system of beliefs": Kluckhohn and Leighton, *The Navaho*, p. 166.

224 "Knowing a good story": Ibid., p. 167.

"On the existential plane": Eliade, *The Sacred and the Profane,* p. 94.

227 "It is quite possible": Kluckhohn and Leighton, *The Navaho,* p. 176.

"The People blame": Ibid., p. 177.

Navajos believe . . . blameless: Ibid., p. 175.

244 Participation in . . . family's income: Clyde Kluckhohn, "Participation in Ceremonials in a Navaho Community," *American Anthropologist,* 40 (1938), pp. 359–69.

One fifth to one-sixth . . . ceremonies: Kluckhohn and Leighton, *The Navaho,* p. 160.

The origin of . . . enduring and popular: David F. Aberle, *The Peyote Religion Among the Navajo* (Norman: University of Oklahoma Press, 1966), p. 17.

It has been estimated . . . of the NAC: David Aberle, "Peyote Religion Among the Navajo," in *Handbook of North American Indians,* vol. 10 (Washington: Smithsonian Institution, 1983), p. 558.

245 Peyote contains . . . not addictive: Ibid.

"something is being done": Aberle, *The Peyote Religion Among the Navaho,* p. 11.

246 "Peyotism provides . . . by the majority": Ibid., p. 15.

247 "Superficially then": Farella, *The Main Stalk,* p. 201.

248 "In all but": Aberle, *The Peyote Religion Among the Navaho,* p. 6.

248–9 "I used just to" . . . "dimension of meaning": Ibid., p. 8.

249 "You can use": J. S. Slotkin, *The Peyote Religion: A Study in Indian-White Relations* (Glencoe, Ill.: Free Press, 1956), p. 76.

"Peyote is a symbol": Aberle, in *Handbook,* p. 559.

250 "It is very probable": David M.'Brugge, *Navajo Pottery and Ethnohistory* (Window Rock, Ariz.: Navajoland Publications, Navajo Tribal Museum, 1963), pp. 22–23, as cited in Farella, *The Main Stalk,* p. 196.

251 "is redemptive": Aberle, in *Handbook,* p. 558.

"the only permanence": Farella, *The Main Stalk,* p. 195.

264 sometimes rearranging . . . heart: Aberle, in *Handbook,* p. 560.

268 "The stones are said": Sidney M. Calloway and others, *Grand-*

father Stories of the Navahos (Rough Rock, Ariz.: Rough Rock Demonstration School, 1968), p. 63.

305–6   But Indians make good use . . . to enter school: Bergman, in *Handbook*, p. 672.

329   "Children, I want": Farella, *The Main Stalk*, pp. 24–25.

A NOTE ON THE TYPE

The text of this book was composed in Palatino, a type face designed by the noted German typographer Hermann Zapf. Named after Giovanbattista Palatino, a writing master of Renaissance Italy, Palatino was the first of Zapf's type faces to be introduced in America. The first designs for the face were made in 1948, and the fonts for the complete face were issued between 1950 and 1952. Like all Zapf-designed type faces, Palatino is beautifully balanced and exceedingly readable.

Composed by PennSet, Inc.,
Bloomsburg, Pennsylvania

Printed and bound by Quebecor Martinsburg,
Martinsburg, West Virginia

Typography and binding design by
Dorothy Schmiderer Baker